Thank you, Wendy and my family, for always being by my side; my heart will always be yours. Scott Joseph, thanks for having my back.

To all operators—active, retired, or having paid the ultimate sacrifice for this nation. You are an inspiration to me and this nation for your dedication, motivation, and desire to serve. Your families suffer greatly when you are away in training or combat. I hope all who serve in our military understand our gratitude.

table of contents

part 1:

overview

introduction

When I first started writing fitness books in the 1990s, there were no other manuals based upon the Navy SEAL workout out on the market. Ten years after the first printing, these books are a dime a dozen. Just like any other profession there is progress, growth, and change. I have also learned quite a bit since my first book and decided to bring something unique and different to the market.

For this reason, you will receive nothing but the most informative and effective fitness guidance the market has to offer. Backed by my experience in the fitness industry and military, *Special Ops Fitness Training* will take you to the next level.

In this book, I've taken the best exercises from various Special Forces units to create a program that will generate peak performance. I've also added multiple routines so that your body will never plateau, taking your fitness levels off the charts. The alternative weightlifting program combines calisthenics with free weights to build speed, power, endurance, and size. This book leaves no stone unturned as far as training the upper body, lower body, and abs—you'll also see how the Special Forces include running, swimming, cardio, and weights in their fitness regimens. Whether you're male or female, a beginner or a pro, the exercises and routines in this book will help you achieve results beyond your expectations.

Author Mark De Lisle (right) makes some adjustments.

striving for peak performance

You've probably purchased this book because you're not satisfied with being average—you're looking for something that will take you to the next level of fitness. *Special Ops Fitness Training* will definitely help you get there, but not in the way you might think. The majority of clients I work with are more concerned with how many reps they do rather than performing the exercises correctly. The physical aspect is just a small portion of the peak-performance picture.

In addition, during the training sessions, someone will invariably say, "I can't do any more!" I refuse to let them quit and tell them that they better perform or we're going to be there all day. Take a guess whether they're able to squeeze out those last couple of reps. Sure enough, they do, and they just smile when I remind them that they had nothing left a few reps ago.

Mental domination is essential—you must rise above your body and any weakness in order to function at your peak. Our first reaction while exercising is to listen to our body, and our body's first reaction is to quit under stress. DON'T LISTEN TO IT! From this point forward, you will train like a Special Ops operator and dominate your body so your body can't dominate you. Nobody wants to be a slave to anyone so why let yourself be a slave to your body? It's a weakness, and *Special Ops Fitness Training* eliminates weakness like a bad habit.

Every Special Ops operator has a unique mindset. Failure is not an option so they must find a way to succeed no matter what the cost. You, too, can acquire this mentality by eliminating all doubt from your mind. Not everyone can reach the levels of mental and physical dominance of a Special Ops operator (if anyone could, there wouldn't be anything special about Special Ops), but you can get mighty close. You have to want something so bad that you can taste it, otherwise your motivation will be short-lived. When you begin to feel failure, weakness, or discomfort, take the operator stance and attack it until it becomes a strength. When it comes to your mental strength, take no prisoners and do not look back.

history of special operations

Modern-day Special Forces can be traced back to Italian assault units, called Arditi, and the German storm trooper of World War II. Both units were specially trained and received extensive training beyond that of the normal infantry; they also had distinct uniforms that separated them from the normal soldiers.

During World War II, British prime minister Winston Churchill formed an elite group of troops known as Special Air Service (SAS), along with the Long Range Desert Group, the Special Boat Service, and the Small Scale Raiding. All were used in unconventional formats, with duties such as reconnaissance, guerrilla tactics, hostage rescue, and assaults.

Many have asked about the difference between U.S. Special Forces and special forces. In most cases, "U.S. Special Forces" refers to Army Green Berets, while the latter refers to all forces within this community. Army or U.S. Special Forces were around as early as World War II, under the direction of Strategic Services; this special group of men performed missions behind enemy lines and gathered intelligence in various locations throughout the world. But the actual origins of modern Special Forces go back a little further.

Major Robert Rogers commanded a unique group of men utilizing unconventional tactics during the French and Indian War. These men enjoyed working in environments that others avoided. Rogers often told his men to "move fast and hit hard." Thanks to these courageous men, later known as Roger's Rangers, the foundation for modern special warfare was laid.

Another pioneer that used the element of surprise to

harass and demoralize the enemy was Francis Marion in the late 18th century. Even though his troop numbers were small, they were very successful on their missions. These units evolved and became the Devil's Brigade, Darby's Rangers, Merrill's Marauders, and Alamo Scouts.

William Donovan, a seasoned veteran of World War I, was able to convince President Franklin D. Roosevelt that a new type of soldier was needed, one who could run secret missions behind enemy lines while collecting intelligence. In 1941 Roosevelt granted Donovan the opportunity to form Coordinator of Intelligence (COI); this organization was soon changed to Office of Strategic Services Society (OSS). In 1952 Special Forces was officially launched.

Air Force Pararescue

Motto: "That others may live."

Air Force Special Operations Command has an elite group of men known as Pararescues, or PJs, who are specially equipped to conduct unconventional and conventional rescue operations behind enemy lines or wherever needed. They can perform down-pilot or personnel rescue. These men are incredible combat medics and can handle most situations or injuries they may encounter during a rescue operation. Since they have no idea what they may find in a rescue operation, they have to be on top of all the latest medical skills available, which makes them the most qualified emergency trauma experts in the U.S. military. Because of the need to infiltrate from any scenario, all PJs must be proficient in free-fall sky diving and air operations, as well as skilled in scuba and various other insertion techniques.

The Pararescue unit was purportedly born during World War II, with the China-Burma-India Theater considered the birthplace. Captain John L. Porter organized the first rescue unit, which flew out of India using two C-47s. Porter's men were able to locate 20 people who had bailed out of a crippled C-46. Having to avoid local Japanese troops and head hunters, they parachuted in one flight surgeon, two combat surgeons, and supplies, while ground troops headed their way. All 20 men were able to find their way out to safety. Realizing a great need for an officially organized command in 1946, Air Rescue Service (ARS) was founded. ARS would eventually change its name to Air Force Pararescue. If you've seen the movie *Air Force One*, Harrison Ford's character was rescued by PJs.

Army Rangers

Motto: "Rangers lead the way."

Army Rangers are a light infantry special operations force based out of Fort Benning, GA. Heeding their motto "Rangers lead the way," they can be deployed anywhere in the world with just an 18-hour notice. This makes them a valuable asset to the Special Forces. The force specializes in airborne; air assaults; light infantry and direct action operations; raids; infiltration and exfiltration by air, land, or sea; airfield seizure; recovery of personnel and special equipment; and support of general purpose forces (GPF). Throughout the decades there have been scenarios where groups of 18 men or less did not provide enough fire or man power to handle the mission. Rangers are trained to work in large numbers while maintaining group integrity and fire superiority, and are also much respected for their reconnaissance and land navigation skills.

The Rangers' origins go back to pre–Revolutionary War days, when colonists surveyed the frontier fortifications, conducting reconnaissance and gathering early warnings of raids from the American Indians. Benjamin Church first organized the group, combining white frontiersman and Indian scouts. His journal was later used as a military manual. During the French and Indian War, Robert Rogers organized a group of New England woodsman to form full-time English auspices (military men) paid under British funds. Roger's Rangers' wilderness skills were so well respected that other military units called upon them for training.

The first group of Army Rangers was hand-picked to perform during World War II. Formed in 1942 as the 1st Ranger Battalion, it began training under Scottish and English commandos. After World War II, the Rangers were disbanded but the training regimen was kept in place, open only to senior non-commissioned officers (NCOs, soldiers who achieved a higher ranking in the military without a college degree) and officers. In 1969, the Rangers were needed in Vietnam and formed into the 75th Ranger Infantry Regiment.

Green Berets

Motto: "De Oppresso Liber" (to free the oppressed)

U.S. Special Forces, or Green Berets, like the Navy SEALs, are generally the first on the ground or at a location when

the situation gets hot. Their ability to master foreign languages, customs, and cultures enables them to train foreign troops or insurgents. In order for them to do this, they must be well versed in tactics, weapons, and every facet of war. President John F. Kennedy called Green Berets "a symbol of excellence, a badge of courage, a mark of distinction in the fight for freedom."

Green Berets were officially launched in 1952, evolving from the Coordinator of Intelligence (COI) that World War I veteran William Donovan convinced President Roosevelt to form in 1941. Fort Bragg became the home for Psychological Warfare and Special Forces Center. The 10th Special Forces Group was officially launched with Aaron Bank as their commander. The 10th Special Forces took their ranks from ex-OSS officers, ex-Ranger troops, Airborne, and combat veterans. In 1961 President Kennedy had a unique interest in Special Forces and this led to the adoption of Green Berets.

Marine Force Recon

Motto: "Swift, Silent, Deadly."

Marine Force Recon skills include scout swimming, small boat operations, close-quarter combat (CQB), helicopter and submarine insertion/extraction capabilities, demolition, reconnaissance, and airborne and waterborne insertion missions. Force Recon received its start in the South Pacific during World War II and was known as Amphibious Reconnaissance Battalion. The Marine Corps merged the Amphibious Reconnaissance Company with an experimental team in 1957 to form 1st Force Reconnaissance Company. Like the SEALs, Force Recon received its first military action during Vietnam, but was deactivated shortly after the conflict ended. The need for Force Recon arose once again in 1986 during the Gulf War. Force Recon has now grown to four units and represents the best of the Marines. Force Recon became an official member of U.S. Special Operations Command in February 2006 and will be a part of the new

Marine Corp Forces Special Operation Command (MARSOC), which will be fully commissioned by 2010.

Navy SEALs

Motto: "The more you sweat in peacetime, the less you bleed in war."

Navy SEALs (SEAL stands for "sea, air, and land") have the ability to strike from anywhere and at any time. They continue to be a key asset to U.S. Special Operations Command (SOCOM) because they can deploy from ships, submarines, aircraft, helicopters, and small boat operations. Extremely well respected for their clandestine and stealth capabilities, SEALs perform a wide range of special operations. They originally were known only to strike from the sea, but over the years they have proven that their skills are not limited to just the sea. Their versatility is augmented by their skills in small arms, demolition, reconnaissance, unconventional warfare, foreign languages and cultures, and combat martial arts. Their expertise allows them to embark on assault and direct-action missions, as well as engage in close-quarter battle and hostage rescue.

John F. Kennedy saw the direction the world was taking when it came to military struggles and tactics. He envisioned the future would be engaged in more small conflicts rather than larger-scale conflicts. In 1963, he announced that he wanted to form a group that could demoralize and fight the enemy with intense guerilla tactics. Thus the SEALs were formed and received their first opportunity to prove themselves in Vietnam. During the Vietnam War, the SEALs appeared and disappeared in the jungles, which established great fear in the Viet Cong. The SEALs became so feared and respected by their enemies that they were given the nickname "devils with green faces."

Although the SEALs were officially started by President Kennedy, they actually originated during World War II with the Underwater Demolition Teams (UDT), or Frogmen. The UDTs went through some of the most grueling training the military had to offer at that time. During World War II, UDT teams were used to clear beach landing with the demolition they swam in with.

special ops training

Each branch of the Special Forces has a specialty and each depends on one muscle group more than others. Still, they have to be ready for anything, which requires peak physical conditioning of the entire body. SEALs, for example, need good upper body strength for the amount of swimming they do and possible shipboard attacks; at the same time, if their legs and core are not strong, their swimming will falter.

Marine Force Recon have similar physical needs as the SEALs, and cannot perform and excel if any part of their physical training routine is lacking. Army Rangers and Green Beret are well known for their land capabilities, which demand incredible stamina and leg strength. Yet in an urban arena they could be called upon for anything, so once again they have to be ready. Air Force PJs never know what kind of environment they will encounter due to the wide variety of combat rescue missions that are found in both non-wartime and wartime campaigns.

To give you a better idea of the excellent shape Special Operations members must be in, this book compiles the minimum physical requirements applicants must meet before they're even considered for recruitment. (You are welcome to visit the following websites for more information: www.bragg.mil, www.specialoperations.com, and www.specialoperations.military.com.) This section also highlights the mental attitude required to endure the demands and responsibilities of being in the Special Forces and get the job done.

Air Force Pararescue

Pararescue undergo some extremely tough and rigorous training, which earns them the right to wear the maroon beret. PJs first must pass a two-week prep course at Lackland Air Force Base in Texas that prepares them to succeed physically in the indoctrination course. Trainees are instructed in physiological training, dive physics, dive tables, metric manipulations, medical terminology, cardiopulmonary resuscitation, weapons qualifications, PJ history, and leadership reaction. They also engage in obstacle courses and rucksack marches. Afterward, they go through standard EMT training.

Candidates then take a three-week jump school course at Fort Benning. Afterwards, they spend six weeks in Air Force Dive School, where they learn about open- and closed-circuit diving and conduct sub-surface searches and basic recovery missions. A one-day course teaches candidates how to safely escape from a water-bound aircraft. This is followed by a two-and-a-half-week sur-

PAST Test

SWIM	RUN	CALISTHENICS (with 3-minute breaks in between)
• Underwater 20 meters • Rest 5–10 minutes	• 1.5 miles (no maximum time limit) • Rest 10 minutes	• Chin-ups/pull-ups (1 minute)
• Surface swim 500 meters using freestyle, breaststroke, or sidestroke • Rest 30 minutes		• Flutter kicks (2 minutes)
		• Push-ups (2 minutes)
		• Sit-ups (2 minutes)

POINTS SCALE FOR PARARESCUE PAST

Note: *You must receive a combined total of 270 points and complete the 20-meter underwater to successfully pass the PAST.*

SWIM		RUN		CALISTHENICS					
				CHIN-UPS		Note: *Points are awarded for each area*			
500m Time	Points	1.5-mile Time	Points	Chin-ups Repetitions	Points	Sit-Ups Repetitions	Push-Ups Repetitions	Flutter Kicks Repetitions	Points
16:01 or higher	10	14:01 or higher	10	1	3	1–5	1–5	1–5	3
15:41–16:00	20	13:01–14:00	20	2	5	6–10	6–10	6–10	4
15:21–16:40	40	12:21–13:00	30	3	7	11–15	11–15	11–15	5
15:01–15:20	60	12:11–12:20	40	4	10	16–20	16–20	16–20	8
14:41–15:00	70	12:01–12:10	50	5	15	21–25	21–25	21–25	11
14:21–14:40	75	11:51–12:00	60	6	20	26–30	26–30	26–30	14
14:01–14:20	80	11:41–11:50	70	7	23	31–35	31–35	31–35	17
13:41–14:00	85	11:31–11:40	75	8	25	36–40	36–40	36–40	20
13:21–13:40	90	11:21–11:30	80	9	26	41–45	41–45	41–45	23
13:01–13:20	95	11:11–11:20	85	10	27	46–50	46–50	46–50	25
12:01–13:00	100	11:01–11:10	90	11	28	51–55	51–55	51–55	26
11:01–12:00	103	10:51–11:00	95	12	29	56–60	56–60	56–60	27
11:00 or below	105	10:31–10:50	100	13 or more	30	61–65	61–65	61–65	28
		10:11–10:30	103			66–70	66–70	66–70	29
		10:10 or below	105			71 or more	71 or more	71 or more	30

vival course. Candidates then attend a five-week free-fall school conducted by the U.S. Army. Pararescue finish their training by attending two very intense medical courses, a 22-week paramedic course and a 24-week Pararescue Recovery Specialist Course.

All candidates must be proficient swimmers and meet specific physical fitness standards as noted in the PAST Test (see page [illegible]).

Army Rangers

Army Ranger training involves several phases, beginning with a two-week pre-Ranger course to test a candidate's physical and leadership skills and determine whether or not he has what it takes to be a Ranger; Pre-Ranger School also teaches small-unit tactics and land navigation to active and reserve units. Essentially, if you're not already in good physical condition prior to arriving at Ranger School, you'll have a difficult time keeping up.

The Fort Benning Phase incorporates a number of physical challenges. The Army Physical Fitness Test (APFT) requires candidates to do a minimum of 49 push-ups in two minutes, 59 sit-ups in two minutes, and 6 chin-ups. Part of the test includes running five miles, while wearing BDUs and running shoes, in formation in under 40 minutes; if at any point during the run soldiers fall more than 15 meters behind the formation, they will be considered a run fall-out.

Candidates must also take the Combat Water Survival Test (CWST). The CWST starts with a 15-meter swim while wearing BDUs (camouflage pants), boots, and a load-bearing harness (LBE) with full canteens, and maintaining control of a rubber M16. The test continues in the same uniform; blindfolded, the candidate uses full 30-inch steps until he steps off the diving board and drops three meters into the pool. Once he surfaces, he must confidently swim back to the edge of the pool. In another portion of the test, wearing the same uniform, the candidate steps backward into the pool and releases his rubber M16 and LBE while fully submerged. If the candidate surfaces and any part of the weapon or LBE is still touching his body, this is a "NO-GO." Candidates must receive a "GO" in all events in order to receive a "GO" for CWST.

In addition to the water test, candidates endure a 16-mile foot march along with day and night land navigation courses, and 3-mile runs with an obstacle course. They're also trained in hand-to-hand combat, basic combat medical skills, terrain association, demolition, and patrol base, and given a refresher parachute jump.

Potential Rangers then move on to Camp William O. Darby in Georgia for their second phase. Here they begin to work on their combat patrol skills in a squad atmosphere. Patrolling skills include boxing, fieldcraft training, Darby Queen obstacle course, communications, and the basics of warning order/operations order format. Ranger candidates must learn battle drills, ambushes, reconnaissance patrols, close-quarters battle (CQB), air operations, and air assault operations. The last step is a final training mission (FTX), where everything is done as realistically as possible.

In the Mountain Phase, adverse weather, rugged terrain, fatigue, and stress challenge Army Ranger candidates mentally, emotionally, and physically. This is where they further develop their survival skills, learn military mountaineering skills, and hone their leadership and soldier skills. They also train how to work with squads and platoons during combat patrol missions in mountainous environments. Candidates must complete a 200-foot night rappel at Yonah Mountain, followed by two FTXs. Over a four-day period, they perform a variety of missions against a conventionally equipped force. They then work as a platoon over a five-day FTX, where they move across the country over mountains, rugged terrain, ambush vehicles, and communications sites using various means such as air assaults or a grueling ten-mile march.

The Final, or Florida, Phase takes place in a jungle or swamp, where candidates work on crossing rivers and streams, as well as other skills necessary for survival in this unique environment. Candidates continue to develop their combat arms skills and leadership abilities; they can also perform a variety of operations, including air, small boat, ship to shore, and dismounted combat control. After a ten-day grueling FTX that incorporates everything they have learned up to that point, they finish their training by parachuting into Fort Benning in an airborne insertion.

Green Berets

Candidates for Green Beret must score a minimum of 229 points on the Army Physical Fitness Test (APFT), which requires candidates to do a minimum of 49 push-ups in two minutes, 59 sit-ups in two minutes, and 6 chin-ups, as well as run five miles in under forty minutes. They must also be able to meet medical fitness standards. All candidates are given a 50-meter swim assessment, conducted in uniform, during Special Forces Assessment School (SFAS) to determine whether their swimming skills are sufficient to make it through training.

Candidates must first pass a 30-day indoctrination course that allows the Special Forces instructors to ascertain whether or not the soldier has the mental, physical, and emotional stamina to make it through the next phase of training. This also gives the soldier a chance to see if this is truly what he wants. Following this is the Special Forces Qualification Course, which has several phases involving physical training as well as skill acquisition.

Phase One determines a candidate's ability to navigate, operate, and survive in rugged environments day or night. Special skills include land navigation, patrolling, survival air operations, special operations techniques, and small-unit tactics.

Phase Two is geared towards more specialty training, based upon the candidate's unit's needs and the candidate's aptitude toward various skills. There are five categories. SF Detachment Commander [illegible] 20 weeks and teaches candidates how to direct and employ other members of his group and best utilize them. SF Weapons Sergeant (24 weeks) educates candidates in all weapons foreign and domestic, weapons tactics, utilization of anti-armor weapons, indirect fire operations, man-portable air-defense weapons, emplacement of weapons, and how to integrate combined-arms fire control. Engineer Sergeant (24 weeks) combines construction and fortification skills along with demolition and explosives. SF Medical Sergeant (57 weeks) provides advanced medical training in the subjects of trauma management and surgical procedures. SF Communications Sergeant (32 weeks) is where candidates learn about radio theory, radio waves, radio communications, and how to apply this in a combat environment.

Phase Three is a culmination of everything candidates have learned up to this point: special operations, air operations, unconventional warfare, and direct action isolation. The phase consists of 38 days in which they integrate and reinforce specialty and common skills training. Candidates are organized into detachments to practice in a realistic environment, where they are hunted

Marine Corps Physical Fitness Test Points

Points	Pull-Ups	Crunches (within 2 minutes)	3-Mile Run
100	20	100	18:00
99		99	18:10
98		98	18:20
97		97	18:30
96		96	18:40
95	19	95	18:50
94		94	19:00
93		93	19:10
92		92	19:20
91		91	19:30
90	18	90	19:40
89		89	19:50
88		88	20:00
87		87	20:10
86		86	20:20
85	17	85	20:30
84		84	20:40
83		83	20:50
82		82	21:00
81		81	21:10
80	16	80	21:20
79		79	21:30
78		78	21:40
77		77	21:50
76		76	22:00
75	15	75	22:10
74		74	22:20
73		73	22:30
72		72	22:40
71		71	22:50
70	14	70	23:00
69		69	23:10
68		68	23:20
67		67	23:30
66		66	23:40
65	13	65	23:50
64		64	24:00
63		63	24:10
62		62	24:20
61		61	24:30
60	12	60	24:40
59		59	24:50
58		58	25:00
57		57	25:10
56		56	25:20
55	11	55	25:30
54		54	25:40
53		53	25:50
52		52	26:00
51		51	26:10
50	10	50	26:20
49		49	26:30
48		48	26:40
47		47	26:50
46		46	27:00
45	9	45	27:10
44		44	27:20
43		43	27:30
42		42	27:40
41		41	27:50
40	8	40	28:00
39		x	28:10
38		x	28:20
37		x	28:30
36		x	28:40
35	7	x	28:50
34		x	29:00
33		x	29:10
32		x	29:20
31		x	29:30
30	6	x	29:40
29		x	29:50
28		x	30:00
27		x	30:10
26		x	30:20
25	5	x	30:30
24		x	30:40
23		x	30:50
22		x	31:00
21		x	31:10
20	4	x	31:20
19		x	31:30
18		x	31:40
17		x	31:50
16		x	32:00
15	3	x	32:10
14		x	32:20
13		x	32:30
12		x	32:40
11		x	32:50
10		x	33:00

Round up all values (e.g., 18:01 to 18:09 equals 99 points). 300 points is excellent.

and attack live targets to simulate live missions they will encounter as a member of a Special Forces unit.

Marine Force Recon

After a Marine finishes School of Infantry, he is assigned to an eight-week Basic Recon Course (BRC). Recruits acquire all the skills necessary to operate in a basic reconnaissance environment. Once he has completed BRC, he proceeds to the eight-week Combatant Dive Course, which includes open- and closed-circuit scuba diving, dive laws and physics, underwater searches, and medicine. Upon successful completion of dive school, he advances to Army Airborne Jump School. In this three-week program, new Recon members learn the basics of static line jumping (static line means that the chute automatically opens up as the soldier leaves the plane or helicopter) and get their initial five jumps under their belts. From this point, the Recon can attend many advanced schools such as Freefall, Army Ranger School, Applied Explosives Course, and Helicopter Rope Suspension Training (HRST).

Before soldiers can apply for Marine Force Recon, they must obtain a first-class score (300 points or more) on the Marine Corps Physical Fitness Test (page 14).

Navy SEALs

SEALs are known to have the toughest military training in the world. What sets the SEALs apart from other military outfits is the fact that their entrance training begins and ends in one place: BUD/S (Basic Underwater Demolition/SEAL School) in San Diego, CA. (Many elite groups receive their training in various locations at various times.) From day one, SEAL wannabes must survive the rigors of acquiring their skills while resisting the on-going pressure from instructors to quit—this creates a scenario where only the best make it through BUD/S. The first phase of training (two months) is very physical, with running, swimming, obstacle courses, physical training (PT) sessions, and daily hammer sessions (wherein instructors push students out of their comfort zones using surf torture, intense exercise, and other team-building drills). SEALs candidates are also introduced to hydro-reconnaissance, stealth, and concealment. It's better known for its infamous Hell Week, when candidates undergo daily training without a wink of sleep. The second phase is the Dive Phase (two months), followed by another two months in the third phase, Land Warfare. Keep in mind that it's not always the strongest and fastest that make it through, but rather the mentally robust. Once the third phase is completed, candidates continue with one month at Parachute Jump School and six months in advanced sea, air, and land training.

Navy SEAL Physical Screening Test Requirements

- Swim 500 yards within 12:30 minutes.
- Rest 10 minutes.
- Do 42 push-ups within 2 minutes.
- Rest 2 minutes.
- Do 50 sit-ups within 2 minutes.
- Rest 2 minutes.
- Do 6 pull-ups (no time limit).
- Rest 10 minutes.
- Run 1.5 miles within 11 minutes.

Before they can even be considered for recruitment, Navy SEALs candidates must pass a medical and diving physical examination in addition to completing the Physical Screening Test Requirements.

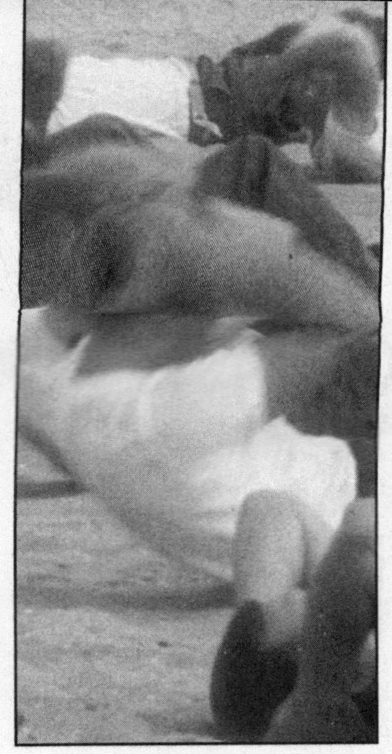

mental attitude

In this book you'll find everything you need to succeed physically, but there's only one thing that will make you successful with this program—attitude! When any elite soldier's physical abilities have been depleted due to the stresses of training, elements of weather, and intense training schedules, he looks deeply within himself for the necessary motivation—failure is not an option for these individual warriors. No heart, no drive, no desire? Go home.

Similarly, you have to go after your objective like a bull out of the gate. New levels of conditioning, strength, and size don't come easy. You'll have to push yourself hard, but the rewards will be amazing. As you change physically and mentally, you'll acquire higher planes of self-confidence, self-esteem, and drive that will cross over into your relationships and career. You only have one body so take care of it and treat it like a temple—once it's gone, you can't replace it.

During a cross-training session with some Marines, our assistant officer of Bravo Platoon was getting fired up and ready to go. Then one of the Marine officers said to him, "Stand down, hard charger." That phrase has stuck with me ever since. I don't want you to stand down—I want you to be a hard charger in every aspect, from mental dedication to physical performance to mental motivation. This is what separates the top notch from the rest. The words "I can't" no longer exist in your vocabulary.

Whether you're a Navy SEAL, Green Beret, Recon, or weekend warrior, you can't live without goals, roadmaps, or motivation. All the motivation in the world won't account for much unless you channel it towards a specific direction or goal. Goals give you a mental destination to focus on while roadmaps show you how to get there. Roadmaps also provide checklists. For example, let's say you want to put on 20 pounds of lean muscle mass. So where do you want to put on this extra weight? Will this require modifying your diet to either gain or lose weight? All this information has to be transferred to paper to make it legit. This checklist covers your diet, exercises (along with reps), and goals, and gives you something to refer to on a daily basis. Nothing brings greater satisfaction than checking off an item on a to-do list. Visual tools such as this are extremely effective in helping you accomplish your goal, so be sure to keep your checklist in a visible place. (You'll find a sample chart on page 20. Make copies to use, or create your own.)

Remember that intelligence plays a major factor in the Special Forces. Physical excellence is just one piece of the puzzle.

before you begin

Before you begin any exercise routine, it is recommended you consult a physician. Find out what your limitations are, if any. A doctor most likely will give you the green light, or he may have you modify something based upon your physical conditioning. Either way, don't let ego get in the way of proper exercising. Stepping into this program intelligently allows your body to benefit and develop the way you want it to.

Equipment

Special Operations incorporate a combination of calisthenics and weight training so that operators have quick-burst strength and energy as well as long-distance or endurance strength that is called upon in many missions. You cannot achieve optimal conditioning with weight training alone; it is not practical and is not always available. In fact, I have operator friends who have never touched weights in their entire lives or stopped after getting into Special Warfare (Spec War). Though numerous soldiers stay in phenomenal shape just by sticking to their own body weight, many say that size and sheer strength cannot be achieved without weights. I know that ever since I strapped on a 50-pound weight vest from weightvest.com and performed push-ups, pull-ups, and dips with it, my training regimens were never the same again.

As far as *Special Ops Fitness Training*, access to a pull-up bar and dip bar is helpful, but you can also use the monkey bars at your local park. You'll just need to be a little creative.

Injury Prevention

Nothing is more heart wrenching when you're training hard than encountering an injury. In many cases the injury could have been prevented. Although some people say that you don't need to stretch prior to exercising, I disagree and strongly encourage warm-ups and stretching. This does not mean bending over, touching the ground, and saying, "Ahh, that feels good. Let's exercise."

It's important to get the blood flowing into the muscle groups you are going to work, which is where warm-up comes into play. Do not neglect this aspect of your training. Remember, warm up first to get blood flowing into your muscles, then stretch. Your stretching routines should be no less than ten minutes per session.

In many cases there is confusion when it comes to how far you should push yourself when stretching. Whether you're stretching or exercising, there's a distinction between pain and discomfort. Too many people will begin to stretch and stop as soon as they feel just the slightest bit of tightness. The ideal stretch is to go to the point of discomfort, bordering on low-intensity pain, and holding it for a couple of seconds. This discomfort will generally last for ten seconds before it begins to dissipate.

If you have severe lower back pain, consult a doctor to understand the extent of your pain and what your capabilities are. If your lower back is simply tight, however, you will want to stretch out your calves, hamstrings, and glutes, in addition to your lower back.

When it comes to your joints, it's important to listen to your body. Know when to push it and know when to back off. Once again, do not let your ego get in the way. I have seen people push their bodies too hard because they think they're still 21 years old, or they think that after not working out for a couple of years they can start off right where they left off. So put your ego aside and take things slow. This will be your greatest prevention of injuries that you could ever apply.

Get to know your range of motion. For example, when you're working through your pull-up exercises, go slow in the downward movements. Always remember, when it comes to the speed of exercises, use the same speed going up as the same speed going down. Maintain consistency, whether you've moving forward, back, up, or down.

"Smooth is fast" is what we were taught in the SEAL teams. The reasoning behind it was that when we went too fast, our technique went out the door. So we focused on proper technique and pushed the envelope as hard as we could, as long as technique was not broken. This same principle would be applied to exercises. There really is no benefit in doing exercises as fast as you can. Your technique will suffer and you're opening yourself up to injury. Remember to consider the range of motion when it comes to your joints. I guarantee that when you perform your exercise at too fast a pace, you will push the limits of your range of motion. Is it worth it to get those extra reps and make the exercise easier yet spend two to six weeks out with torn ligaments?

The Core of the Matter

The key to a well-conditioned warrior is his core. Without a strong core we are useless. A strong core does not mean only having great upper abs, but rather the upper abs, lower abs, obliques, lower back, and glutes. To achieve optimal conditioning, you must hit every region of your core, from every angle possible. This book includes many kinds of abdominal exercises to provide you with the knowledge base to create your own routines. By changing up these exercises, the intensity, the reps, and the routine, you, too, can achieve a Special Forces core. Take what you have learned here and add it to other routines. The growth is unlimited.

GOAL & MEASUREMENT CHARTS

Name ______________________ Body Fat % ____________

Start Date ______________ Start Weight ______________

Every 30 Days Date ____________

Neck ________ Shoulders ________ Chest ________

Waist ________ Thigh ________ Calves ________

Weight (Goal)________ Weight (Current) ________ Body Fat %________ Body Fat (Current)________

Exercise Calisthenics Max

Pull-Ups (Goal) ________ Pull-Ups ________ Sit-Ups (Goal) ________ Sit-Ups ________

Push-Ups (Goal) ________ Push-Ups ________ Lunges (Goal) ________ Lunges ________

Dips (Goal) ________ Dips ________

Free-Weight Exercise Max

Bench (Goal) ________ Bench ________ Curl (Goal) ________ Curl ________

Squat (Goal) ________ Squat ________ Military Press (Goal) ________ Military Press ________

Every 30 Days Date ____________

Neck ________ Shoulders ________ Chest ________

Waist ________ Thigh ________ Calves ________

Weight (Goal)________ Weight (Current) ________ Body Fat %________ Body Fat (Current)________

Exercise Calisthenics Max

Pull-Ups (Goal) ________ Pull-Ups ________ Sit-Ups (Goal) ________ Sit-Ups ________

Push-Ups (Goal) ________ Push-Ups ________ Lunges (Goal) ________ Lunges ________

Dips (Goal) ________ Dips ________

Free-Weight Exercise Max

Bench (Goal) ________ Bench ________ Curl (Goal) ________ Curl ________

Squat (Goal) ________ Squat ________ Military Press (Goal) ________ Military Press ________

GOAL & MEASUREMENT CHARTS

Every 30 Days Date ____________

Neck ____________ Shoulders ____________ Chest ____________

Waist ____________ Thigh ____________ Calves ____________

Weight (Goal) ________ Weight (Current) ________ Body Fat % ________ Body Fat (Current) ________

Exercise Calisthenics Max

Pull-Ups (Goal) ________ Pull-Ups ________ Sit-Ups (Goal) ________ Sit-Ups ________

Push-Ups (Goal) ________ Push-Ups ________ Lunges (Goal) ________ Lunges ________

Dips (Goal) ________ Dips ________

Free-Weight Exercise Max

Bench (Goal) ________ Bench ________ Curl (Goal) ________ Curl ________

Squat (Goal) ________ Squat ________ Military Press (Goal) ________ Military Press ________

Every 30 Days Date ____________

Neck ____________ Shoulders ____________ Chest ____________

Waist ____________ Thigh ____________ Calves ____________

Weight (Goal) ________ Weight (Current) ________ Body Fat % ________ Body Fat (Current) ________

Exercise Calisthenics Max

Pull-Ups (Goal) ________ Pull-Ups ________ Sit-Ups (Goal) ________ Sit-Ups ________

Push-Ups (Goal) ________ Push-Ups ________ Lunges (Goal) ________ Lunges ________

Dips (Goal) ________ Dips ________

Free-Weight Exercise Max

Bench (Goal) ________ Bench ________ Curl (Goal) ________ Curl ________

Squat (Goal) ________ Squat ________ Military Press (Goal) ________ Military Press ________

GOAL & MEASUREMENT CHARTS

Every 30 Days Date ____________________

Neck ____________________ Shoulders ____________________ Chest ____________________

Waist ____________________ Thigh ____________________ Calves ____________________

Weight (Goal) __________ Weight (Current) __________ Body Fat % __________ Body Fat (Current) __________

Exercise Calisthenics Max

Pull-Ups (Goal) __________ Pull-Ups __________ Sit-Ups (Goal) __________ Sit-Ups __________

Push-Ups (Goal) __________ Push-Ups __________ Lunges (Goal) __________ Lunges __________

Dips (Goal) __________ Dips __________

Free-Weight Exercise Max

Bench (Goal) __________ Bench __________ Curl (Goal) __________ Curl __________

Squat (Goal) __________ Squat __________ Military Press (Goal) __________ Military Press __________

Before & After Photos

BEFORE

AFTER

part 2:

the workouts

how to use this book

Special Ops Fitness Training will provide you with a complete lifestyle change. The workout routines in this section will help you achieve optimal performance and conditioning, whether you're trying to maintain a certain conditioning level, lose weight, gain muscle, or take your performance to a professional level. Take the routines that I have developed for you and combine them with the workout charts on pages 20–22 to create your own fitness journals.

I recommend performing any of the three Special Ops Routines (pages 28–39) Monday, Wednesday, and Friday for at least 12 solid weeks; the one day of rest in between each workout allows your muscle fibers to build and repair themselves. Each Special Ops Routine takes about 45 to 60 minutes to complete, depending on skill and conditioning. If you don't have that much time in a day to devote to exercise, you can break up the routines into upper body and lower body sessions and alternate them. In this case, you'd do lower body and abs on Monday, upper body on Tuesday, lower body and abs on Wednesday, upper body on Thursday, lower body and abs on Friday, and upper body on Saturday. In addition to doing these routines on their own, you can also combine them with other exercises or incorporate the appropriate Alternative Workout (pages 50–52).

After at least 12 weeks, you can break up the program by utilizing any of the five individual branch programs. Switching up the routines you do will make it very difficult for your body to plateau, which means it can only get stronger in order to keep up with your demands.

Focusing is a major factor in peak performance. Many times I'll watch a client work out and catch him looking off in one direction then another—right in the middle of his rep. That same person then attempts to complete six pull-ups but wants to quit at number four. That's when I make him choose a spot on the wall or ceiling, depending on the position of his body. He takes that spot and looks at it like a site on a gun. When he sees that object in perfect focus and everything else goes blurry, he's ready to perform his exercise. Try it—the difference it makes in your training will be significant.

Stretching

Stretching is one of the most neglected categories in any exercise routine. Whether you're a Navy SEAL, Green Beret, Army Ranger, Recon, or PJ, you will need incredible flexibility so make sure to stretch after every workout and take your time. This does not mean getting into position, going to the point of discomfort, and then releasing it. The key to stretching is to go to the point of discomfort then wait until that discomfort dissipates. Proper breathing is another important part of stretching. Once you reach the point of discomfort, take a deep breath and exhale slowly and audibly; try to relax every fiber in the muscle you are stretching. Another key point to effective stretching is not to bounce. This does not help you to get the most out of your stretch routine; in some cases it can even cause injury.

Increase the effectiveness of your stretching routine by spending a good five to ten minutes doing so at the end of your routine. Remember that your greatest gains in flexibility occur post-workout. You might also consider spending 60 to 90 seconds stretching the specific muscles you just worked out. For example, if I'm performing push-ups, I'll do chest stretches after the third set or at the peak of my pyramid. I seem to be able to push myself a little harder afterwards while alleviating the stress on the muscle at the same time.

Abdominal stretches should be performed every third abs exercise. This helps prevent the muscles in your stomach from tightening up. Perform the Cobra Stretch (page 75) when exercising your upper, middle, and oblique muscles. Lower Back Stretch (page 78) is excellent for loosening up your lower back; it can also be used to alleviate lower back strain if you enlist a partner to help you stretch.

When it comes to your back, always take extra care. I have been in two major car accidents. Add to that the stresses that Special Ops can play on your body and my back can act up. If it were not for these exercises and stretches I could be in a lot of pain. I have also noticed that if I back off of my training for a certain period of time, my back can act up. Therefore, if you have back problems, seek permission from your doctor before performing these exercises. Once again, take your

TAKING IT OUTSIDE

If you want to apply physical fitness in a more practical environment or if you wish to help your body adapt to the rigors of a Special Ops mission, then find a local park that has monkey bars, an obstacle course, a ropes course, or a physical fitness course. This kind of equipment will allow your body to experience muscle exertion under higher stress levels. There's nothing like running a mile and then performing push-ups and pull-ups, or maneuvering a monkey bar. If you come across a log while doing a long-distance run, increase your hand-eye coordination by running down it. Hopping over obstacles and hurdles can greatly enhance your quick-burst muscle. When it comes down to it, you must be well-rounded if you expect to succeed. If you want to train like the Special Forces, then train for the unexpected.

VISUALIZATION

Sometimes if you have difficulty getting your muscles to exercise and perform at their optimum level, try visualizing. For example, when I perform a Behind-the-Neck Pull-Up, I picture just my inner back and back muscles working. I visualize perfect form before and while I do my exercise. You'll soon see improvement in your technique.

time when it comes to stretching and take advantage of the lower back stretch.

Special Ops Exercises & Free Weights

Navy SEALs have always joked about heavy body builders as having useless muscles. If you're going to incorporate weights into your routine, then be smart about it and create useful muscles. It means nothing if you have incredible strength for 30 to 60 seconds. I want you to have incredible strength that will last for 30 minutes to whatever it takes to get the job done. That's why I've included the Alternative Workout (pages 50–52).

To get the most out of your weigh training while maximizing your calisthenics, I've laid out a complete routine that combines the best calisthenics and free weights exercise for optimum results. It's generally best to do a related calisthenics exercises at the end of your weights exercises. For example, start on a flat bench to work the chest and triceps. Next, move on to butterflies with either dumbbells or the butterfly machine. Your chest is now primed to maximize a push-up routine (the calisthenics).

Routine Cycling

No matter what kind of shape you're in and regardless of how successful your existing exercise program may be, your body's natural reaction to any intense training program is to get bored over a certain period of time and plateau, adjusting to the workload and making it easier to perform. Your body is an amazing instrument, and it's smart. It has a survival mechanism and its first priority is to protect itself from stress and strain. For this reason, I lay out the Alternative Workout routine over a three-day period. The example below shows which body parts to work each week. Unlike calisthenics, which require one day of rest, weightlifting routines need two to three days' rest between body parts.

By rotating your workout patterns, *Special Ops Fitness Training* creates an environment in which you're able to confuse your body and keep it in a state of shock. Take this book and grow, adapt, and expand. This may be the greatest exercise routine you've ever experienced.

Pyramid & Burnout

For about six weeks, perform the routines as laid out. The next six weeks, you may pyramid: for instance, doing 4 reps/rest/6 reps/rest/8 reps/rest/6 reps/rest/4 reps. You may start to peak as the reps get higher; this is when you should reduce the number of reps, which helps you keep good form as your body gets tired.

Before your body gets used to the pyramid, perhaps the week after, you might incorpo-

WEEK ONE	
MONDAY	Chest / Triceps
TUESDAY	Legs / Biceps
WEDNESDAY	Shoulders / Back
THURSDAY	Chest / Triceps
FRIDAY	Legs / Biceps

WEEK TWO	
MONDAY	Shoulders / Back
TUESDAY	Chest / Triceps
WEDNESDAY	Legs / Biceps
THURSDAY	Shoulders / Back
FRIDAY	Chest / Triceps

rate burnouts, where you go as hard as you can for as long as you can during one exercise. When you have nothing left, switch to the next exercise and burn out on this one. Burnout won't take as long as other routines but they leave you even more exhausted. Never perform burnouts over an extended period of time. If you do need to perform burnouts, do them several days in a row but then go back to another routine. You don't want to make yourself prone to injury. Burnouts have a tendency to stress the muscle groups dramatically and you'll need a certain period of time to repair.

As you can see, there are many ways to keep the body guessing. With this manual, you'll have sufficient routines and exercises to keep you going for a very long time.

SPECIAL OPS ROUTINE 1

WARM-UP	p. 56	Jumping Jacks	1 x 30 secs
	p. 57	Half Jumping Jacks	1 x 30 secs
	p. 58	Iron Mikes	1 x 30 secs
STRETCHES	p. 65	V Stretch	1 x 30 secs
	p. 60	Upper Back Stretch	1 x 30 secs
	p. 78	Partner-Assisted Lower Back Stretch	1 x 30 secs each side
	p. 68	Hamstring Stretch	1 x 30 secs
	p. 69	Trunk Stretch	1 x 30 secs each side
	p. 70	Groin Stretch	1 x 30 secs each side
	p. 72	Quad Stretch	1 x 30 secs each side
	p. 66	Straight-Leg Stretch	1 x 30 secs
	p. 67	ITB Stretch	1 x 30 secs each side
	p. 62	Tricep Stretch	1 x 30 secs each side
	p. 61	Forearm Stretch	1 x 30 secs each side

SPECIAL OPS ROUTINE 1

STRETCHES	p. 71	Partner Butterfly	1 x 30 secs
	p. 73	Calf Stretch #1	1 x [illegible] secs each side
	p. 75	Cobra Stretch	1 x 30 se[illegible]
	p. 76	Cat Back Stretch	1 x 30 secs
	p. 59	Chest Stretch	1 x 30 secs each side
	p. 63	Partner-Assisted Upper Body Stretch	1 x 30 secs
	p. 64	Side-to-Side Stretch	1 x 30 secs each side
UPPER BODY	p. 80	Pull-Up: Regular	*Set 1:* max reps/*Set 2:* 75% of last set/ *Set 3:* 75% of last set/*Set 4:* 75% of last set
	p. 83	Pull-Up: Behind the Neck	*Set 1:* max reps/*Set 2:* 75% of last set/ *Set 3:* 75% of last set/*Set 4:* 75% of last set
	p. 84	Dip	*Set 1:* max reps/*Set 2:* 75% of last set/ *Set 3:* 75% of last set/*Set 4:* 75% of last set
	p. 85	Push-Up: Regular	*Set 1:* max reps/*Set 2:* 75% of last set/ *Set 3:* 75% of last set/*Set 4:* 75% of last set
	p. 86	Push-Up: Diamond	*Set 1:* max reps/*Set 2:* 75% of last set/ *Set 3:* 75% of last set/*Set 4:* 75% of last set
	p. 87	Push-Up: Ranger Diamond	*Set 1:* max reps/*Set 2:* 75% of last set/ *Set 3:* 75% of last set/*Set 4:* 75% of last set
	p. 88	Push-Up: Triple Sets	*Set 1:* max reps/*Set 2:* 75% of last set/ *Set 3:* 75% of last set/*Set 4:* 75% of last set

SPECIAL OPS ROUTINE 1

UPPER	p. 90	Push-Up: Elevated	max reps at each position
	p. 85	(Optional) Partner-Assisted Push-Up	4 x max reps
	p. 92	Eight-Count Body Builders	*Set 1:* 60 secs/*Set 2:* 45 secs/ *Set 3:* 30 secs/*Set 4:* 15 secs
LOWER BODY	p. 94	Walking Lunge	*Set 1:* 50 yards at medium pace (timed)/ *Set 2:* 50 yards 15 secs faster/*Set 3:* 50 yards 10 secs faster
	p. 97	Wall Sit	10 minutes
	p. 95	Frog Hop	3 x 50 yards
	p. 96	Star Hop	3 x 20 reps
	p. 102	Ruck Sack March (to be done after leg routine or abs workout)	6 miles
ABDOMINALS	p. 116	Fly My Airplane	*Set 1:* 60 secs/*Set 2:* 45 secs/*Set 3:* 30 secs
	p. 101	Bench Back Exercise	*Set 1:* 60 secs/*Set 2:* 45 secs/*Set 3:* 30 secs
	p. 104	Hand to Toes	1 x 60 reps
	p. 106	Ranger Crunch	1 x 60 reps
	p. 105	X Sit-Up	1 x 60 reps
	p. 107	Supine Bicycle	1 x 60 reps

SPECIAL OPS ROUTINE 1

ABDOMINALS

Page	Exercise	Sets x Reps
p.108	Hibberty Jibberty	1 x 60 reps
p. 109	Cross Crunch	1 x 60 reps
p. 112	Sky Hop	1 x 60 reps
p. 111	Flutter Kick	1 x [illegible] reps
p. 113	Lower Ab Crunch	1 x 60 reps
p. 114	Scissor Lift	1 x 60 reps
p. 115	(Optional) Bench Sit-Up	1 x 60 reps

SPECIAL OPS ROUTINE 2

WARM-UP	p. 56	Jumping Jacks	1 x 30 secs
	p. 57	Half Jumping Jacks	1 x 30 secs
	p. 58	Iron Mikes	1 x 30 secs
STRETCHES	p. 65	V Stretch	1 x 30 secs each side
	p. 60	Upper Back Stretch	1 x 30 secs
	p. 77	Partner-Assisted Lower Back Twist	1 x 30 secs each side
	p. 68	Hamstring Stretch	1 x 30 secs
	p. 69	Trunk Stretch	1 x 30 secs each side
	p. 70	Groin Stretch	1 x 30 secs each side
	p. 72	Quad Stretch	1 x 30 secs each side
	p. 66	Straight-Leg Stretch	1 x 30 secs
	p. 67	ITB Stretch	1 x 30 secs each side
	p. 62	Tricep Stretch	1 x 30 secs each side
	p. 61	Forearm Stretch	1 x 30 secs each side

SPECIAL OPS ROUTINE 2

STRETCHES	p. 71	Partner Butterfly	1 x 30 secs
STRETCHES	p. 74	Calf Stretch #2	1 x 30 secs each side
STRETCHES	p. 75	Cobra Stretch	1 x 30 secs
STRETCHES	p. 76	Cat Back Stretch	1 x 30 secs
STRETCHES	p. 63	Partner-Assisted Chest Stretch	1 x 30 secs each side
STRETCHES	p. 63	Partner-Assisted Upper Body Stretch	1 x 30 secs
STRETCHES	p. 64	Side-to-Side Stretch	1 x 30 secs each side
UPPER BODY	p. 80	Pull-Up: Regular	8–10–12–14–16–14–12–10–8
UPPER BODY	p. 83	Pull-Up: Behind the Neck	4–6–8–10–8–6–4
UPPER BODY	p. 84	Dip	4 x 25 reps
UPPER BODY	p. 85	Push-Up: Regular	12–14–16–18–20–22–24–26–24–22–20–18–16–14–12
UPPER BODY	p. 86	Push-Up: Diamond	8–10–12–14–16–14–12–10–8
UPPER BODY	p. 87	Push-Up: Ranger Diamond	4 x 10 reps
UPPER BODY	p. 88	Push-Up: Triple Sets	4 x 20 wide, 15 regular, 10 diamond

SPECIAL OPS ROUTINE 2

UPPER	p. 90	Push-Up: Elevated	*Position 1:* 20 reps/*Position 2:* 25 reps/ *Position 3:* 30 reps
UPPER	p. 85	(Optional) Partner-Assisted Push-Up	*Set 1:* 60 secs/*Set 2:* 45 secs/ *Set 3:* 30 secs/*Set 4:* 15 secs
LOWER BODY	p. 92	Eight-Count Body Builders	*Set 1:* 20 reps/*Set 2:* 15 reps/ *Set 3:* 10 reps/*Set 4:* 5 reps
LOWER BODY	p. 94	Walking Lunge	*Set 1:* 50 yards 40 lbs/*Set 2:* 50 yards 30 lbs/ *Set 3:* 50 yards 20 lbs
LOWER BODY	p. 97	Wall Sit	10 minutes
LOWER BODY	p. 95	Frog Hop	3 x 50 yards
LOWER BODY	p. 96	Star Hop	3 x 20 reps
LOWER BODY	p. 102	Ruck Sack March (to be performed after your leg routine or abs workout)	6 miles
ABDOMINALS	p. 116	Fly My Airplane	*Set 1:* 60 secs/*Set 2:* 45 secs/ *Set 3:* 30 secs
ABDOMINALS	p. 101	Bench Back Exercise	*Set 1:* 60 secs/*Set 2:* 45 secs/ *Set 3:* 30 secs
ABDOMINALS	p. 104	Hand to Toes	1 x 60 reps
ABDOMINALS	p. 106	Ranger Crunch	1 x 60 reps
ABDOMINALS	p. 105	X Sit-Up	1 x 60 reps
ABDOMINALS	p. 107	Supine Bicycle	1 x 60 reps

SPECIAL OPS ROUTINE 2

ABDOMINALS

p. 108	Hibberty Jibberty	1 x 60 reps
p. 109	Cross Crunch	1 x 60 reps
p. 112	Sky Hop	1 x 60 reps
p. 111	Flutter Kick	1 x 60 reps
p. 113	Lower Ab Crunch	1 x 60 reps
p. 114	Scissor Lift	1 x 60 reps
p. 115	(Optional) Bench Sit-Up	1 x 60 reps

SPECIAL OPS ROUTINE 3

WARM-UP	p. 56	Jumping Jacks	1 x 30 secs
	p. 57	Half Jumping Jacks	1 x 30 secs
	p. 58	Iron Mikes	1 x 30 secs
STRETCHES	p. 65	V Stretch	1 x 30 secs each side
	p. 60	Upper Back Stretch	1 x 30 secs
	p. 78	Partner-Assisted Lower Back Stretch	1 x 30 secs each side
	p. 68	Hamstring Stretch	1 x 30 secs
	p. 69	Trunk Stretch	1 x 30 secs each side
	p. 70	Groin Stretch	1 x 30 secs each side
	p. 72	Quad Stretch	1 x 30 secs each side
	p. 66	Straight-Leg Stretch	1 x 30 secs
	p. 67	ITB Stretch	1 x 30 secs each side
	p. 62	Tricep Stretch	1 x 30 secs each side
	p. 61	Forearm Stretch	1 x 30 secs each side

SPECIAL OPS ROUTINE 3

STRETCHES	p. 71	Partner Butterfly	1 x 30 secs
	p. 73	Calf Stretch #1	1 x 30 secs each side
	p. 75	Cobra Stretch	1 x 30 secs
	p. 76	Cat Back Stretch	1 x 30 secs
	p. 59	Chest Stretch	1 x 30 secs each side
	p. 63	Partner-Assisted Upper Body Stretch	1 x 30 secs
	p. 64	Side-to-Side Stretch	1 x 30 secs each side
UPPER BODY	p. 80	Pull-Up: Regular	*Set 1:* 60 secs/*Set 2:* 45 secs/ *Set 3:* 30 secs/*Set 4:* 15 secs (contraction)
	p. 83	Pull-Up: Behind the Neck	*Set 1:* 60 secs/*Set 2:* 45 secs/ *Set 3:* 30 secs/*Set 4:* 15 secs (contraction)
	p. 84	Dip	*Set 1:* 60 secs/*Set 2:* 45 secs/ *Set 3:* 30 secs/*Set 4:* 15 secs (contraction)
	p. 85	Push-Up: Regular	*Set 1:* 60 secs/*Set 2:* 45 secs/ *Set 3:* 30 secs/*Set 4:* 15 secs (contraction)
	p. 86	Push-Up: Diamond	*Set 1:* 60 secs/*Set 2:* 45 secs/ *Set 3:* 30 secs/*Set 4:* 15 secs (contraction)
	p. 87	Push-Up: Ranger Diamond	*Set 1:* 60 secs/*Set 2:* 45 secs/ *Set 3:* 30 secs/*Set 4:* 15 secs (contraction)
	p. 88	Push-Up: Triple Sets	*Sets 1–3:* 20 secs wide, 15 secs regular/10 secs diamond/ *Set 4:* same as Sets 1–3, but all with contraction

SPECIAL OPS ROUTINE 3

UPPER	p. 90	Push-Up: Elevated	*Position 1:* 60 secs/*Position 2:* 45 secs/ *Position 3:* 30 secs
	p.85	(Optional) Partner-Assisted Push-Up	*Set 1:* 60 secs/*Set 2:* 45 secs/ *Set 3:* 30 secs
LOWER BODY	p. 92	Eight-Count Body Builders	*Set 1:* 60 secs/*Set 2:* 45 secs/ *Set 3:* 30 secs/*Set 4:* 15 secs
	p. 94	Walking Lunge	*Set 1:* 50 yards medium pace (timed)/ *Set 2:* 50 yards 15 secs faster/*Set 3:* 50 yards 10 secs faster
	p. 97	Wall Sit	10 minutes
	p. 95	Frog Hop	*Set 1:* 60 secs/*Set 2:* 45 secs/ *Set 3:* 30 secs
	p. 96	Star Hop	*Set 1:* 45 secs/*Set 2:* 30 secs/ *Set 3:* 15 secs
	p. 102	Ruck Sack March (to be performed after your leg routine or abs workout)	6 miles
ABDOMINALS	p. 116	Fly My Airplane	*Set 1:* 60 secs/*Set 2:* 45 secs/ *Set 3:* 30 secs
	p. 101	Bench Back Exercise	*Set 1:* 60 secs/*Set 2:* 45 secs/ *Set 3:* 30 secs
	p. 104	Hand to Toes	1 x 60 secs
	p. 106	Ranger Crunch	1 x 60 secs
	p. 105	X Sit-Up	1 x 60 secs
	p. 107	Supine Bicycle	1 x 60 secs

SPECIAL OPS ROUTINE 3

ABDOMINALS

p. 108	Hibberty Jibberty	1 x 60 secs
p. 109	Cross Crunch	1 x 60 secs
p. 112	Sky Hop	1 x 60 secs
p. 111	Flutter Kick	1 x 60 secs
p. 113	Lower Ab Crunch	1 x 60 secs
p. 114	Scissor Lift	1 x 60 secs
p. 115	(Optional) Bench Sit-Up	1 x 60 secs

AIR FORCE PARARESCUE

Air Force PJs may be required to haul their objective out of enemy territory. This requires excellent upper body strength and good leg endurance for the long haul. At the same time, PJs require a lot of quick-burst muscles to get in and out fast.

Page	Exercise	Sets/Reps
p. 56	Jumping Jacks	1 x 60 secs
p. 57	Half Jumping Jacks	1 x 60 secs
pp. 59–79	Stretches	1 x 30 secs each
p. 80	Pull-Up: Regular	*Set 1:* 60 secs/*Set 2:* 45 secs/ *Set 3:* 30 secs/*Set 4:* 15 secs
p. 84	Dip	4 x 25 reps
p. 85	Push-Up: Regular	*Set 1:* 100 reps/*Set 2:* 30 secs burn-out/ *Set 3:* 20 (4 count)
p. 86	Push-Up: Diamond	*Set 1:* 30 reps/*Set 2:* 30 secs burn-out/ *Set 3:* 15 (4 count)
p. 88	Push-Up: Triple Sets	30 secs burn-out at each position
p. 94	Walking Lunges	4 x 45 secs as fast as you can

CARDIO

- Monday 3-mile run
- Wednesday 1-mile swim (freestyle)
- Friday 3-mile run

AIR FORCE PARARESCUE

The following are all performed in burn-out mode—as many as you can in 30 seconds

p. 104	Hand to Toes	1 x 30 secs
p. 105	X Sit-Up	1 x 30 secs
p. 108	Hibberty Jibberty	1 x 30 secs
p. 109	Cross Crunch	1 x 30 secs
p. 110	Obliques	1 x 30 secs
p. 112	Sky Hop	1 x 30 secs
p. 113	Lower Ab Crunch	1 x 30 secs
p. 114	Scissor Lift	1 x 30 secs
p. 111	Flutter Kick	1 x 30 secs

ARMY RANGER

Of all the Special Forces, Army Rangers require the highest level of endurance due to their missions involving deep enemy territory penetration. They must have high levels of strength in all parts of their body, but especially in their legs.

Page	Exercise	Sets/Reps
p. 56	Jumping Jacks	1 x 60 secs
p. 58	Iron Mikes	1 x 60 secs
pp 59–79	Stretches	1 x 30 secs each
p. 80	Pull-Up: Regular	*Set 1:* 10 reps/*Set 2:* 8 reps/ *Set 3:* 6 reps/*Set 4:* 4 reps
p. 84	Dip	*Set 1:* 25 reps/*Set 2:* 20 reps/ *Set 3:* 15 reps/*Set 4:* 10 reps
p. 85	Push-Up: Regular	4 x 20 reps (4 count)
p. 87	Push-Up: Ranger Diamond	4 x 20 reps
p. 92	Eight-Count Body Builders	4 x 90 secs
p. 94	Walking Lunge	4 x 90 secs

CARDIO

- Monday 10-mile Ruck Sack March
- Wednesday 3-mile run
- Friday 15-mile Ruck Sack March

ARMY RANGER

The following are all performed in a controlled pace—do as many as you can with perfect technique.

p. 105	X Sit-Up	1 x 60 secs
p. 106	Ranger Crunch	1 x 60 secs
p. 108	Hibberty Jibberty	1 x 60 secs
p. 109	Cross Crunch	1 x 60 secs
p. 112	Sky Hop	1 x 60 secs
p. 113	Lower Ab Crunch	1 x 60 secs
p. 114	Scissor Lift	1 x 60 secs

GREEN BERET

Green Beret/Delta Force require high levels of strength and endurance.

Page	Exercise	Sets/Reps
p. 56	Jumping Jacks	1 x 60 secs
p. 58	Iron Mikes	1 x 60 secs
pp 59–79	Stretches	1 x 30 secs each
p. 80	Pull-Up: Regular	*Set 1:* Burn-out/*Sets 2–7:* 8 reps
p. 84	Dip	4 x 15 reps
p. 85	Push-Up: Regular	1 x 20 reps (5 count)
p. 87	Push-Up: Ranger Diamond	4 x 20 reps
p. 88	Push-Up: Triple Sets	1 x 20 reps
p. 92	Eight-Count Body Builders	1 x 30 reps
p. 94	Lunges (Standing—step left, step right = 1 rep)	1 x 100 reps

CARDIO
- Monday 3-mile run
- Wednesday 15-mile Ruck Sack March
- Friday 3-mile run

GREEN BERET

The following are performed with 20 seconds of rest in between each set.

Page	Exercise	Sets x Reps
p. 104	Hand to Toes	1 x 65 reps
p. 106	Ranger Crunch	1 x 65 reps
p. 108	Hibberty Jibberty	1 x 65 reps
p. 109	Cross Crunch	1 x 65 reps
p. 112	Sky Hop	1 x 65 reps
p. 113	Lower Ab Crunch	1 x 65 reps
p. 114	Scissor Lift	1 x 65 reps

MARINE FORCE RECON

The operators in Marine Special Forces units (Marine Special Operations Command, or MARSOC) have similar requirements as SEALs.

Page	Exercise	Sets/Reps
p. 56	Jumping Jacks	1 x 60 secs
p. 57	Half Jumping Jacks	1 x 60 secs
pp. 59–79	Stretches	1 x 30 secs each
p. 80	Pull-Up: Regular	*Set 1:* 30 reps/*Set 2:* 25 reps/ *Set 3:* 20 reps/*Set 4:* 15 reps
p. 82	Pull-Up: Close Grip	*Set 1:* 20 reps/*Set 2:* 15 reps/*Set 3:* 10 reps
p. 83	Pull-Up: Behind the Neck	*Set 1:* 15 reps/*Set 2:* 10 reps/*Set 3:* 5 reps
p. 84	Dip	4 x 25 reps
p. 85	Push-Up: Regular	*Set 1:* 100 reps/*Set 2:* 75 reps/ *Set 3:* 50 reps/*Set 4:* 25 reps
p. 86	Push-Up: Diamond	*Set 1:* 25 reps/*Set 2:* 20 reps/ *Set 3:* 15 reps/*Set 4:* 10 reps
p. 92	Eight-Count Body Builders	4 x 15 reps
p. 94	Walking Lunge	4 x 50 yards

CARDIO

- Monday 3-mile run
- Wednesday 1-mile swim (freestyle)
- Friday 1-mile interval sprints (sprint on straightaway and jog the corners)

MARINE FORCE RECON

p. 104	Hand to Toes	1 x 65 reps
p. 105	X Sit-Up	1 x 65 reps
p. 106	Ranger Crunch	1 x 65 reps
p.108	Hibberty Jibberty	1 x 65 reps
p.110	Obliques	1 x 65 reps
p. 113	Lower Ab Crunch	1 x 65 reps
p. 111	Flutter Kicks	1 x 45 reps (4 count)

NAVY SEAL

SEALs need quick-burst energy but sometimes have to swim up to three hours at a time. High levels of upper body strength could be needed at any given moment. Combine this workout with the other workouts provided in this book and there is no excuse for not being ready physically for BUD/S.

Page	Exercise	Sets/Reps
p. 56	Jumping Jacks	1 x 60 secs
p. 57	Half Jumping Jacks	1 x 60 secs
pp. 59–79	Stretches	1 x 30 secs each
p. 80	Pull-Up: Regular	*Set 1:* 30 reps/*Set 2:* 25 reps/ *Set 3:* 20 reps/*Set 4:* 15 reps
p. 82	Pull-Up: Close Grip	*Set 1:* 20 reps/*Set 2:* 15 reps/*Set 3:* 10 reps
p. 83	Pull-Up: Behind the Neck	*Set 1:* 15 reps/*Set 2:* 10 reps/*Set 3:* 5 reps
p. 84	Dip	4 x 25 reps
p. 85	Push-Up: Regular	*Set 1:* 100 reps/*Set 2:* 75 reps/ *Set 3:* 50 reps/*Set 4:* 25 reps
p. 86	Push-Up: Diamond	*Set 1:* 25 reps/*Set 2:* 20 reps/ *Set 3:* 15 reps/*Set 4:* 10 reps
p. 92	Eight-Count Body Builders	4 x 15 reps
p. 94	Walking Lunge	4 x 50 yards

CARDIO

- Monday 3-mile run
- Wednesday 1-mile swim (freestyle)
- Friday 1-mile interval sprints (sprint on straightaway and jog the corners)

NAVY SEAL

NAVY SEAL

	p. 104	Hand to Toes	1 x 65 reps
	p. 105	X Sit-Up	1 x 65 reps
	p. 106	Ranger Crunch	1 x 65 reps
	p. 108	Hibberty Jibberty	1 x 65 reps
	p. 110	Obliques	1 x 65 reps
	p. 113	Lower Ab Crunch	1 x 65 reps
	p. 111	Flutter Kick	1 x 45 reps (4 count)

ALTERNATIVE WORKOUT: WEIGHT-TRAINING PROGRAM

MONDAY—Chest & Triceps		
p. 117	Bench Press	4 x 8 reps (75–80% of max)
p. 118	Dumbbell Fly	4 x 8 reps (75–80% of max)
p. 85	Weight Vest Push-Up	*Set 1:* max reps/*Set 2:* 10 less/ *Set 3:* 5 less/*Set 4:* same
p. 119	Triceps Pull-Down	4 x 8 reps (75–80% of max)
p. 120	Skull Crusher	4 x 8 reps (75–80% of max)
p. 86	Push-Up: Diamond	*Set 1:* 20 reps/*Set 2:* 15 reps/ *Set 3:* 10 reps/*Set 4:* 10 reps
TUESDAY—Legs & Biceps		
p. 127	Weighted Lunge	3 x 50 yards
p. 97	Wall Sit	3 mins (10-min goal)
p. 98	Calf Raise: Regular	1 x 45 secs
p. 99	Calf Raise: Toe to Toe	1 x 45 secs
p. 100	Calf Raise: Heel to Heel	1 x 45 secs
p. 95	Frog Hop	3 x 50 yards

ALTERNATIVE WORKOUT: WEIGHT-TRAINING PROGRAM

Page	Exercise	Sets/Reps
p. 128	Preacher Curl	4 x 8 reps (75–80% of max)
p. 129	Seated Dumbbell Curl	4 x 8 reps (75–80% of max)
p. 130	Curl Bar—Inner Grip	4 x 8 reps (75–80% of max)

WEDNESDAY–Shoulders & Back

Page	Exercise	Sets/Reps
p. 80	Pull-Up: Regular	8-10-12-14-12-10-8
p. 82	Pull-Up: Close Grip	6-8-10-8-6
p. 83	Pull-Up: Behind the Neck	2-4-6-4-2
p. 122	Lat Pull-Down	3 x 8 reps (75–80% of max)
p. 123	Military Press	3 x 8 reps (75–80% of max)
p. 125	Shoulder Raise	3 x 8 reps (75–80% of max)
p. 124	Shoulder Rotation	3 x 8 reps (75–80% of max)

THURSDAY—Chest & Triceps

Page	Exercise	Sets/Reps
p. 117	Bench Press (Super Sets)	*Set 1:* 80% of max/*Set 2:* take off 20 lbs/ *Set 3:* take off 20 lbs/*Set 4:* take off 20 lbs (no rest between sets)
p. 118	Dumbbell Fly (Super Sets)	*Set 1:* 80% of max/*Set 2:* take off 20 lbs/ *Set 3:* take off 20 lbs/*Set 4:* take off 20 lbs (no rest between sets)
p. 85	Weight Vest Push-Up (Super Sets)	*Set 1:* max reps in full vest/*Set 2–n:* take 1 weight out of front & back each set and perform max reps until vest is empty

ALTERNATIVE WORKOUT: WEIGHT-TRAINING PROGRAM

p. 84	Dip	4 x 15–20 reps
p. 120	Skull Crusher (Super Sets)	4 x 8–10 reps
p. 121	Triceps Kickback	4 x 8 reps
p. 119	Triceps Pull-Downs	4 x 8–10 reps
p. 86	Push-Up: Diamond	1 x to failure
	FRIDAY—Legs & Biceps	
p. 127	Weighted Lunge	3 x 50 yards
p. 97	Wall Sit	3 mins (10-min goal)
p. 98	Calf Raise: Regular	1 x 45 secs
p. 99	Calf Raise: Toe to Toe	1 x 45 secs
p. 100	Calf Raise: Heel to Heel	1 x 45 secs
p. 95	Frog Hop	3 x 50 yards
p. 128	Preacher Curl	4 x 8 reps (75–80% of max)
p. 129	Seated Dumbbell Curl	4 x 8 reps (75–80% of max)
p. 130	Curl Bar—Inner Grip	4 x 8 reps (75–80% of max)

Every 30 Days Date ______________________

Neck ______________________ Shoulders ____________________ Chest ______________________

Waist ______________________ Thigh ______________________ Calves ______________________

Weight (Goal) __________ Weight (Current) ________ Body Fat % ________ Body Fat (Current) ________

Exercise Calisthenics Max

Pull-Ups (Goal) ____________ Pull-Ups __________ Sit-Ups (Goal) __________ Sit-Ups __________

Push-Ups (Goal) ___________ Push-Ups _________ Lunges (Goal) __________ Lunges __________

Dips (Goal) __________ Dips _______________

Free-Weight Exercise Max

Bench (Goal) ______________ Bench ___________ Curl (Goal) ____________ Curl ___________

Squat (Goal) _________ Squat ________ Military Press (Goal) _________ Military Press ___________

Every 30 Days Date ______________________

Neck ______________________ Shoulders ____________________ Chest ______________________

Waist ______________________ Thigh ______________________ Calves ______________________

Weight (Goal) ________ Weight (Current) ________ Body Fat % ________ Body Fat (Current) ________

Exercise Calisthenics Max

Pull-Ups (Goal) ____________ Pull-Ups __________ Sit-Ups (Goal) __________ Sit-Ups __________

Push-Ups (Goal) ___________ Push-Ups _________ Lunges (Goal) __________ Lunges __________

Dips (Goal) __________ Dips _______________

Free-Weight Exercise Max

Bench (Goal) ______________ Bench ___________ Curl (Goal) ____________ Curl ___________

Squat (Goal) _________ Squat ________ Military Press (Goal) _________ Military Press ___________

part 3:

the exercises

jumping jacks

There's nothing fancy about Jumping Jacks. They're a great vehicle to get the blood pumping through our muscle groups without dramatic strain to the muscle fibers. All Special Operation branches utilize this warm-up.

STARTING POSITION: Stand with your feet together, keeping a slight bend in your knees. Place your hands by your sides and look straight ahead.

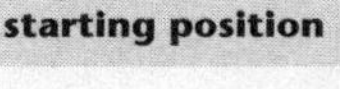

1 With a light thrust upward, open your feet past the width of your shoulders. At the same time, raise your hands and touch them lightly above your head. Do not cheat yourself by not touching your hands.

2 Return to starting position, making sure not to slap yourself when your hands return to your hips.

TIP

You do not have to jump very high to perform a perfect jumping jack.

half jumping jacks

Half Jumping Jacks are a quicker-paced modification of Jumping Jacks to help get the blood flowing. The main differences are that your arms do not go above your shoulders and your pace is two to three times the regular speed. Keep in mind that if you pick up the pace you still must maintain good technique.

STARTING POSITION: Stand with your feet together, keeping a slight bend in your knees. Place your hands by your sides and look straight ahead.

starting position

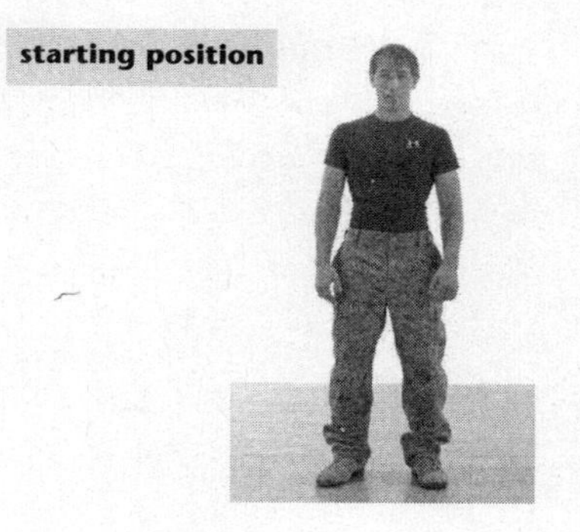

1

2

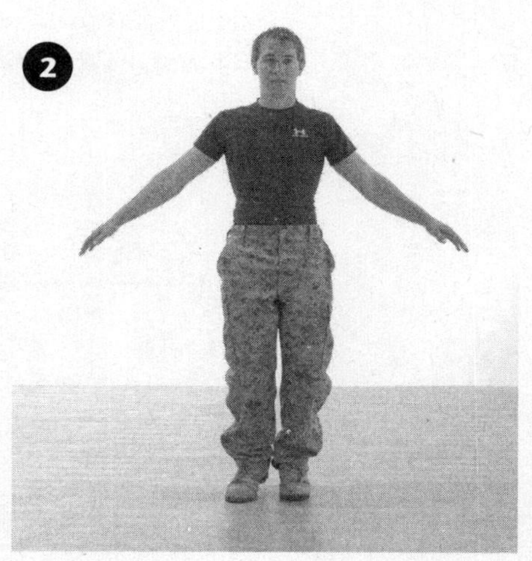

1 With a light spring, open your feet a little past shoulder width while raising your arms to shoulder height.

2 Immediately bring your arms and legs back together to starting position.

iron mikes

Iron Mikes are identical to lunges and are utilized by the Army Rangers as a warm-up. Although I prefer lower-impact exercises for warm-ups, Iron Mikes are a great leg exercise. Iron Mikes are a four-count exercise (e.g., 1-2-3-1, 1-2-3-2), and I highly recommend taking this exercise slow to make sure that when you step out, you don't let your knees go past the front of your toes.

STARTING POSITION: Stand with your feet parallel and place your hands on your hips. Look straight ahead.

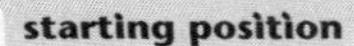

starting position

1

2

1 Step straight forward with your left foot, trying not to come down too hard or too fast. Maintain a straight back and keep looking straight ahead. Do not take too large or too short of a step: If you take too short of a step, your knee will go past your toes; if you take too long of a step, you put added stress on your legs for a warm-up.

2 Return to starting position and step forward with your right leg. Remember to step forward and not back.

> **TIP**
> Try not to look down at your feet as this will cause your shoulders to lean forward. I recommend practicing in front of a mirror to watch your form.

chest stretch

Special Operations relies a lot on the chest. If you don't stretch out your chest, you could end up pulling a muscle, which can affect your entire upper-body routine. Keep in mind that your chest can tighten up during any exercise routine so restretch as you feel necessary.

STARTING POSITION: Stand with your left side to a sturdy, tall object (wall, doorframe), about one foot away, and place your left hand on the object so that it's behind your shoulder and one to two feet above. Make sure your arm is locked straight.

starting position

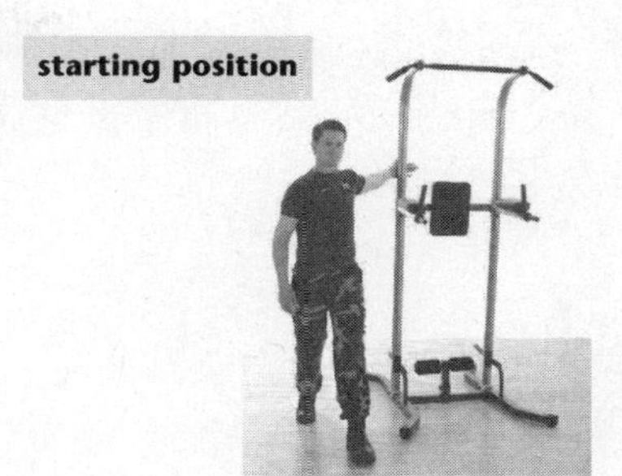

1 Step your left foot 1–2 feet forward.

2 Bend your left knee and drop down while pressing forward until you feel the stretch in your chest.

3 Gently release and switch sides.

TIP
Experiment by dropping more forward or downward to get the best stretch. At the same time, you can also adjust your hand position up or down.

upper back stretch

STARTING POSITION: Stand with your feet about hip-width apart. Interlock your fingers in front of you with your palms facing in.

starting position

1 Facing your palms outward, drive your hands forward until your arms are locked straight. Hold and maintain this position for at least 10 seconds. As you finish this stretch, take a deep breath and let your shoulders roll forward. This will allow you to further relax and get the most out of this stretch.

TIP
For better balance, you can widen your stance.

forearm stretch

You will be surprised how much your forearm can tighten up during exercise, especially during pull-ups. This is a simple stretch but well worth it.

STARTING POSITION: Stand with your feet shoulder-width apart.

starting position

1 Extend your right hand in front of you and point your fingers straight up. Keep your arm as straight as possible.

2 Grasp your right fingers with your left hand and slowly pull your fingers and hand towards you.

triceps stretch

Triceps are essential in your upper body workouts so take the time to stretch them out to prevent injury. Do not rush this stretch which not only hits your triceps but also the entire side of your back and core; you need to completely relax your back and shoulders while stretching your triceps.

STARTING POSITION: Stand with your feet wider than shoulder-width apart. Adjust the width of your stance to get the most out of this stretch

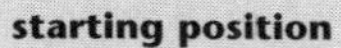

starting position

1 Reach your right hand over your head and touch your upper spine. Place your left hand on your right elbow.

2 Slowly lean to your left, continuously applying pressure to your right elbow. Go to the point of discomfort but not pain; do not twist your upper body.

3 Slowly return to starting position and switch sides.

partner-assisted upper body stretch

upper and lower back, core, chest, shoulders

With the assistance of a partner, you can stretch out your upper and lower back while your partner stretches his core, chest, and shoulders at the same time. It is important to take your time on this stretch and lift each other slowly. Pay attention to each other's commands.

STARTING POSITION: Stand back to back and interlock your arms at the elbows. Keep your feet shoulder-width apart for balance.

starting position

1

2

1 Slowly bend forward to lift your partner's feet just a foot or two off the ground. Don't bend too far forward, which will cause your partner's weight to ride high on your upper body.

2 Return to starting position and switch roles.

TIP
Instead of just interlocking your arms, you can also grab your hands to secure this position even better.

partner-assisted chest stretch

chest, shoulders

This is a great stretch but requires slow movements and relaxation.

STARTING POSITION: *Stand with your feet wider than hip-width apart and raise your arms until they're about shoulder height. Your partner stands behind you with one leg forward and one leg back for balance. He then grabs both of your wrists from underneath for more control.*

starting position

1

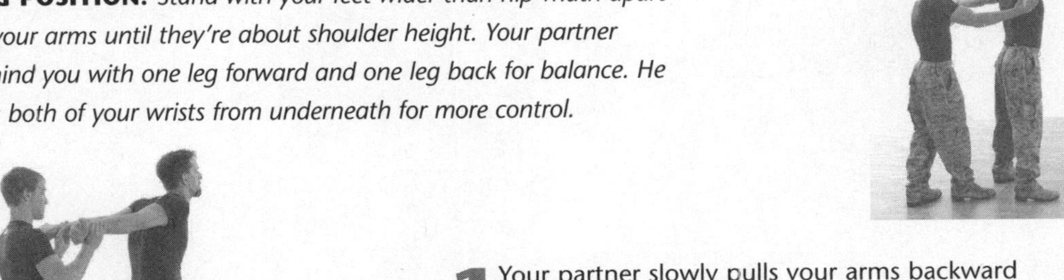

1 Your partner slowly pulls your arms backward while maintaining them at shoulder height. Tell your partner when you get close to your peak—go to the point of discomfort but not to the point of pain.

Return to starting position and switch roles.

side-to-side stretch

STARTING POSITION: Stand with your feet wider than shoulder-width apart.

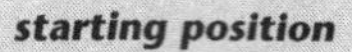

starting position

1 Place your left hand on your left hip and reach your right hand over your head. Keep your right arm a foot or two above your head with a slight bend in your elbow.

2 Lean to your left while maintaining your right hand above your head; keep driving with this arm. Do not rotate your hip during this movement.

3 Return to starting position and switch sides.

v stretch

STARTING POSITION: Sit on the floor with your legs extended in front of you and your feet a foot or two wider than shoulder width. Sit up tall, bending your knees slightly if necessary to release any tension in your back and knees.

starting position

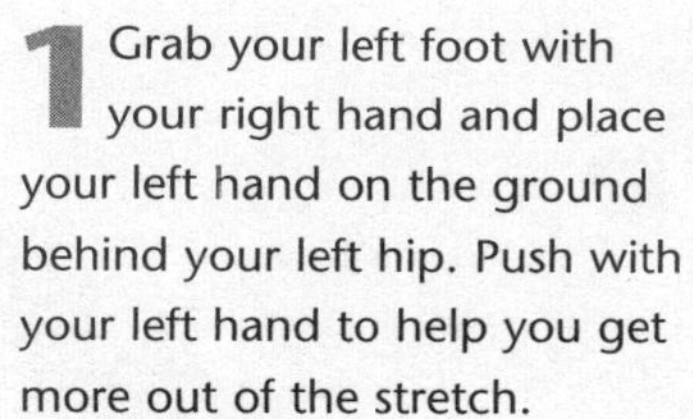

1 Grab your left foot with your right hand and place your left hand on the ground behind your left hip. Push with your left hand to help you get more out of the stretch.

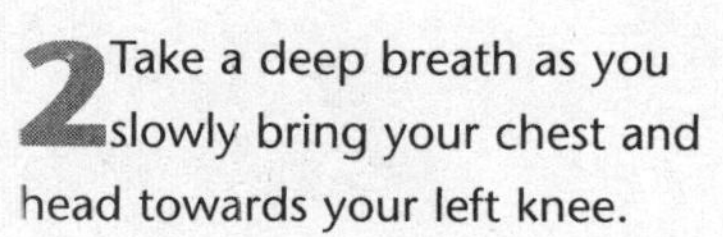

2 Take a deep breath as you slowly bring your chest and head towards your left knee.

3 Slowly return to starting position and switch sides.

straight-leg stretch

Straight-leg stretches are a great transition from V stretches (page 65).

STARTING POSITION: Sit on the floor with your legs together and extended in front of you. Bend your knees slightly.

starting position

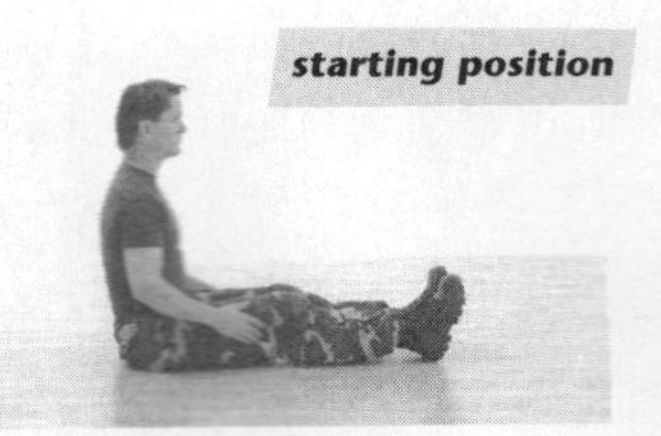

1 Grab your toes with your fingers and relax your entire upper body. This will allow you to stretch your hamstrings better.

2 Bring your chest and head toward your knees.

TIP

As you become more flexible, walk your fingers down the bottom of your shoes or place your hands over the tops of your feet. Eventually your fingertips will hit the floor near the base of your heels.

ITB stretch

If you have a tight lower back, you need to stretch more than just your lower back muscles. Even though the iliotibial band (ITB) is a good place to start, you'll still need to target your hamstrings and calves. This version allows you to get more leverage.

STARTING POSITION: Sit on the floor with your legs straight out in front of you.

starting position

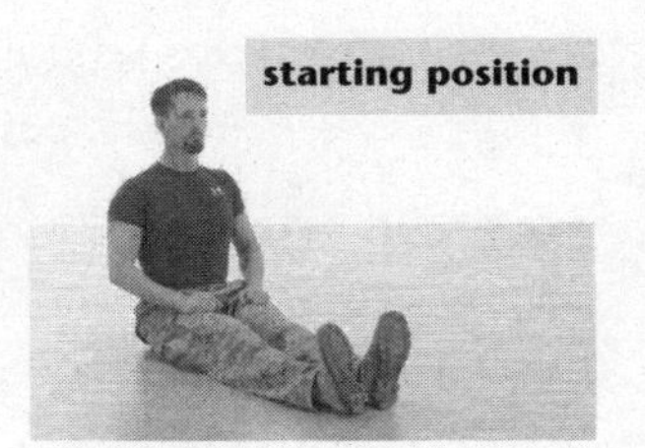

1

2

3

1 Place your right foot on the outside of your left knee. Wrap your arms around your right knee; you can also grab your right elbow with your left hand for leverage. Apply pressure by squeezing your leg to your chest. Don't be afraid to put a good squeeze on your leg. The glute muscle is very resilient and needs a lot of pressure to loosen up.

2 Slowly release and place your left arm on the outside of your right knee while locking your arm straight. Place your right arm behind your right hip. Now look over your right shoulder as you apply pressure to your right leg with your left arm. Rotate your right shoulder to the right until you feel tension in the lower back. Hold this position until the tension releases. Take a deep breath to get your lower back to stretch a little more.

3 Return to starting position and switch sides.

MODIFICATION FOR TENDER KNEE
Place your left hand on your right ankle and place your right hand on your left knee. Squeeze with even pressure while lifting the right foot off the ground.

hamstring stretch

Rangers utilize a three-part hamstring stretch and top it off by stretching the calves. Your hand position helps you maintain control.

STARTING POSITION: Sit on the floor with your legs straight out in front of you, keeping a slight bend in your knees. Place one hand beneath each leg. Take a deep breath and relax your entire upper body and legs. Slowly lower your chin down towards your thighs.

starting position

1

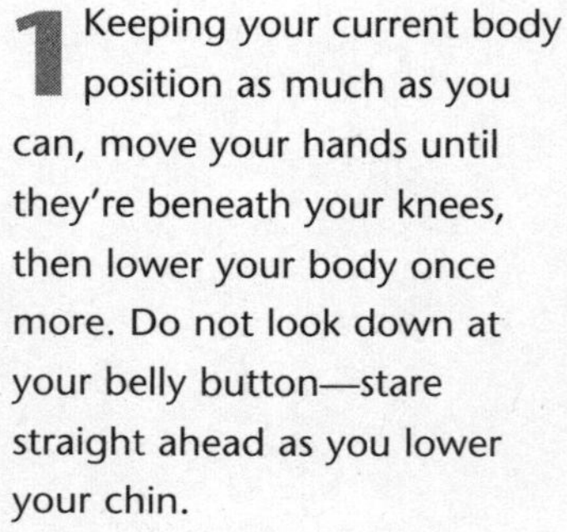

1 Keeping your current body position as much as you can, move your hands until they're beneath your knees, then lower your body once more. Do not look down at your belly button—stare straight ahead as you lower your chin.

2 Release the pressure slightly and move your hands until they're beneath your lower calves. Lower your head towards your knees and let your gaze fall to your knees. If possible, grab your toes and pull them towards you.

2

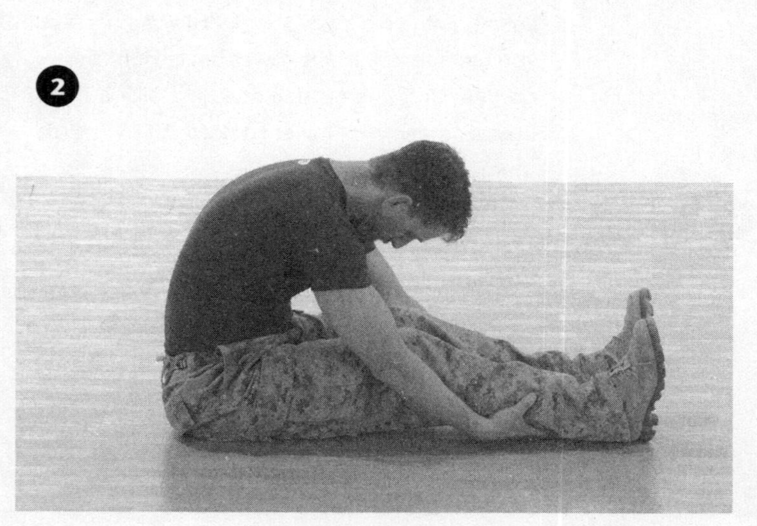

trunk stretch

Proper breathing will definitely enhance your stretch. So remember to take a deep breath and let it out slowly after you have reached the peak of your stretch. This will allow you to go a little further.

STARTING POSITION: Lie on your back with your legs extended along the floor and your arms by your sides.

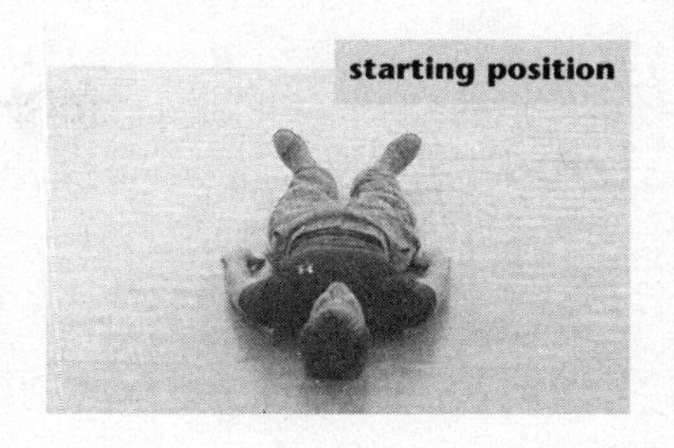
starting position

1 Cross your left leg to your right side, extending your arms into a "T" position. Keep both shoulders on the ground.

Once you have reached and maintained your peak position during the stretch, switch sides.

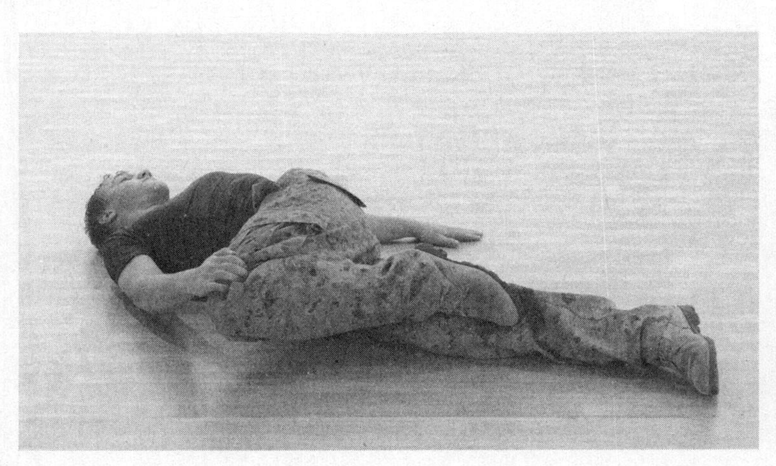

MODIFICATION
This can also be done with a bent leg by placing your left foot on the inside of your right knee and then pulling your left knee to your right by using your right hand.

groin stretch

There is nothing worse than a pulled groin so take advantage of this stretch and do it as often as you can. The key to groin stretches is taking your time dropping into position and raising up and out of the down position.

STARTING POSITION: Stand with your feet one to two feet wider than shoulder width. Make sure both feet are pointing straight ahead.

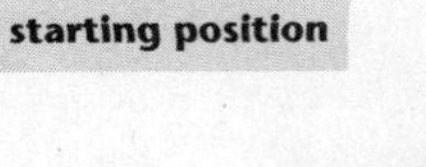

1 Bend your left knee and place your left elbow on that knee; lean to your left. Once you reach the point where your right foot wants to lift off the ground, lower your hips until you feel discomfort but not pain. Keep your back straight and look forward.

2 Slowly return to starting position and switch sides.

TIPS

- Do not sit down too much—it is not necessary to sit all the way down on your heel.
- Keep both feet flat on the ground.

partner-assisted butterfly stretch

STARTING POSITION: Sit with the bottoms of your feet pressed together with your hands on your shoelaces.

starting position

1 Press your elbows into your inner knees.

2 From behind, your partner begins to slowly, lightly push forward and down on your lower shoulder blades.

quad stretch

STARTING POSITION: Stand with your feet shoulder-width apart.

starting position

1 Grab your left foot with your right hand. Keep your back straight and look straight ahead.

2 Slowly raise your left foot up towards your lower middle back. Take a deep breath, let it out slowly, then apply a little more pressure.

Slowly return to starting position and switch sides.

TIP
Keep your abs tight to maintain a straight torso while you stretch.

VARIATION
For an additional stretch, once you begin to feel pressure as you're raising your foot, slowly bend over and try to lift your knee higher than your hip. You can use a chair for support.

calf stretch #1

STARTING POSITION: Place your hands on the floor as if you were going to perform a push-up.

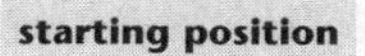

starting position

1 Place the tip of your right foot on top of your left heel.

2 Lower your left heel to the ground by pushing with your legs and walking your hands towards your feet. Try not to raise your butt too high in the air because this will take away from the stretch.

Return to starting position and switch sides.

TIP

If you can touch your heel to the ground but still don't feel the stretch, bend your elbows and lower your chest towards the ground.

calf stretch #2

The key to this stretch is maintaining good balance. Do not place your right and left foot on a single line—allow some distance between the two (width not length).

STARTING POSITION: Stand with your feet shoulder-width apart.

starting position

1

2

1 Step your left leg forward and bend your left thigh 90 degrees; place both hands on your left thigh. Extend your right leg further behind you so that your heel is elevated. You should feel tightness in your calf at this point. Lower your heel until it is flat on the ground. As you do so, bring your hips forward and lower them slightly, keeping your back straight.

2 Switch sides.

TIPS

- Use your forward leg for support but do not put all your balance forward on the leg.
- Try to keep your weight centered over your hips.

cobra stretch

I like to perform this stretch after every three ab exercises.

STARTING POSITION: Lie flat on your front with your hips firmly down and your hands on the floor, slightly wider than your shoulders. Your feet can be together or shoulder-width apart.

starting position

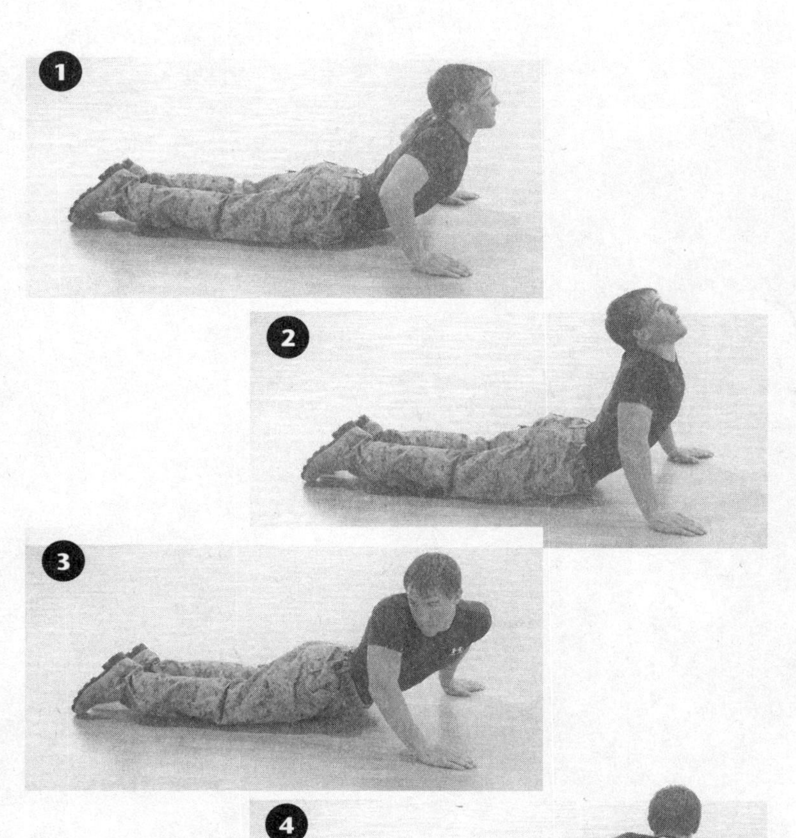

1–2 Slowly raise your upper body by straightening your arms, exhaling at the point of discomfort. Once you have fully extended your arms, you can tilt your head backwards. Begin to shrug your shoulders towards your ears.

3 Lower down halfway and drive your left shoulder to the right. Look over your right shoulder until you see your left foot. Hold this position for a few seconds.

4 Return to center and switch sides.

TIP
Perform the Cat Back Stretch (page 76) after this stretch to really stretch out your core.

cat back stretch

Always perform this stretch right after the Cobra Stretch.

STARTING POSITION: Come to all fours, placing your hands on the floor and your knees shoulder-width apart.

starting position

1

1 Round your back towards the ceiling like a cat, walking your hands slightly inward toward your knees to raise your lower back.

partner-assisted lower back twist

STARTING POSITION: Lie on your back with both legs straight along the floor.

starting position

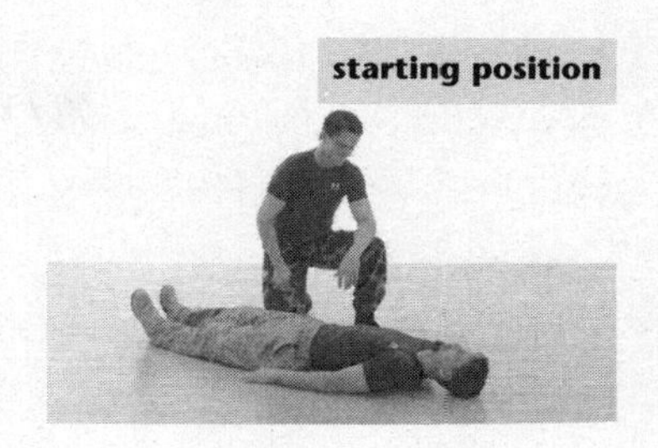

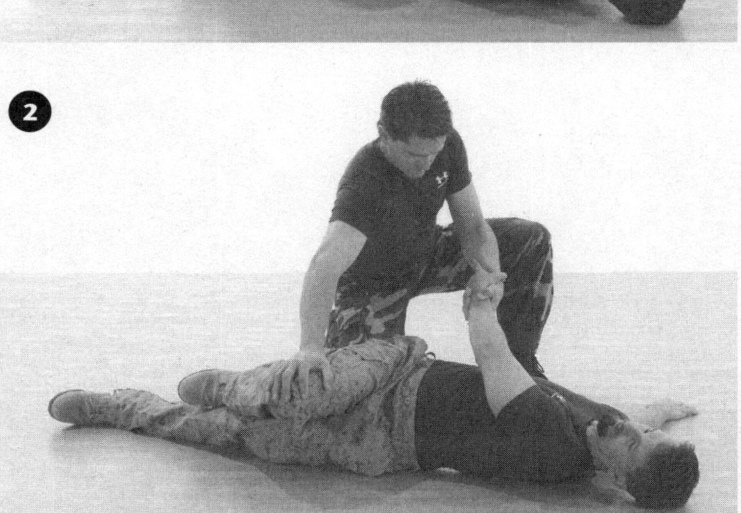

1 Place your right foot on the inside of your left knee. Your partner kneels down behind your right knee and places his right hand on your right knee. At the same time, he grabs your left arm by the wrist while you grab his arm by his wrist.

2 He slowly pulls on your left arm while applying pressure to your right knee. Let him know if he needs to apply more pressure or back off.

partner-assisted lower back stretch

This is one of the best stretches to alleviate lower back pain. Your partner must watch your facial expression to determine that he is taking you to the point of discomfort but not pain.

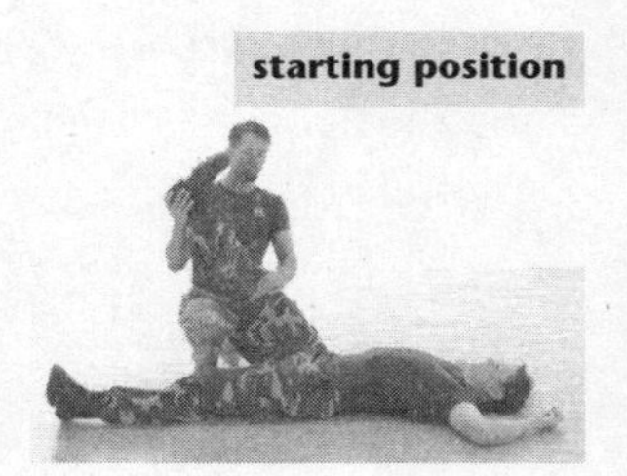
starting position

STARTING POSITION: Lie on your back with both legs straight along the floor. Your partner kneels on your right side and raises your right leg by placing one hand behind your right heel and his other hand on top of your right knee. The key is to elevate your leg without bending it.

1

1 Your partner lifts your leg to the point of discomfort. Hold this position for 3 to 5 seconds.

2 He lowers it down by one foot to relieve the tension. Hold for 3 to 5 seconds.

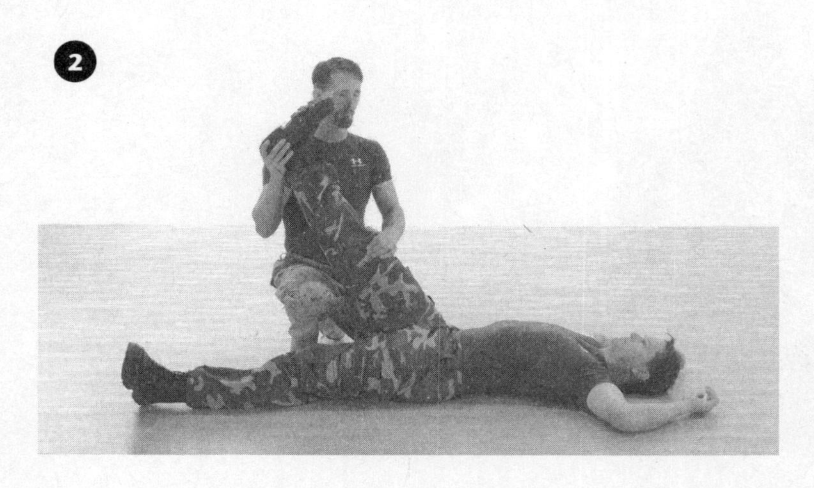
2

3 As he lifts the leg again, inhale deeply and exhale slowly at the point of discomfort. As you exhale, your partner applies just a little more pressure. Repeat three times total.

4 Once he has stretched out your hamstrings and lower back three times, he will lower your leg just six inches. Keeping one hand behind your heel, he places the other hand over the tips of your toes. Maintaining the heel securely, he applies pressure to your toes to stretch your calf.

Switch legs; partner will move to the other side.

3

VARIATION

This can also be done without a partner by looping a strap or towel around your foot.

4

pull-up—regular

Special Ops Spin: Pull-ups are so important that every branch of Special Forces incorporates them into their routines. Navy SEALs must be able to lift themselves up onto enemy ships for ship attacks. When fast-roping out of a helicopter, Force Recon and Green Berets must have the upper body strength to slow down their descent. Army Rangers and PJs must scales walls to rescue hostages or downed pilots.

STARTING POSITION: Place your hands on the bar six inches wider than your shoulders; either tuck your thumbs underneath or wrap them around the bar. Drive your elbows down while keeping your chest forward. Cross your ankles and bend your knees 90 degrees.

starting position

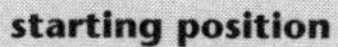

1 Raise your chin to bar level, keeping your abs tight to help maintain a straight back.

2 Lower down slowly to starting position.

1

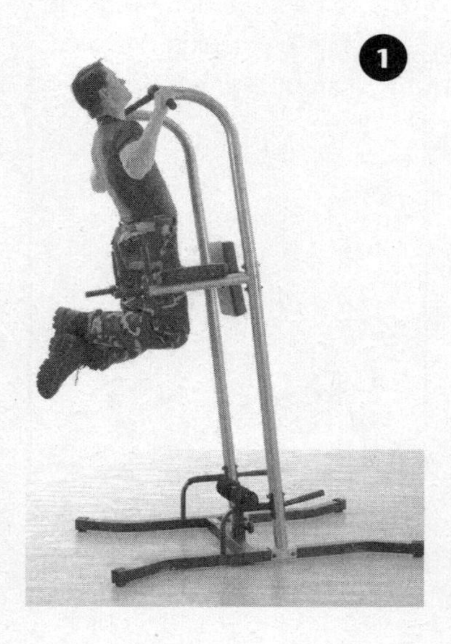

2

TIPS

- If you look in a mirror and see that your arms and hands form a good V, you're in the right position.
- Bending your knees and crossing your ankles keep you from losing proper form while performing a perfect pull-up.
- Do not come down too fast—swinging puts extra pressure on your shoulder joints.
- Make sure not to cheat yourself of excellent back development by doing half pull-ups.

VARIATION—PARTNER ASSIST

Your partner places his left hand beneath your ankle or right on your shoelaces. His right hand grabs the tip of the shoe so that his palm rests against the sole of the shoe. He now lays his forearm and elbow against his right thigh, allowing the leg to bear the brunt of the pressure. You will push into him when you perform the pull-ups—if he has proper form, this will not be a strain for him.

VARIATION—CHAIR ASSIST

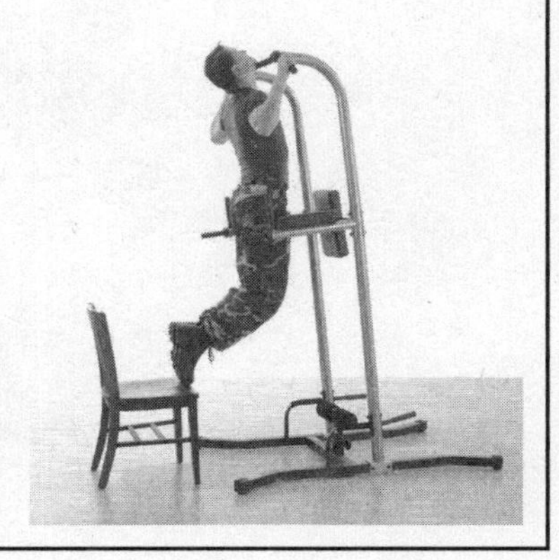

The most difficult part about chair assist is trying not to rely too much on your legs. If your arms are not shaking by your second-to-last rep, you are using your legs too much.

#1 Cross your ankles and place the ball of your lower foot on the chair. To perform the pull-up, use your thigh muscles to drive your body upward while contracting your back muscles.

#2 Place your feet together on the chair and drive off the ball of your feet, using your thigh muscles to assist in the pull-up. Keep your abs tight to prevent your back from bowing.

pull-up—close grip

Special Ops Spin: Special Ops operators use the shoulder blades, forearms, and triceps in a number of scenarios, including cast and recovery, enemy takedowns, and crawling along the jungle floor.

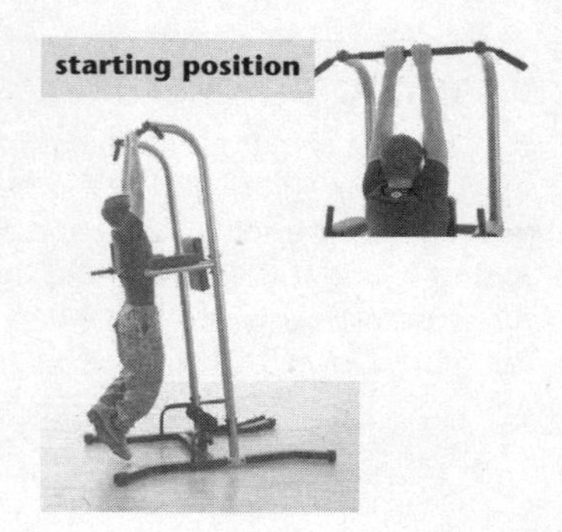

STARTING POSITION: Place your hands on the bar one to two inches apart; either tuck your thumbs underneath or wrap them around the bar. Bring your elbows in tight and maintain this position throughout the movement.

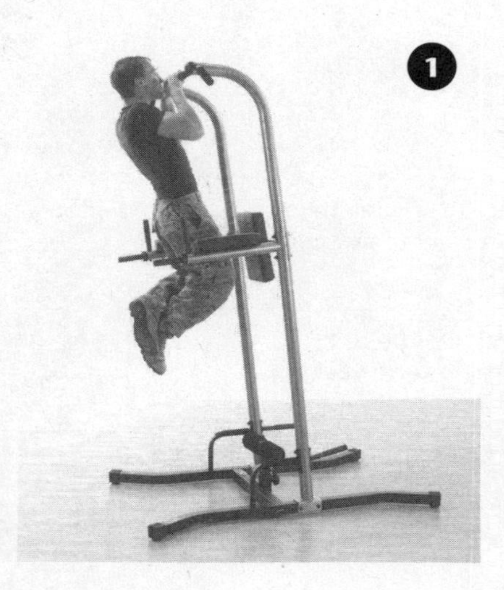

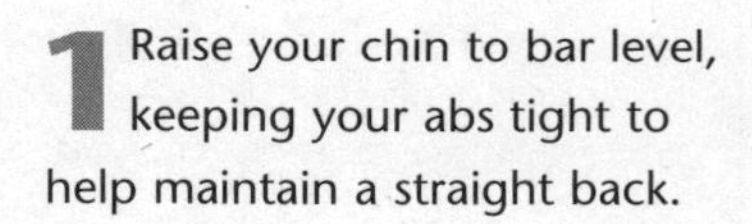

1 Raise your chin to bar level, keeping your abs tight to help maintain a straight back.

2 Slowly lower down to starting position.

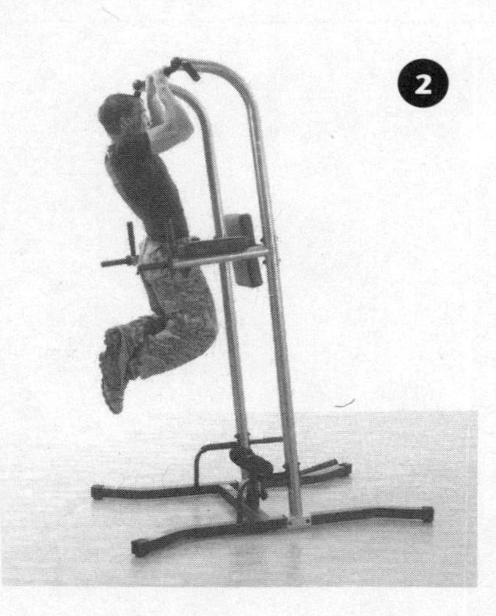

pull-up—behind the neck

Special Ops Spin: The inner back and shoulder blade muscles play a key role in any climbing or elevating movement, which is a common activity in Special Operations.

This is also one of the toughest pull-up exercises you'll ever do.

STARTING POSITION: Place your hands on the bar so that they're slightly wider than your regular pull-up grip; either tuck your thumbs underneath or wrap them around the bar. Cross your ankles and bend your knees 90 degrees.

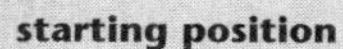

starting position

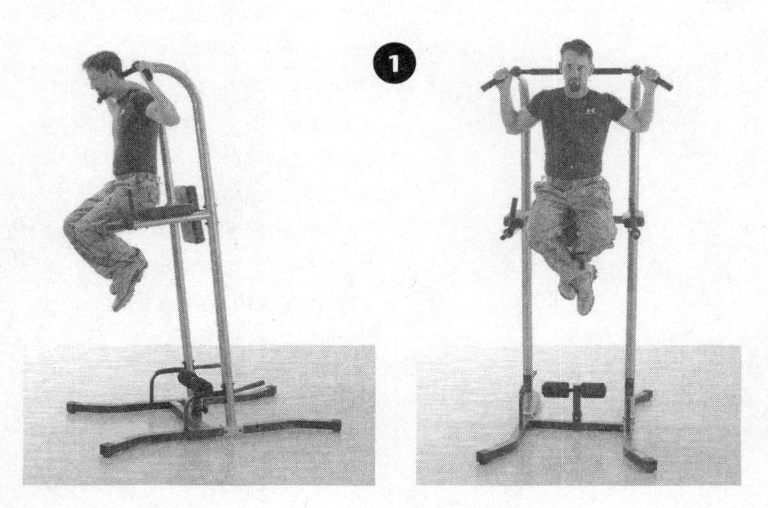

1 With your head tilted slightly forward, raise yourself up until the base of your skull is at bar level. Aim for your hair line and keep your abs tight to help maintain a straight back

2 Slowly lower down to starting position.

TIP

Maintain a smooth, fluid motion throughout the entire movement, both up and down.

dip

Special Ops Spin: During shipboard attacks, the dip movement is a key element when it comes to transitioning from climbing the side of a ship to boarding it. Any movement that would require a soldier to climb a wall or obstacle incorporates similar muscular exertion.

When doing dips, the height from which you drop down is really important. Most people either do not drop low enough or drop too low. The former will not allow you to get the most out of this exercise, and the latter puts too much strain on the shoulders.

starting position

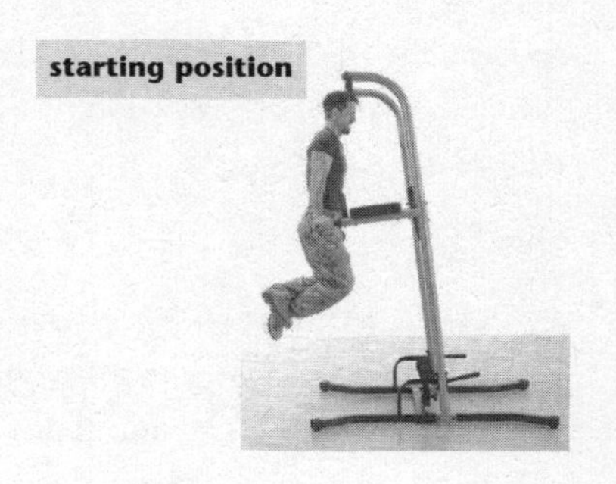

1

2

STARTING POSITION: Place your hands on the bars so that your hands are directly under your shoulders. Keep your shoulders away from your ears. Cross your ankles and keep your abs tight throughout the movement to help keep you from swinging. Look straight ahead and maintain a straight back.

1 Lower yourself at a controlled pace, stopping when your elbows are bent 90 degrees.

2 Apply pressure with your triceps to push yourself back up, stopping once your arms are fully extended.

TIP

- Look in a mirror while you perform this so you can get an idea of the correct dip height.
- Do not position yourself too far back on the bar.

push-up—regular

Special Ops Spin: The military has been utilizing regular push-ups for decades since they're essential for developing the frequently used chest muscles, triceps, and abs. Imagine an operator in the middle of a fire-fight with 80 pounds of gear on his back when someone yells out, "I have an exit!" This operator requires chest and triceps muscles to help him spring to his feet.

starting position

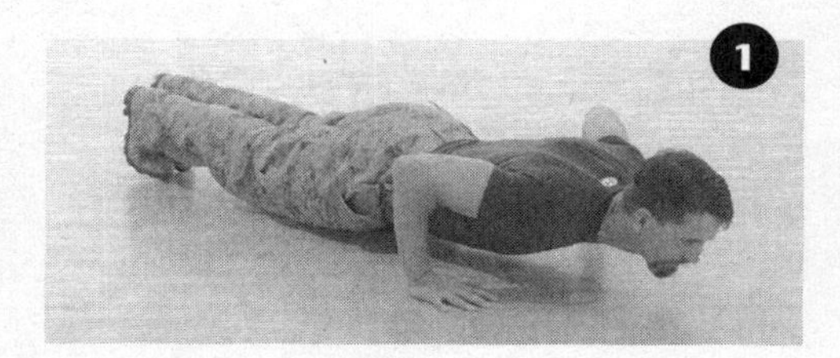

STARTING POSITION: Place your hands on the floor so that they're slightly wider than shoulder width. Your elbows should not flare out past your hands. Place your feet side by side or one foot on top of the other. Maintain a straight line from your shoulders to your feet by keeping your abs tight; do not let your back sag or raise your seat too high in the air. Imagine you have a 2 x 4 down your back.

1 Lower down until your chest is one or two inches from the ground.

2 Press up to starting position.

VARIATION

If you have trouble doing this from your feet, start from your knees until you develop the strength to get off your knees.

VARIATION—PARTNER ASSIST

Keep your abs very tight during this one. Your partner stands in front of you and places one hand on each shoulder blade. As you drop down to the halfway mark, your partner applies medium pressure on your shoulders. Your partner must maintain a consistent level of pressure throughout the exercise; he may even have to ease off if you start to drop, or else yell encouragement. If you run out of strength and drop down to the ground, don't stop. Get back up and last as long as you can. If you fall during the first 15 of 60 seconds, then it just means that you have to keep getting back up for 45 more seconds.

push-up—diamond

Special Ops Spin: Triceps are important in any pushing or pulling movement. Just about every operation will require great strength from this muscle group.

The key to getting the most out of Diamond Push-Ups is hand position. If you have your hands too far forward, you'll feel it more in your shoulders.

STARTING POSITION: Place your hands on the ground and touch your fingers and thumbs together. Extend your legs behind you and place your feet a little wider than shoulder-width apart. Keep your abs tight as you bring your hands just under your lower chest.

starting position

2

1 Lower yourself down to within one inch of the ground—come as close as you can to your sternum with your hands. Let your elbows flare out to hit your triceps harder.

2 Press up to starting position.

> **TIP**
>
> If you get a cramp in your hip, position your feet closer together.

push-up—ranger diamond

Special Ops Spin: Just about every Special Ops mission depends on triceps strength. This is a favorite of the Army Rangers.

Ranger Diamond Push-Ups differ from normal Diamond Push-Ups in that only your thumbs touch; here, your fingers are extended forward and your hand position looks like a U. In addition, your elbows are tucked in instead of flared out.

STARTING POSITION: Place your hands on the ground and touch your thumbs together, letting your fingers extend forward. Your hands should be under your chest. Extend your legs behind you and place your feet together. Keep your abs tight and your elbows close to your sides throughout the movement.

starting position

1 Lower down until you are one or two inches from the ground, making sure your elbows stay in.

2 Press up to starting position.

1

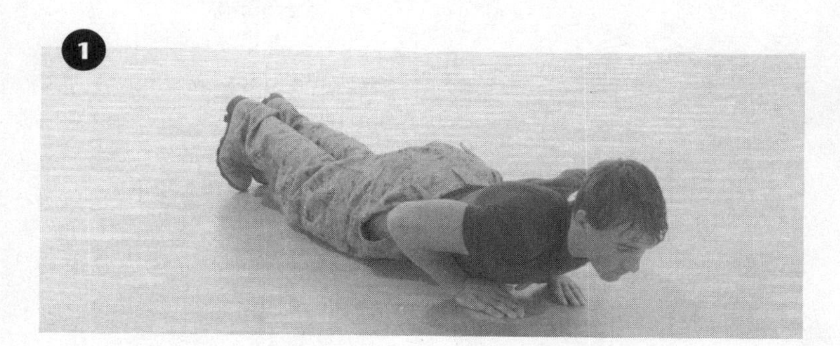

2

push-up—triple sets

This is a combination of wide-angle, regular, and diamond push-ups. You perform each exercise as one rep then move onto the next position. Wide Angle counts as rep 1, Regular as rep 2 and Diamond as rep 3—this completes one cycle or 1-2-3-1, 1-2-3-2, 1-2-3-3, etc.

STARTING POSITION: Place your hands six inches wider than regular push-ups and your legs side by side. Keep your abs tight to maintain a straight back.

starting position

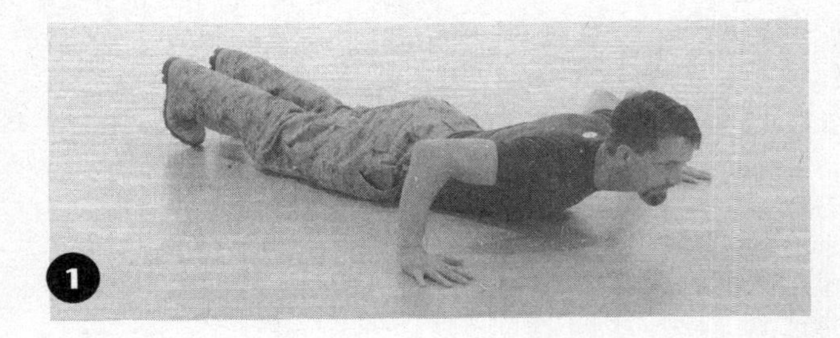

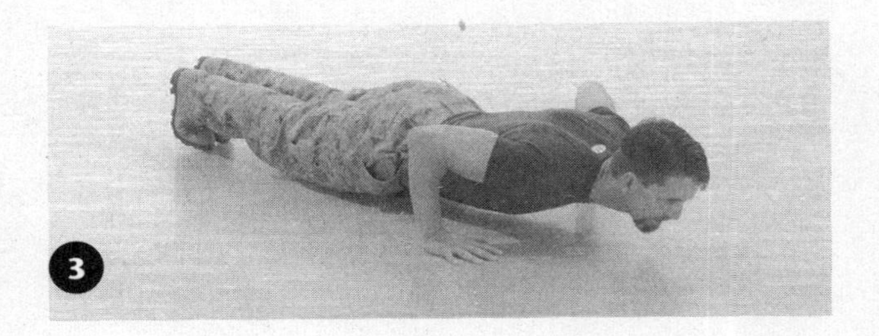

1 From this wide-angle push-up position, drop down until you're one to two inches from the ground.

2 Immediately switch to a regular push-up as you press up, making sure hands are directly to the sides of your shoulders.

3 Lower down until you're one to two inches from the ground.

4 Immediately switch to a diamond push-up as you press up, touching your fingers and thumbs together and moving your feet a little wider than shoulder-width apart. Your hands should be just under your lower chest.

5 Lower yourself down to within one inch of the ground, coming as close as you can to your sternum with your hands. Let your elbows flare out.

6 Press back up to the wide-angle push-up position.

push-up—elevated

Special Ops Spin: Just about every Special Ops mission depends on triceps strength.

This exercise requires strong abs so if you're just beginning, you might want to hold off on this one until you're stronger. Basically, you perform push-ups from three different positions. A chair or bench is good for the top position, and stairs or a crate can work for the middle position. It is very important to maintain tight abs throughout the entire movement to prevent your back from sagging.

starting position

STARTING POSITION: Place your hands in a regular push-up position (hands directly to the sides of your shoulders, legs together). Start with your feet at least 3 feet up in the air.

1. Lower down and touch your nose to the floor.

2. Press back up and continue with your reps at this level.

3. Once you've completed your set and taken the prescribed rest, lower your feet until they're 1.5 to 2 feet from the ground.

4 Lower down and touch your nose to the floor.

5 Press back up and continue with your reps at this level.

6 Once you've completed your set, release your feet to the ground so that you're in regular push-up position.

7 Lower down until you're one inch from the floor.

8 Press back up and finish your reps.

TIP
I recommend performing this exercise in front of a mirror so you can watch your form.

eight-count body builders

Special Ops Spin: Eight-Count Body Builders are an excellent way to develop the muscles used when crawling on your belly or engaging in a firefight that requires getting up and down a lot.

This is a great way to incorporate cardio, upper body, and lower body and also develop your quick-burst muscle fibers while working on endurance.

STARTING POSITION: Stand with your feet together and place your hands on your hips.

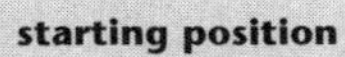

1. Squat down and place your hands on the ground.

2. Thrust your feet back until you're in a push-up position.

3. Open your feet until they're wider than shoulder-width apart.

4. Jump your feet back to push-up position.

5 Lower down for a regular push-up.

6 Press yourself back up.

7 Jump your feet back to the squat position.

8 Return to starting position.

walking lunge

Special Ops Spin: Walking Lunges enable any Special Ops platoon to have one leg up on the enemy. Rangers and Green Beret are known for long patrols where leg strength and endurance are essential for completing the mission. Recon could be called upon for missions that require everything from long dives to reconnaissance deep within enemy territory. SEALs may have to swim half a mile onto shore and then take on the enemy. If a downed pilot is injured, PJs literally have to carry him out with the enemy bearing down on them. These lunges are going to help them get there.

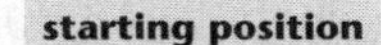

STARTING POSITION: Stand with your feet together and hands on your hips.

1 Step your left foot forward into a lunge, making sure that your knee does not cross over the tip of your shoe; keep your back straight and chin up. Bend your right arm up.

2 Without stopping in the middle or standing up, step your left foot forward into a lunge.

Continue alternating legs.

frog hop

Special Ops Spin: When you're in a firefight and your right-hand man finds an exit to the left, you must be able spring to your feet, utilizing every fast-twitch muscle in your lower body, in order to get out of there quickly.

Frog Hops are a good exercise to get your lungs burning.

STARTING POSITION: Stand with your legs shoulder-width apart and your arms in front of you like a downhill skier.

starting position

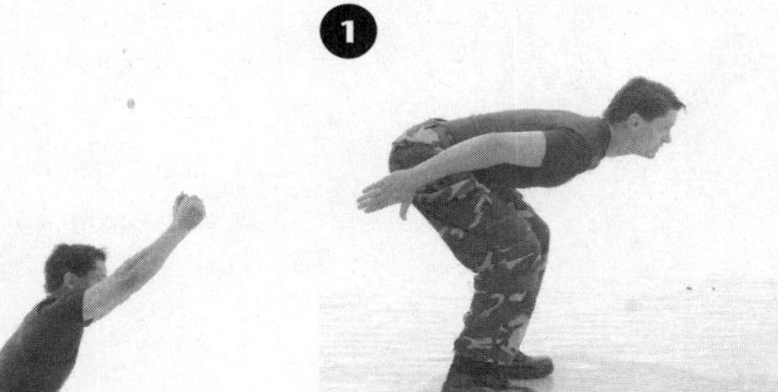

1 Move your arms back into the exploding position and squat down slightly to coil your legs.

2 Bring your arms forward and simultaneously explode forward, not up. Be sure to land with your knees soft, not stiff.

3 Bring your arms back to prepare for the next jump.

TIP

Do not recoil your arms back until after you have landed.

star hop

Special Ops Spin: Leg strength and speed is essential after you've eliminated your target. You must get out of there quickly and efficiently, running, hopping over obstacles, and hurdling ditches in an attempt to return to your evac (evacuation) point as fast as you can.

Star Hops work the quick-burst/fast-twitch muscles and will increase your vertical leap and lung capacity.

starting position

STARTING POSITION: Stand with your legs shoulder-width apart.

1

2

3

4

1 Squat down so that you can place your hands on the outside of each ankle.

2 Explode upward as high as you can, reaching up with your hands, which are slightly wider than your shoulders. Keep your back straight, your chin up, and your rear end down.

3 Land softly with your knees bent to absorb any recoil.

4 Squat back down and prepare to explode again.

wall sit

Special Ops Spin: During an ambush, squatting for hours at a time is a reality that requires much endurance that can be gained through Wall Sits.

THE POSITION: With your back flush against a wall, walk your feet forward until your knees are bent 90 degrees and do not cross over your toes. Your knees should be shoulder-width apart. You can cross your arms across your chest. Hold the position, making sure to keep your back straight and not lean forward.

TIP
Do not place your hands on your knees—this is cheating.

calf raise—regular

Special Ops Spin: Any type of long march, run, or swim requires strong calves; any weakness in this area can jeopardize your ability to contribute to your squad or platoon.

To get the most out of calf raises, you must keep your legs completely straight. If you bend your knees at all, your quads kick in.

STARTING POSITION: Stand with your feet shoulder-width apart and place your hands on your hips.

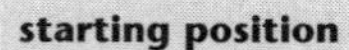

starting position

1 Rise onto the balls of your feet so that your heels are up at least 2 inches.

2 Lower down with control. Try to maintain the same speed both up and down.

calf raise—toe to toe

STARTING POSITION: Stand with your toes touching each other with your heels flared out; make sure your toes touch throughout the exercise. Hands can be at your sides or on your hips.

starting position

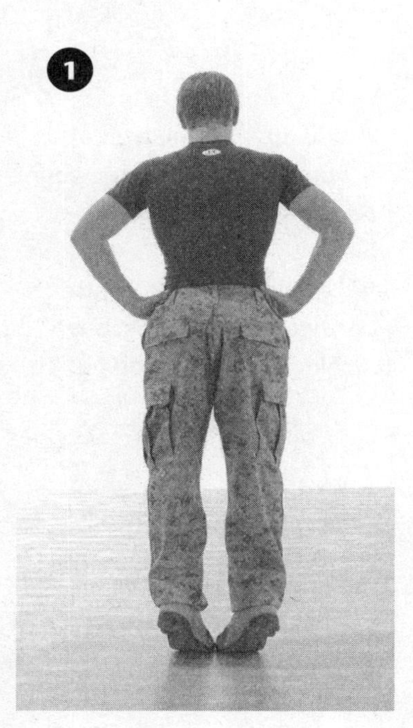

1 Rise up onto the balls of your feet, making sure your toes keep touching.

2 Lower down with control. Check that your toes are touching before continuing.

TIP
If you have balance issues, you can hold on to a pole or wall until you are able to shift your hands to your hips.

calf raise—heel to heel

STARTING POSITION: Stand with your heels touching each other with your toes pointed outward. Try to keep your legs as straight as possible throughout this movement. Hands can be at your sides or on your hips.

starting position

1

1 Rise up onto the balls of your feet, making sure your heels keep touching.

2 Lower down with control. Check that your heels are touching before continuing.

2

TIP

- The degree of difficulty can be increased by reps, time, and weight, or by utilizing a box, step, or other object to increase the range of motion.
- If you have balance issues, you can hold on to a pole, chair, or wall until you are able to shift your hands to your hips.

bench back exercise

Special Ops Spin: The lower back definitely comes into play when your buddy goes down and you have to lift him up over your shoulders or over an obstacle. If your lower back is not strong enough, you'll put yourself in jeopardy of hurting yourself and further sacrifice the mission.

This exercise can be performed off the ground or a bench. I recommend beginning on the ground and working your way up to the bench.

STARTING POSITION: Lie belly-down on a bench and interlock your fingers behind your head. Your partner grips behind your heels or ankles; he must maintain a solid grip throughout the exercise.

starting position

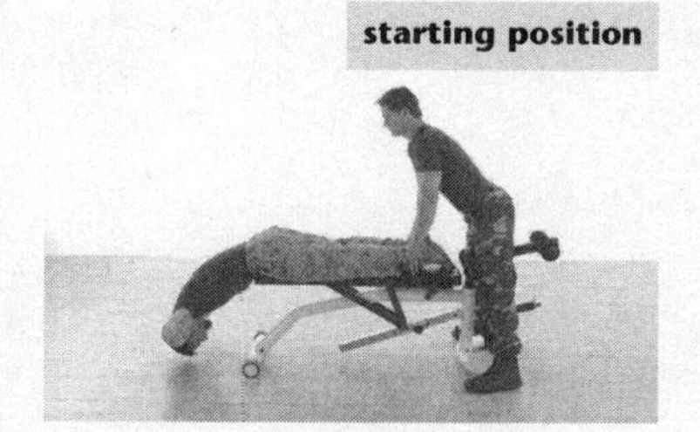

1 Raise your upper body as high as you feel comfortable by contracting your lower back.

2 Maintain control as you come back down.

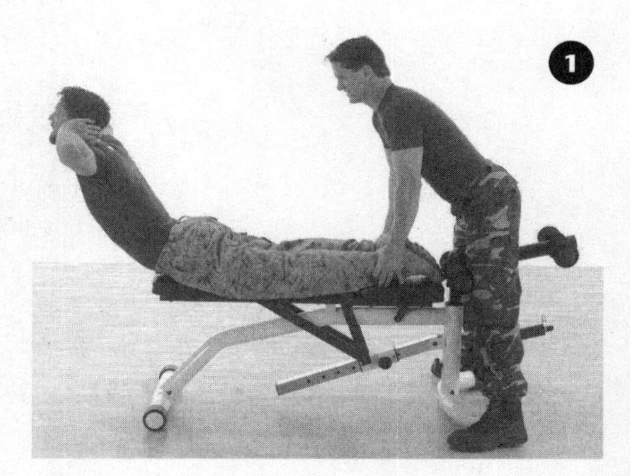

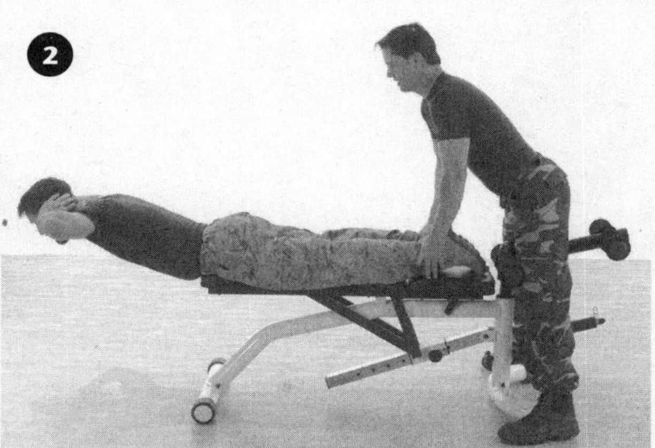

GROUND VARIATION
This can also be done on the ground.

MODIFICATION
When performing this on the bench, your partner can also sit on your lower legs.

ruck sack march (with airborne shuffle)

Special Ops Spin: This is a terrific exercise to help prepare your legs for the rigors of patrolling.

Equipment:

- *A sand bag filled with 30 pounds of sand. Make sure it's not filled all the way to the top; leave a quarter of the bag empty so that you can tie it up nice and tight. There's nothing worse than your bag breaking or opening up during a march.*
- *A daypack that fits snug against your back and does not have any slack in it. Fill it with the 30-pound sand bag.*

Footwear: You can start out with tennis shoes or soft hiking boots, but I recommend progressing up to jungle boots.

starting position

STARTING POSITION: Put on the daypack, making sure it fits well. You don't want the backpack bouncing up and down against your back and hips. To avoid any strain on your lower back, carry the bag high on your upper back, not slung low.

1 Begin the Airborne Shuffle, which is a smooth march just under a slow jog. This keeps the impact low and reduces stress on the spine and knees. Basically, lift your feet just enough off the ground to move them without stubbing. Keep your arms relaxed with a 90-degree bend.

TIP
As you get stronger, you can progress from a 30-pound sand bag to 40 pounds to 60 pounds to 80 pounds.

Ill-fitting daypack:

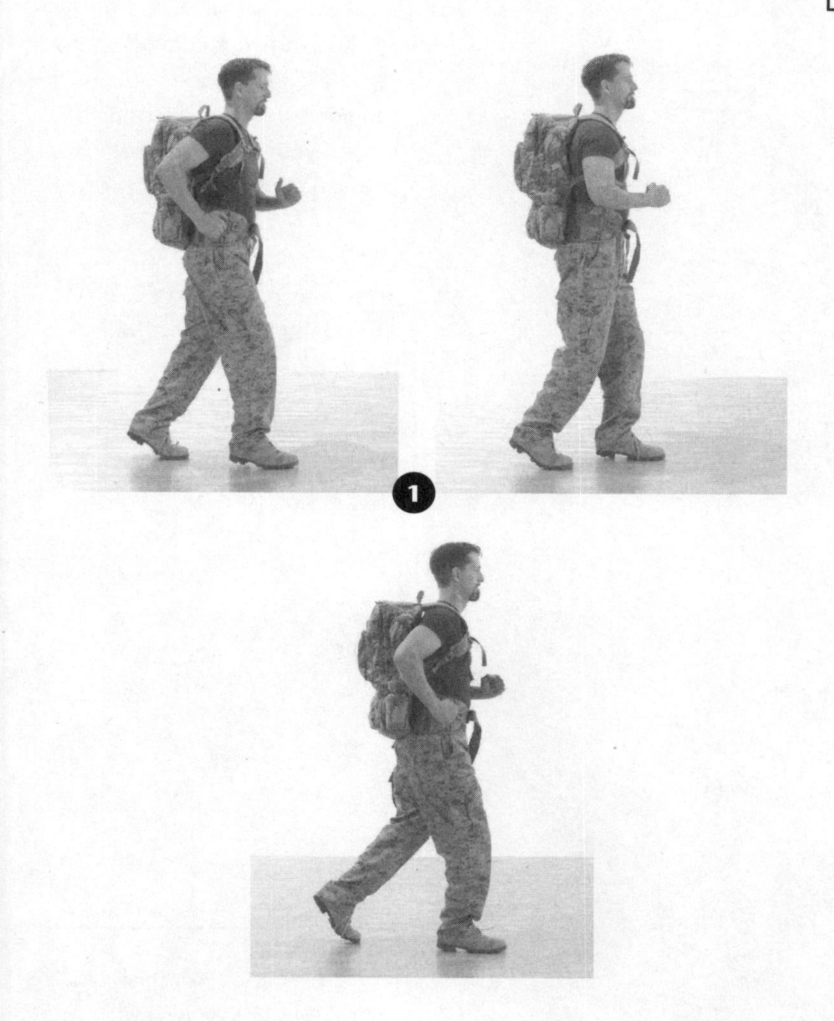

hand to toes

Special Ops Spin: No soldier will succeed during the obstacle course (especially the rope and wall climbs) if his abs are not strong. He won't have the strength to lift his legs to complete the obstacle.

STARTING POSITION: Lie on your back and bring your feet to the ceiling so that your legs are 45 degrees to the floor; you can bend your knees slightly but not too much. Cross your ankles and rest your hands on your chest.

1 Keeping your chin off your chest and driving with your shoulders, reach your hands toward your shoelaces, lifting your shoulder blades off the floor.

2 Lower down to starting position, returning your hands to your chest.

TIP
If you can't reach your shoelaces, aim at least for your lower shins.

x sit-up

Special Ops Spin: Core strength is essential and necessary to become an elite operator. For example, throwing a grenade is not all arm strength. Doing so requires a strong midsection so that you can coil and release for optimum distance and speed.

X Sit-Ups are a good all-round abdominal exercise but you have to reach the high reps to feel the burn. This is a four-count exercise such as 1-2-3-1, 1-2-3-2.

STARTING POSITION: Lie on your back with your knees bent and feet on the ground. Touch your hands lightly to your ears.

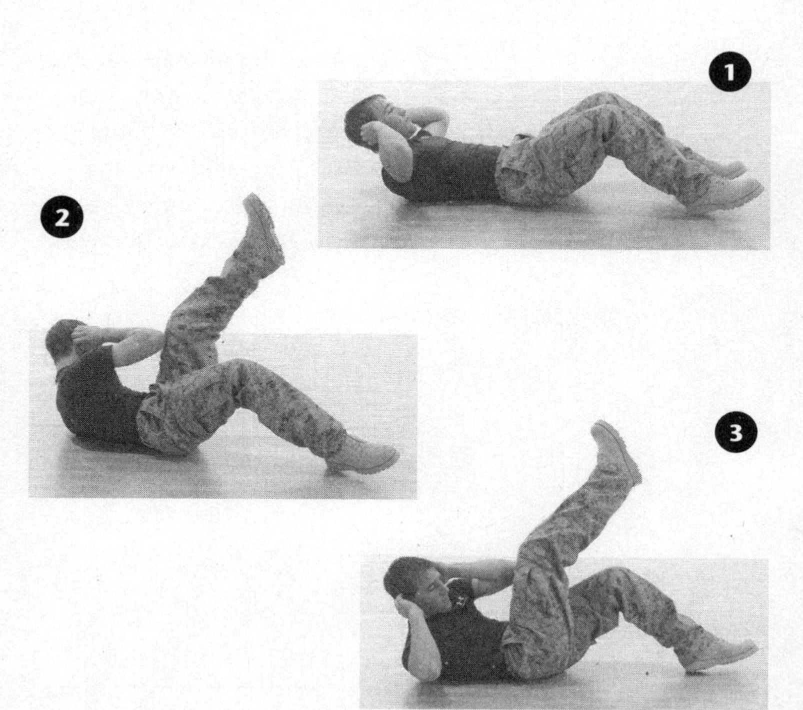

starting position

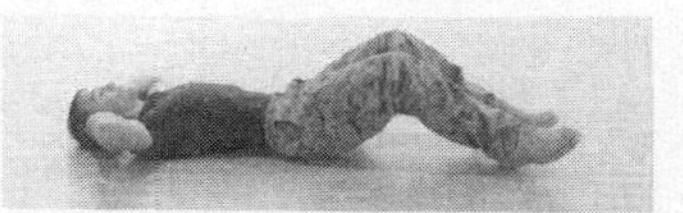

1 Raise your shoulders four to six inches off the ground. Keep your shoulders off the ground during the entire movement.

2 Raise your left leg so that it's 90 degrees from the ground, keeping your foot above your knee. Crunch into the final movement and try to touch your right elbow to your left knee. Do not bring your knee in towards your chest—do not compromise technique just because you cannot reach your elbow to your leg. Work on your strength so that you can eventually bring your elbow to your inner thigh.

3 Keeping your shoulders off the floor, lower your left leg to the floor and then raise your right. Touch your left elbow to your right knee. This is one rep.

TIP

You will rock your shoulders from side to side to complete your crunches but don't drop your shoulders back down at any time during the exercise.

ranger crunch

Special Ops Spin: Think about being loaded down with more gear than usual and fastroping into a hostile situation. You have a tight grip on the rope, your back is straight, and your legs are slightly elevated. Your strong abs and core make this possible.

STARTING POSITION: Lie on the floor with your knees slightly bent and feet flat on the floor. Cross your arms and place your hands on your outer upper chest with your fingers barely touching your shoulders.

starting position

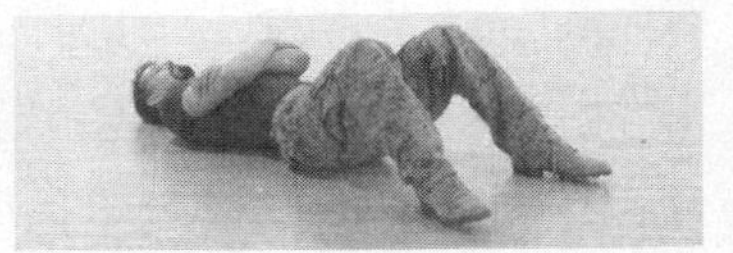

1

1 Leading with your chin and shoulders, drive upward, lifting your shoulder blades just a few inches off the ground as you push your abs downward. Keep your chin away from your chest.

2 Lower down to starting position.

2

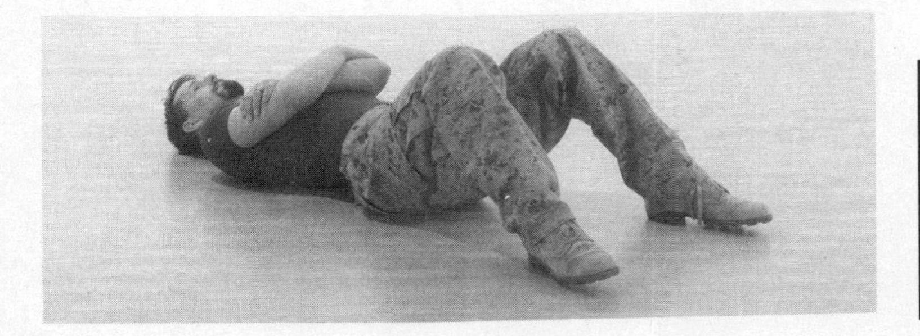

TIP

You don't have to lift your shoulders that high. The burn will be caused by how hard you crunch your ab muscles downward and towards your hips.

supine bicycle

Special Ops Spin: This movement is similar to a Special Ops operator sprinting up the stairs to the top of a building to provide cover fire for his fellow soldiers. You have to be quick and you must have quick core muscles.

This is a four-count exercise: 1-2-3-1, 1-2-3-2.

STARTING POSITION: Lie on your back with your legs extended straight along the floor. Touch your hands lightly to your ears.

starting position

1

1 Bend and lift your right leg 90 degrees towards your chest and raise your left elbow to meet it. Lift your shoulder blades slightly off the ground.

2 Return your right foot to the ground before switching sides.

2

hibberty jibberty

Special Ops Spin: Think about being loaded down with more gear than usual and fastroping into a hostile situation. You have a tight grip on the rope, your back is straight, and your legs are slightly elevated. Your strong abs and core make this possible.

STARTING POSITION: Lie on your back with your legs extended straight in front of you and six inches off the floor. Touch your hands lightly to your ears and lift your shoulder blades off the ground.

starting position

1 As you bring your right leg in to a 90-degree position, simultaneously raise your upper body to meet it halfway. Touch your right knee to your right elbow.

2 Lower your upper and lower body back down to the starting position and then immediately move into the next rep, now using your left leg and elbow.

3 In the final phase of this exercise, lower back down to starting position and then bring both your legs up together to the 90-degree position. Now touch your left elbow to your left knee and your right elbow to your right knee all at the same time. This will constitute one repetition.

TIP
Do not jerk your body to get to the "up" position. This movement should be smooth and fluid.

cross crunch

Special Ops Spin: Core strength is essential and necessary to become an elite operator. For example, throwing a grenade is not all arm strength. Doing so requires a strong midsection so that you can coil and release for optimum distance and speed.

STARTING POSITION: Lie on your back with your knees bent.

starting position

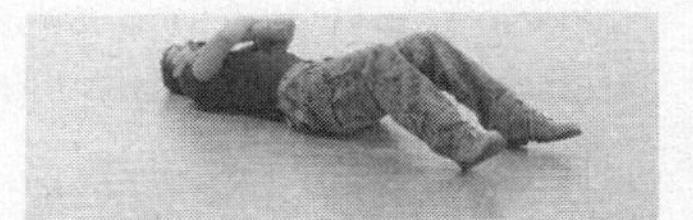

1

1 Extend your right leg straight and raise it about two feet off the ground. Bend your left leg 90 degrees and place the foot on the inside of your right knee. Place your left hand on the ground for balance and your right hand lightly on your right ear. Keep your legs elevated throughout the exercise.

2

2 Drive your right elbow into your left inner thigh so that you are crunching, not rotating, into position. Make sure not to bury your chin into your chest.

3

3 Slowly lower your torso to the floor.

obliques

Special Ops Spin: Core strength is essential and necessary to become an elite operator. For example, throwing a grenade is not all arm strength. Doing so requires a strong midsection so that you can coil and release for optimum distance and speed.

Proper positioning of the hip is really important in terms of getting the most out of this exercise.

STARTING POSITION: Lie on your right side with your legs and feet stacked on top of each other, slightly bent. Prop yourself up with your right elbow, keeping your right hand flat on the ground, and lightly touch your left ear with your left hand. Make sure the top part of your hip is rotated back far enough so that you're resting between your hip bone and your glute muscle. The top shoulder should be tilted slightly backward.

starting position

1

2

1 Keeping your knees and feet together, raise them straight up about two feet and tuck your left elbow into your left thigh. Make sure not to come in towards your chest.

2 Slowly lower down, lightly tapping the ground before moving into the next rep.

TIPS

- Don't lift your legs so high that you don't have to crunch to touch your elbow to your thigh.
- Don't bring your legs in towards your chest.
- If the exercise feels awkward, check your hip positioning.

flutter kick

Special Ops Spin: Navy SEALs, Green Beret, Force Recon, and PJs are all scuba-qualified and need phenomenal leg strength to keep kicking. No one wants to throw off pace count, recovery time, or, worse, the mission.

STARTING POSITION: Lie on your back and raise your hips off the ground. Place your hands underneath your tailbone, touching your fingers and thumbs together to form a diamond; allow a little space between your palms and the floor. Lower your tailbone onto your hands.

starting position

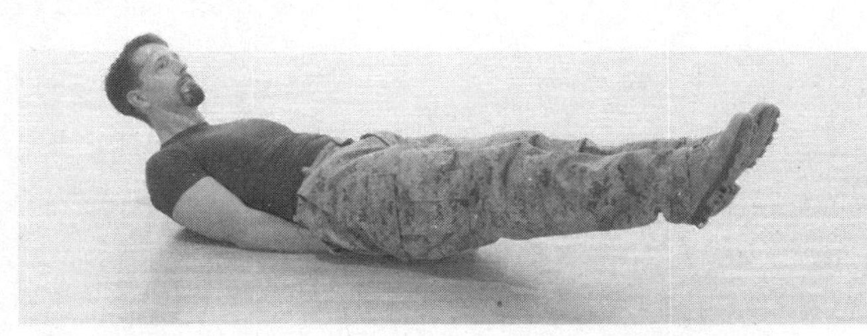

2

3

1 Lift your head and shoulder blades off the ground, keeping your chin away from your chest by looking straight ahead.

2 Straighten your legs and lift them 6 inches off the ground. Raise your left leg 36 inches, keeping your right leg off the ground. Press your abs downward and keep them tight to make this even more effective.

3 Return to Step 1 and switch legs without letting your feet hit the ground. Continue keeping your legs straight and pressing your abs downward.

TIP

It is very important to keep your head and shoulders elevated during this exercise. If you're tired, lower your feet and head instead, rest, and then pick it up again.

sky hop

Special Ops Spin: Core strength is essential and necessary to become an elite operator. For example, throwing a grenade is not all arm strength. Doing so requires a strong midsection so that you can coil and release for optimum distance and speed.

STARTING POSITION: Lie on your back with your knees bent and feet on the floor. Raise your hips and place your hands underneath your tailbone, touching your fingers and thumbs together to form a diamond; allow a little space between your palms and the floor. Now lower your tailbone onto your hands and extend your legs straight six inches off the floor. Lift your head and shoulder blades off the floor so that you can maintain a flat lower back during the entire movement.

starting position

1 Begin lifting your legs until they're perpendicular to the floor.

2 Just as you're about to hit perpendicular, elevate your hips upward as high as you can.

3 Slowly lower your legs to starting position, making sure that they do not drop too fast.

TIP
Use the same speed to raise your legs up and down.

1

2

3

lower ab crunch

Special Ops Spin: Elite operators encounter numerous occasions when they need lower ab strength to lift their legs up and over a wall or object.

STARTING POSITION: Sit with your legs straight and crossed at the ankles. Cross your arms and place your hands on your triceps, keeping your forearms parallel to the ground (*I Dream of Jeannie* style). Keep your abs tight throughout the movement to protect your lower back.

starting position

1 Slowly lower yourself down about 45 degrees, remembering to keep your abs tight. Bring your arms down to your chest.

2 Slowly raise yourself back up to starting position, lifting your arms away from your chest.

1

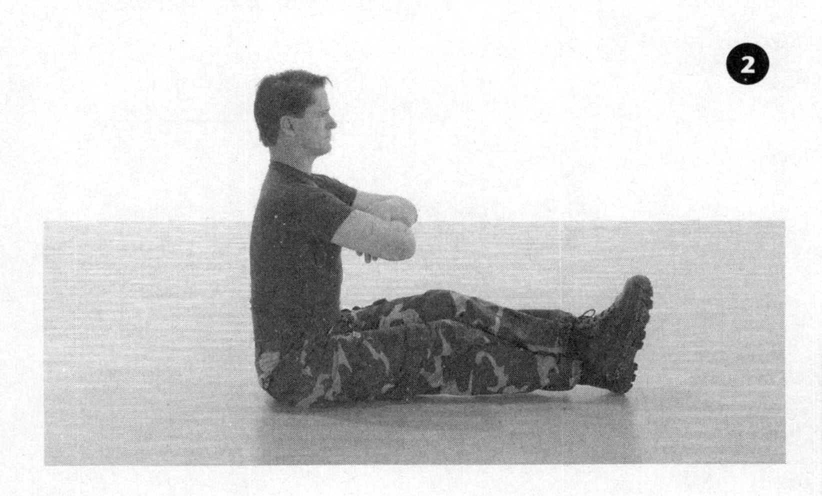

2

TIP

As you get stronger, you can lower all the way to the ground.

scissor lift

Special Ops Spin: Some branches call these Good Morning Darlings. They are extremely useful when it comes to swimming, sprinting, and long-distance running.

STARTING POSITION: Lie on your back with your knees bent and feet on the floor. Raise your hips and place your hands underneath your tailbone, touching your fingers and thumbs together to form a diamond; allow a little space between your palms and the floor. Now lower your tailbone onto your hands and extend your legs along the floor.

starting position

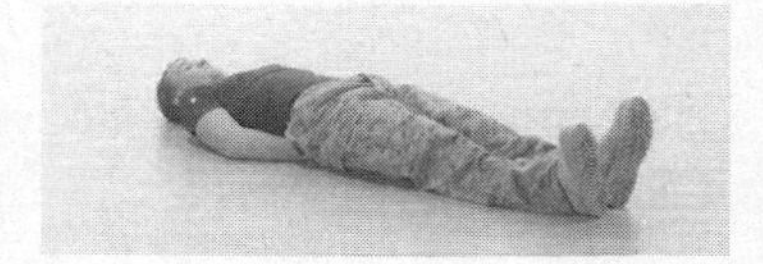

1 Raise your legs six inches off the floor and lift your head and shoulder blades off the floor so that you can maintain a flat lower back during the entire movement. Keep your abs tight throughout the movement.

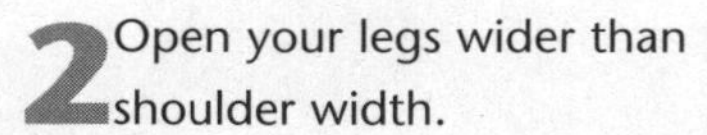

2 Open your legs wider than shoulder width.

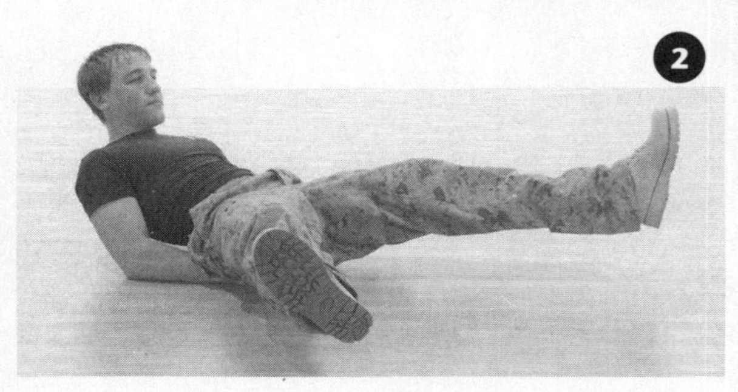

3 Bring your feet back together, just lightly touching your feet together before you open them again.

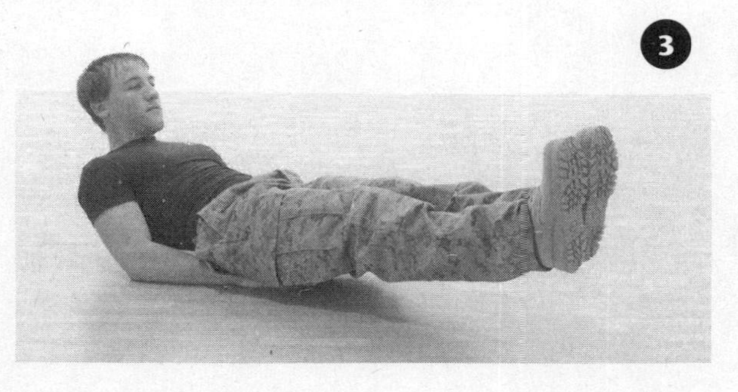

bench sit-up

Special Ops Spin: Long marches, runs, and swims all rely on lower abs and hip flexors strength.

This is a very advanced exercise. If you have any back problems, I do not recommend it.

STARTING POSITION: Sit on a bench so that your legs are extended along it and the upper part of your rear end is at the edge of the bench. Your partner holds onto or sits on your shins for stability. Cross your arms for balance and tighten your abs.

starting position

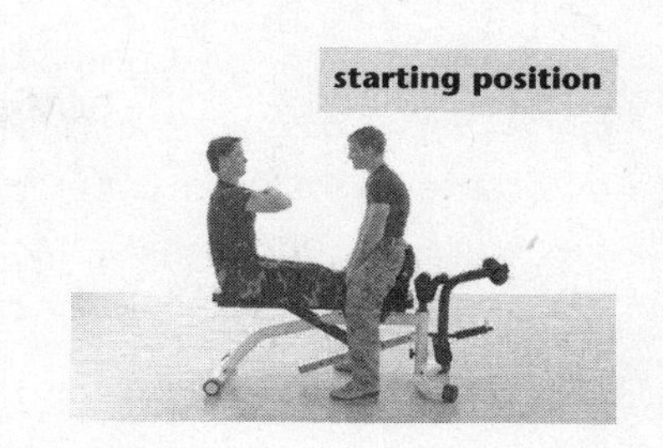

1 Begin lowering your upper body, stopping when it lowers itself just past the level of the bench.

2 Tighten your lower and upper abs to raise yourself back up past the 90-degree mark.

1

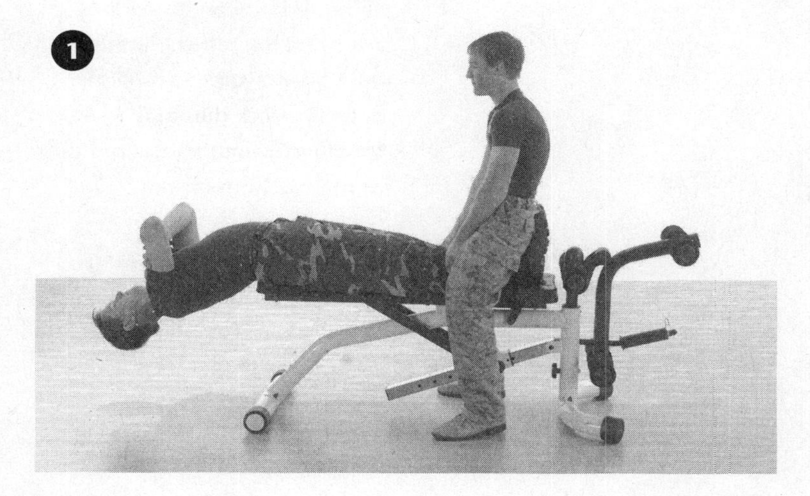

2

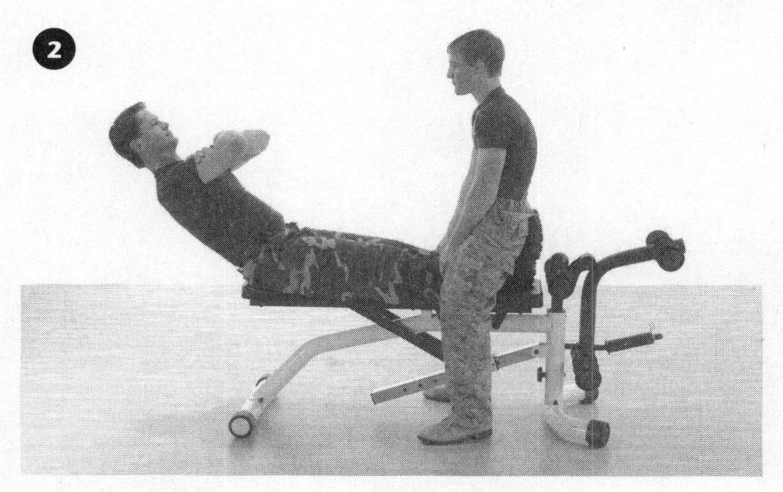

fly my airplane

Special Ops Spin: Fly My Airplane was used as a team-building exercise in the Army. Soldiers would take their helmets and place them under their stomachs. When the drill instructor yelled out "Fly your plane," they would lift every appendage and hold them straight out. If someone did not put out, the entire team would pay and continue suffering until that individual finally put out.

The main point of this exercise is endurance. It can be done on a helmet, medicine ball, or BOSU.

starting position

STARTING POSITION: Lie face down with a helmet or medicine ball under your stomach. Stretch your arms out in front of you and your legs behind.

1

1 Tighten every muscle in your body and then lift your arms and legs off the ground until they're sticking straight out from your hips and shoulders. Don't let them droop or rise too high.

2 Slowly lower to starting position.

2

TIP
This can also be done with a pillow or balance ball.

bench press

The Bench Press is a great old-school exercise that is excellent in developing chest size and strength. Just don't get caught up in maxing all the time. It's not about how much you bench but rather what the bench exercise develops. If it were all about the max then why does the NFL draft focus more on how many times a particular draftee can bench 225 pounds? Key points on the bench are the speed of reps, the intensity with which the bar comes off the chest, and proper positioning.

starting position

STARTING POSITION: Lie on the bench so that the bar is directly above your chest. With your hands slightly wider than your shoulders, wrap your hands and thumbs around the bar for increased hand strength and safety. It's best to be in a position that allows your arms to be 90 degrees once the bar reaches your chest. Keep your back on the bench and your feet on the floor throughout the exercise.

1

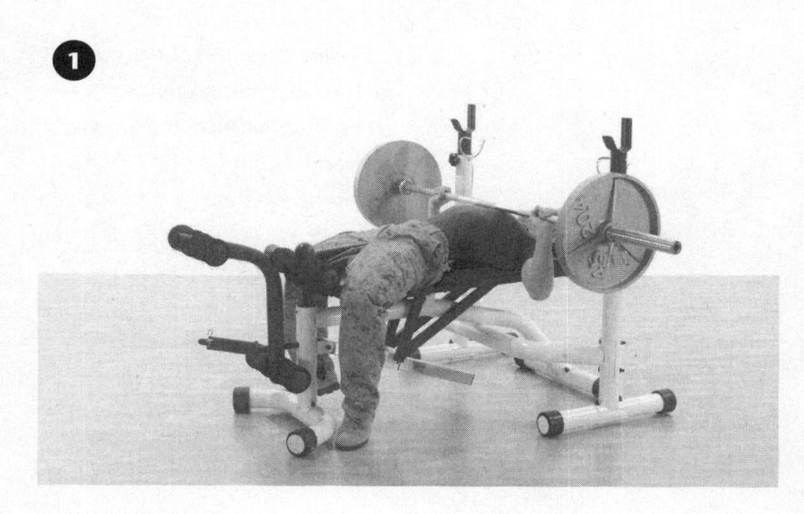

1 Safely lift the bar off the rack and slowly lower the bar to your chest. Do not come down too hard.

2

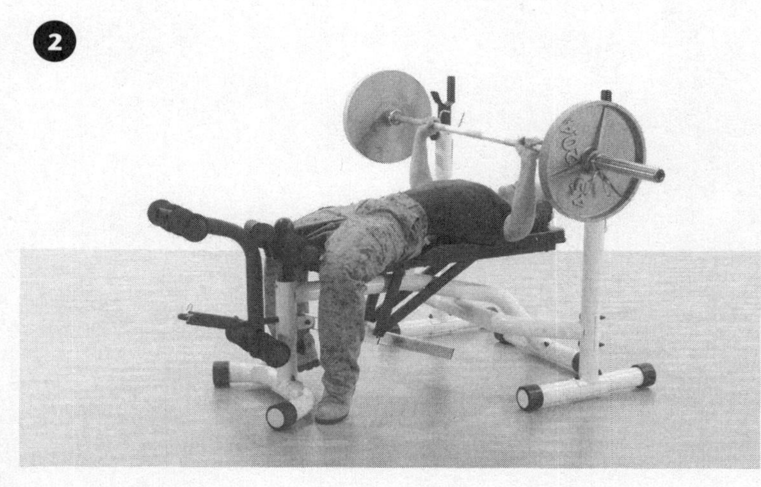

2 Once the bar hits your chest, drive it straight up. If the bar is above your mouth when you finish, readjust so that the bar is over your chest.

TIPS

- Do not lift your head; focus on your chest and triceps.
- Do not let your back raise off the bench.

dumbbell fly

I like to follow up the Bench Press with Dumbbell Flies, which really open up the chest. The emphasis here should be on slow methodical movement, not speed.

STARTING POSITION: With a dumbbell in each hand, lie face up on a bench. Reach both hands to the ceiling, positioning your knuckles inward and keeping a slight bend in your elbows. To keep your arms in the right position throughout the entire movement, imagine that they are wrapping themselves around a barrel. Keep your back on the bench and your feet on the floor throughout the exercise.

starting position

1 Slowly open your arms out to the sides, making sure the dumbbells do not drop below your shoulders. Contract your chest muscles hard toward the end to help in the finishing of the movement and to help reverse your movement back to starting position.

2 Maintaining the same speed, slowly return to starting position.

TIPS

- Do not bend your arms too much.
- Do not let your arms reach above your shoulders as you open up—keep them directly to the sides.

triceps pull-down

Along with dips, Triceps Pull-Down is one of the better exercises for developing your triceps. I like performing it with a solid bar one day and a rope the next to keep my body guessing.

STARTING POSITION: Stand with your feet a little wider than shoulder width and hold the bar, keeping a 90-degree bend in your arms and your elbows tucked against your sides. Keep your hands out and away from your chest and stomach.

starting position

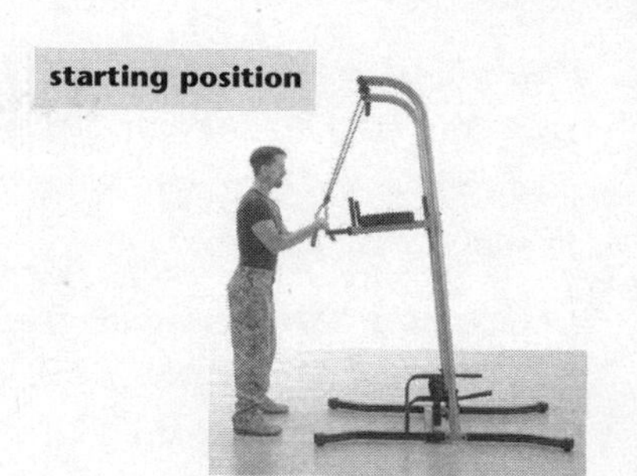

1 Maintaining your elbow position, pull down until your arms are completely straight. The only body parts that move in this exercise are your hands and forearms. At the end of the pull-down, your wrists will flare out.

2 On the way up, bring your wrists back together when you pass your belly button. Stop when your arms are at the 90-degree bend.

TIP

Do not rock or swing to start your next rep.

MODIFICATION

As the weight gets heavier, you might try putting one leg forward and the other leg back.

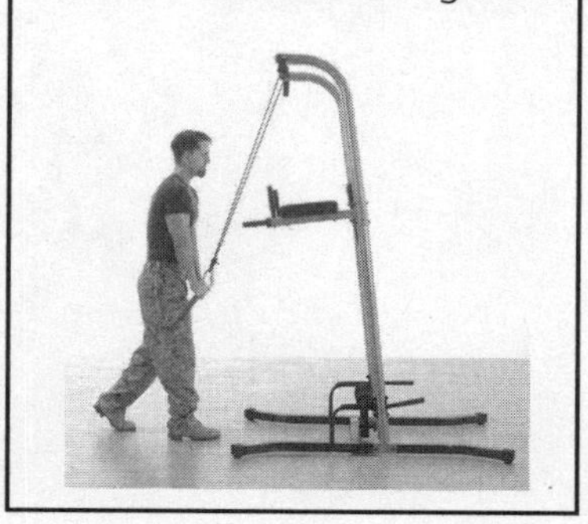

skull crusher

Proper hand, elbow, and ending position are the key to success with Skull Crushers. I like the inner grip better for this exercise, and a standard curl bar will keep your hands and wrists in the proper position throughout the movement.

STARTING POSITION: Holding a curl bar in both hands, lie face up on a bench with your feet on the ground. Position your hands 6 to 8 inches apart on the bar and straighten your arms to the ceiling. Keep your elbows tucked in and your back flat on the bench throughout the exercise.

starting position

1 Keeping your movement smooth and slow, bend your elbows and lower the bar until it's about an inch from your face, directly above your nose or eyebrows; do not bring the bar back over your head.

2 Slowly return to starting position.

1

2

TIPS

- Always take the first rep the slowest to prepare your body for the stop and start.
- Do not let your elbows flare out.

triceps kickback

The key to Triceps Kickback is keeping your elbows in the up position while lowering your dumbbells to starting position. The only body part that should move during this exercise is your forearm. To further isolate the triceps, I like to place a twist at the end of the exercise.

STARTING POSITION: With a dumbbell in your left hand, place your right knee on the edge of a flat bench while placing your right hand further down the bench. Bend your left arm until it's 90 degrees. Keep your elbow up and your shoulders squared throughout the exercise.

starting position

1

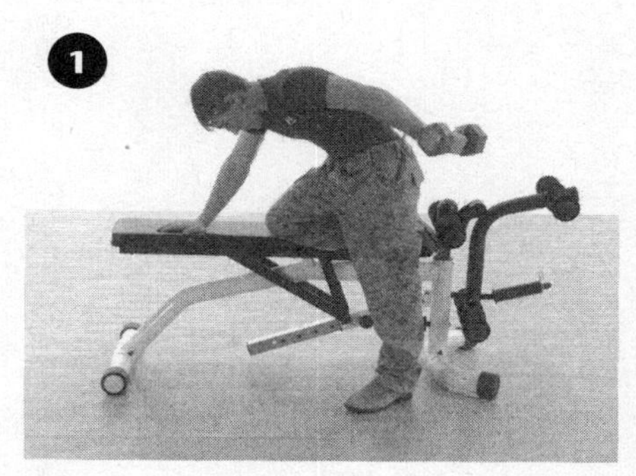

2

3

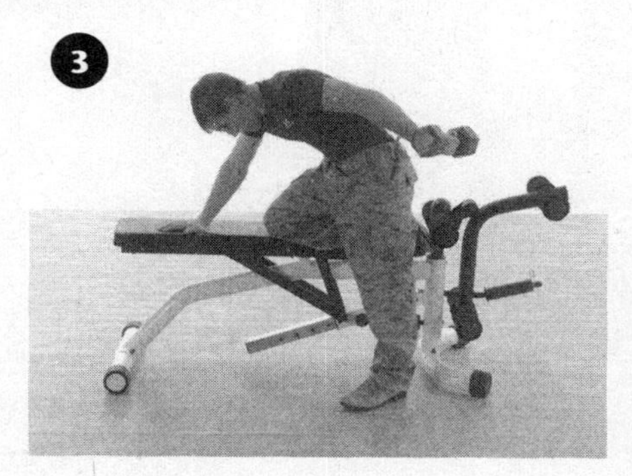

1 Begin straightening your left arm. From the three-quarters position, rotate the top of the dumbbell inward until it forms a "T" with your arm.

2 Straighten your arm completely.

3 Without swinging your arm, return to starting position, making sure to keep your elbow up.

TIP

Do not raise your shoulder as you get tired.

lat pull-down

If you can't perform pull-ups, this exercise will help develop the muscles you need to do so. It is also a great exercise to combine with your pull-ups.

STARTING POSITION: Sitting with your back to the machine, grab the bar about 2 to 4 inches from the end of the bar or, in some cases, where the bar bends. Wrap your thumbs around the bar. Look up and make sure that the point of the shoulders to where your hands rest on the bar form a V.

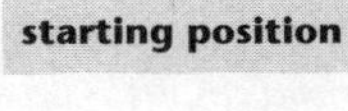

1 Keeping good posture, drive the bar all the way down to the back of the head—rotate your shoulder blades inward while throwing your chest forward (this allows you to contract your back better).

2 Maintaining the same speed, return to starting position; do not let the weight spring up on its own.

TIP
Always bring the bar down to the hairline for proper form.

military press

Military Press requires perfect technique for optimal results. I highly recommend a mirror nearby to see your technique.

STARTING POSITION: Sit on a bench and hold a dumbbell in each hand, palms facing forward. The dumbbells should be above mouth height and touching. Make sure that your elbows are bent 90 degrees and that your elbows are slightly lower than your shoulders.

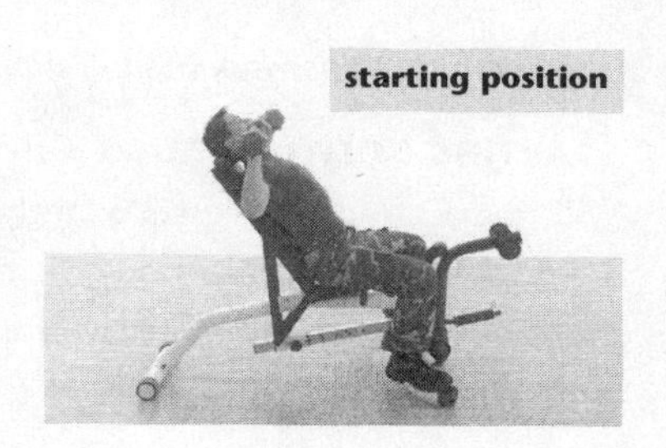
starting position

1 Press up both dumbbells evenly, touching them together above your head; your elbows should have a slight bend at the top. Do not let your hands go too far behind your head.

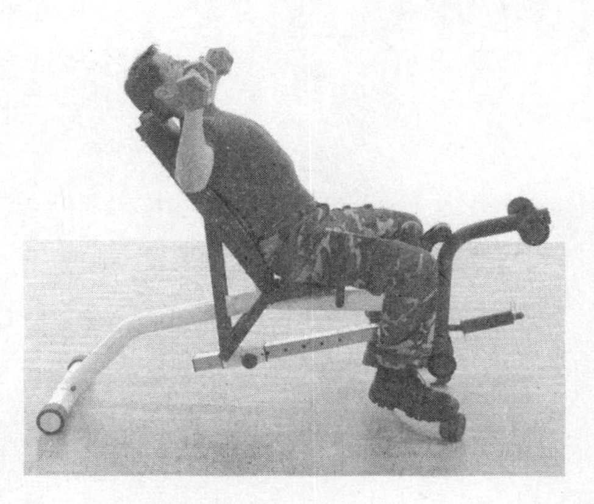

2 Maintaining the same speed, lower the dumbbells to starting position, making sure your hands don't open too wide or drop too low.

shoulder rotation

Shoulder Rotations work the full shoulder, front and back deltoids.

STARTING POSITION: Stand with your feet wider than shoulder-width apart and your knees slightly bent. Your arms are along your sides, palms facing your body; hold a dumbbell in each hand. Tighten your abs to maintain a straight back throughout the exercise.

1 Raise the dumbbells to shoulder height, keeping your arms as straight as possible.

2-3 Once you reach shoulder height, rotate your palms forward and bring your hands together until they're a foot apart.

4-5 When the dumbbells are directly in front of you, rotate your palms down and slowly lower the dumbbells to your sides, keeping your arms as straight as possible. Also make sure not to arch your back by tightening your abs more.

TIP
Fight the tendency to bend your arms, especially when you're tired.

dumbbell shoulder raise

This can be done with three positions—try them all to find out which one works best for your body. If you're lucky and every position feels good, you can hit every position during your repetitions. Go from side to V to front or alternate between sets, focusing on one position per set.

STARTING POSITION: Stand with your feet wider than shoulder-width apart and your knees slightly bent. Your arms are along your sides, palms facing your body; hold a dumbbell in each hand. Tighten your abs to maintain a straight back throughout the exercise.

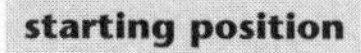

1 Keeping your arms straight, raise the dumbbells out to the side until they're shoulder height.

2 Maintaining the same speed, lower down to starting position.

3 Keeping your arms straight, raise the dumbbells in front of you so that they're slightly wider than your shoulders; stop when they reach shoulder height.

(continued on page 126)

dumbbell shoulder raise (continued)

4 Maintaining the same speed, lower down to starting position.

5 Keeping your arms straight and your palms facing down, raise the dumbbells directly in front of you until they're shoulder height.

6 Maintaining the same speed, lower down to starting position.

VARIATION

This can also be done by alternating arms instead of lifting both simultaneously.

weighted lunge

The Weighted Lunge takes your lunges to another level. The only difference when it comes to weighted lunges is to watch the speed in which you come down into the lunge. There are three ways to do weighted lunges. My preferred method is to use a weighted vest; the best one I've found in terms of comfort and durability is by weightvest.com. Another tool is a curl bar (available at any sporting good store) with a towel wrapped around the middle. The third option is dumbbells, which are a fun way to add diversity to your lunges. With my wrestling team I would have them start out with 40-pound dumbbells in each hand.

starting position

STARTING POSITION: Put on the weighted vest and stand with your feet about shoulder-width apart.

1 Step forward with your left leg and bend your knee until it's 90 degrees—make sure your knee does not pass your toes; bring your right arm up to a 90-degree bend. Your right leg should be bent, with your knee one to two inches from the floor. Keep your shoulders back, your head up, and your back straight with each lunge.

2 Step forward with your right leg, bringing your left arm up.

VARIATION 1
Wrap a towel around the middle of the curl bar and place the bar behind your neck. Your hands should be a little wider than shoulder-width apart.

VARIATION 2
Holding a dumbbell in each hand, let them hang on either side.

preacher curl

Preacher Curls can be done with an inner grip or a shoulder-width grip. Although it can be done with dumbbells, I recommend using a curl bar to get your wrists and hands in the right position. This can also be done on a machine with preacher pads.

STARTING POSITION: Kneel behind a balance ball and place your elbows about shoulder-width apart on it. With your palms facing up, grip a curl bar with your hands shoulder-width apart.

starting position

1 Slowly curl the bar until it's three or four inches from your shoulders; make sure your elbows do not slide inward.

2 Maintaining the same speed, lower down to starting position.

VARIATION

If using a curl bar, you can also switch to the inner grips on the curl bar; if using dumbbells, press them together throughout the entire movement.

seated dumbbell curl

Forming a "T" at the top of your movement isolates your biceps and allows you to get much more out of this exercise.

STARTING POSITION: Using an exercise bench that has an adjustable back, adjust the back of the bench just short of 90 degrees. Have a seat with your back flat against the bench and your abs tight. With your palms facing inward, let the dumbbells dead hang at your sides.

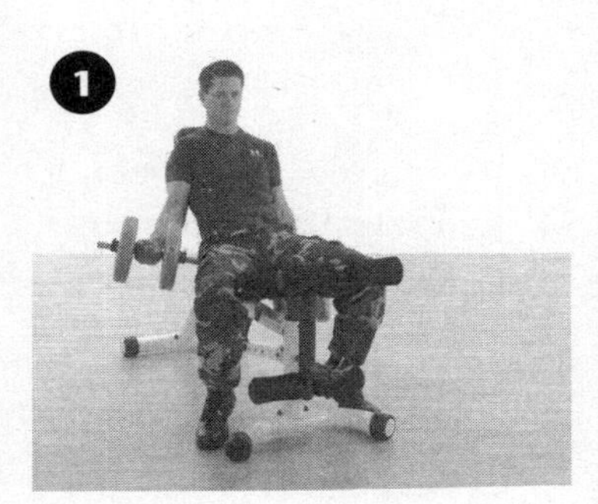

1 Keeping your elbows by your sides, bring the right dumbbell up, leading with the thumb side of your hand.

2 Once you are past your stomach, rotate your palm so that your palm faces your body and the dumbbell forms a "T" with your forearm. Continue curling the dumbbell, stopping a few inches before it touches your shoulder.

3 Rotate your palm so that your thumb is up once again; lead with your pinky to return to starting position.

4 Once your right arm is in starting position, raise the left dumbbell.

VARIATION

To intensify the curl, you can rotate your palms downward before slowly lowering back to starting position.

curl bar—inner grip

Curl Bar is a great way to finish off your biceps.

Putting a little throw forward in your shoulders at the very end helps keep your back straight. In other words, right before you get to the top, quickly and lightly thrust forward with the shoulders.

STARTING POSITION: Stand with your feet wider than shoulder-width apart. Holding a curl bar with both hands, palms up, let your arms hang straight with a slight bend in your elbows. Tighten your abs to keep your back straight throughout the exercise.

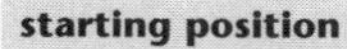

starting position

1 Locking your elbows into your sides, lift the curl bar, stopping a few inches before it touches your shoulders.

2 Slowly release down to starting position, making sure your arms are straight before continuing the next rep.

TIP

Do not arch your back—keep it straight by tightening your abs.

index

acknowledgments

Thanks to Andy Mogg for his exercise photos. It was a pleasure to work with him—he's a true professional and the best in his field.

A big thanks to Mark Divine and Tony Vernetti at www.navyseals.com for helping out with our interior shots. Navyseals.com is the best website for information about Navy SEALs, Special Operations information, products, and gear. Tell them Mark sent you and they will take good care of you.

Thanks to Mike De Lisle and Jeff Stephenson for their help on the photo shoot. They answered my call on a moment's notice and had my back. It was a lot of fun to finally do a project together with my little brother (sorry, Mike, you'll always be my little brother). Jeff, you're the best and I consider you a true friend. Congratulations on being two-time state wrestling champion.

The Golfer's Stroke-Saving Handbook

The Golfer's Stroke-Saving Handbook

CRAIG SHANKLAND
DALE SHANKLAND
DOM LUPO
ROY BENJAMIN

A Sports Illustrated Book
Little, Brown and Company Boston Toronto

FIRST EDITION
T 03/78

LIBRARY OF CONGRESS CATALOGING IN PUBLICATION DATA
Main entry under title:
The Golfer's stroke-saving handbook.
1. Golf. I. Shankland, Craig. II. Lupo, Dom.
GV965.G548 796.352 77-20905
ISBN 0-316-78260-2

Sports Illustrated Books
are published by
Little, Brown and Company
in association with
Sports Illustrated Magazine

Designed by Susan Windheim
Published in cooperation with The Benjamin Company

Published simultaneously in Canada
by Little, Brown & Company (Canada) Limited

PRINTED IN THE UNITED STATES OF AMERICA

Contents

The Golfer's Stroke-Saving Handbook

Introduction

By The Ever-Hopeful Amateur (Roy Benjamin)

At the outset, let's presume that you and I have a great deal in common. We are both hopeful golfing amateurs with limited time to play or practice, and we strive for two obvious goals:

(1) We want to lower our golf scores.
(2) We want to achieve confidence and control over shots and situations we now fear or flub.

Those words represent the essence of this book's concerns.

The aim, concept, and format of this guide to better golf are totally different from any other golf book we, the authors, have ever seen — and we've seen and studied hundreds in the course of the years it has taken us to produce this book.

First of all, we are a *foursome* — working for you, plotting for you, aching for you, thinking of *you* and *your* problems — a foursome that might be loosely identified as teacher-writer-illustrator-amateur. Each of us knows your problems and your capabilities because each of us, in one way or another, identifies with what you are trying to accomplish on the golf course. Before elaborating, let me introduce the authors:

● *The teacher — Craig Shankland.* He's "The Source." Son of one of England's greatest teaching pros — Bill Shankland, a former Ryder Cup player —

Craig is a dedicated, articulate, incisive teacher whose thousands of pupils swear by him and his crystal-clear lessons. He is now the head teaching professional at the Fairview Country Club in Greenwich, Connecticut. For two years president of the New York Metropolitan Professional Golf Association and twice Pro of the Year in that PGA district, Craig knows how to explain and demonstrate golf clearly and simply. He has been on tour, has won the New York Metropolitan PGA championship, was ranked among the "top ten" club professionals for five successive years, and has played in numerous international competitions. (The "here's how" illustrations throughout the book show Craig in action as he wants *you* to be in action.)

- *The writer — Dale Shankland.* Craig's brother Dale knows the game from your point of view because of his years of experience as golf-instruction editor for *Golf Magazine*. Author-collaborator with Johnny Miller on his golf book and a teaching pro himself, Dale has the same knack as his brother for using words, symbols, and images to help you make the golf shots you want, need, and aspire to achieve.
- *The illustrator — Dom Lupo.* He is acknowledged as one of the finest and most understanding graphic interpreters of the golf swing, an expert whose various stop-action techniques help you see and feel the way to make a good golf shot. Dom is a veteran illustrator of hundreds of golf magazine features and numerous books. Many of his paintings hang in the Golf Hall of Fame at Pinehurst, North Carolina.
- *The amateur — Roy Benjamin.* As a weekend player who has enjoyed the game and wrestled with its challenges for more years than I'll admit, I probably face the same curiosities and frustrations about

golf that you do. Having begun at the age of ten caddying and playing in my native Florida, I have had certain head-start advantages that have helped to make me a low-handicap player, an occasional (though not-too-successful) competitor in state, district, and country amateur tournaments, and a twelve-time winner of my own club championship at the Fairview Country Club. But, like most of you, I still turn to books and lessons and extemporaneous on-the-course (hell, sometimes *mid-swing!*) tests and experiments to try to make corrections, add distance, and solve trouble shots.

This book answers many questions we both ask, and no doubt the illustrations and suggestions will help you, as they have helped me. This is a book for *all* golfers. Even if you have played the game for years and have successfully met many of its challenges, you should be able to find in these pages tips, hints, and scraps of advice that will help you achieve that simple but elusive pair of delights — a lower score and the ability to execute one or more shots as you really want them executed.

The number of newly conquered shots and solved situations you can expect to add to your golfing arsenal by reading and applying — and *rereading* and *reapplying* — the lessons from these pages will depend on how conscientious you are, and on how far from perfect you estimate your game to be. Inasmuch as *no* golfer — whether tour superstar, teaching pro, or scratch amateur — can claim the unattainable state of perfection, it stands to reason that the need to find solutions to golfing problems will always exist.

Our desire to help you discover and apply the solutions to your problems motivated the four of us to pool our resources and to assemble, sort out, classify, and set down — in words and pictures — enough practical advice so that on as many occasions as possible — before, after, or during a round — you can say to yourself: "I recognized the challenge and I successfully met it."

Like many amateur golfers, I have experienced the frustrations that come from trying to imitate the playing style of superstars who have written books outlining their personal techniques. "Swing as I do" is the theme of most of these manuals. But only a fortunate few of us part-time golfers have the ability to "follow the stars." Being a book publisher by profession and a golfer by addiction, I had for years searched for a book that would: (1) be the next-best thing to a lesson session on the tee with a wise and understanding teaching professional; and (2) serve as a brushup or review handbook that would provide (away from the golf course, for pregame and postgame study) practical answers, in easy-reference form, to the dozens of challenges we meet in every round of golf we play. No luck in my search — but there may be an answer here. By outlining and developing this new book, in association with my three talented partners, I hope my dual goal has been achieved.

This instruction book focuses the experience and know-how of Craig Shankland, a unique *teaching* professional whose thousands of hours on the lesson tee gives him a keen and sympathetic understanding of the amateur's frailties and limitations; Craig Shankland is the kind of teacher who can articulate advice that you can easily and successfully follow. Furthermore, our authoring team has responded to the kinds of questions you are most likely to ask a golf professional on the practice tee or during a playing lesson.

What are the questions and problems most likely to concern you and me? Adhering to the basics and knowing what goes into making a good shot are obvious fundamentals of learning. That's only the beginning, though. Curing bad shots, conquering trouble shots, executing challenge shots and recovery shots — those are the subtle extras you will find covered in this book. (And to make your search for the answers easier, the contents page conveniently classifies most of the situations that are now likely to concern or baffle you.)

As one amateur to another — and as a collaborator with our teacher, Craig Shankland, on this book — I have briefly introduced each of the seven chapters with my reactions to Craig's instructions. You will find my remarks in italic type, preceded by the caption *Amateur's Note.*

When you analyze golf, you realize that its greatest pleasures are derived from two diametrically opposed situations. One is the positive side, where you execute basics to achieve preplanned results. (We call these the shots that "warm your heart.") The other is the negative side, where the thrill results from overcoming forces that are constantly endeavoring to throw you off balance.

On the negative side, you accept — along with golf's never-monotonous, always-intriguing aspects — those obstacles without which there would be no game: wind, rough, trees, uneven terrain, bunkers, water hazards, undulating greens. You also battle pressure — "choking" and fear. How you overcome these natural, man-made, and mental difficulties ultimately dictates your success in reaching your goals — that lower score and the executed-as-planned shot.

That is why we feel that some of the most important contributions this book can make to your game are contained in chapters five and six, which deal with trouble shots, recovery shots, and challenge shots. In those two chapters you will find a conveniently categorized treatment of nearly one hundred situations that cover most of golf's challenges. Recognize them. Know that *all* who play the game face them — from the lowliest hackers to the gold-laden champions. Approach these trouble shots with confidence and a knowledge of what is required to conquer them. When you do this you'll have taken the most satisfying and rewarding steps possible toward enjoying the game and getting pride from your achievements.

Incidentally, it was the section on trouble shots that first inspired this book. Wouldn't it be valuable, we reasoned, for the reader-golfer to be able to turn to a specific problem (before or after the game) and put his or her finger on the solution to that problem? True, next week's problems may be different, and what you read this week may not be so happily executed next week; but many of your answers do lie in this section.

So skip, jump, search out *your particular momentary needs* in chapters five and six. Don't be afraid to refer again and again to the same bothersome situation. It's no secret that the muscles are not always willing servants of the mind. We won't promise that you'll truly conquer *every* trouble shot. But we'll help you try, because we understand your plight and appreciate your desire to master the game's difficult situations. Examples:

- *Buried lie in a trap near the green.* Many golfers cringe, groan, and curse the fates that give them the "fried-egg lie" in the sand (where the top of the ball is barely visible). That shot — inevitably a "trouble" shot — is just as much a part of the game as setting up the ball for your drive on the first tee. There's no need to go jelly-kneed at the challenge. You *can* extricate yourself and you *can* get close enough to the pin for a one-putt opportunity. (To find out how, turn to chapter five, page 112, "The Buried Lie.")

- *An intentional hook to curl around a tree and reach a green.* The pros do it for you on TV and you marvel at their mysterious abilities. You can do it too. Take this likely situation: You are in the rough and there is a tree between you and the green. Discretion may often call for a safe shot to the fairway. Ah, but in match play — or with a dollar nassau riding — what may be required is an intentional hook to avoid the tree and draw neatly to the green. Luck or misguided hopes are not the answer. And you *can* execute the shot. (Turn to chapter six, page 167, "The Intentional Hook.")

- *Driving into a strong, head-on wind.* This shot baffles, frustrates, and even angers many a golfer, who often finds that the mightier the effort, the punier the result. But there are sound and simple suggestions that will produce very satisfactory results. (Turn to chapter five, page 140, "Hitting Against the Wind.")

Let's face it: golf enthusiasts are too often looking for easy answers when they put their money on the line and buy a golf book. They seem to hope for an impossibility: *The* Secret, The All-Purpose Gimmick, The Mystery "X" Factor, The Fad-of-the-Moment, The Holy Grail, The Shortcut, The Instant Answer, The Painless Solution. They sometimes forget that the complexities, challenges, and variables in golf are what make it the most intriguing game ever contrived.

Our challenge in this book is to present solid,

practical, workable, understandable, and *applicable* instruction. To read a tip and understand it is only the first step; to apply it, as you play, is the acid test.

The nongolfer cannot comprehend the game's bittersweet allure. There is the agony of shanking a simple approach into a trap guarding the green, when winning the match required only that you hit the green and get down in two putts. There is also the ecstasy (particularly when the lie in the trap is a buried one) of recovering from that gaffe with a properly executed, confidently swung, closed-face sand shot that ends up three feet from the hole—enabling you, after all, to execute the winning one-putt stroke.

Good luck, fellow golfers. Welcome to the world of lower scores, achieved because you knew what you were supposed to do . . . and you did it!

1

A Quick Review of the Basics

Amateur's Note

"The grip and the alignment are the foundations of the golf swing!"

That is Craig's undying theme song. The grip is what he first inspects when a player gets on the practice tee for a lesson. In the next few pages, Craig relates your grip to good and bad shots. (Incidentally, unless otherwise indicated, all the discussion, instruction, examples, and illustrations that follow assume a right-handed golfer — left-handers should "transpose" and execute accordingly.)

Remember this basic truth: Whenever you develop a disappointing and erratic pattern in your shots, refer first to your grip before applying any other suggested changes.

Also, check your alignment, setup, and position in relation to the ball. You will see later in this book important references to visualization and feel for the shot you are about to make. But seeing the shot in your mind's eye will not deliver the desired result if you have not mastered your grip and aimed yourself properly.

Your Grip

The foundation of any golf swing is the grip. Only if your hands are positioned correctly initially will it be possible to develop a sound, consistently reliable swing. If you start off with your hands incorrectly positioned, you'll be building your golf swing around a fault and will be forced to compensate in order to return the clubhead to the ball in a desirable square-to-the-target position. As a teacher, I have found that nearly all bad shots are the result of a bad grip.

Say, for example, that your hands are in what is termed a *strong position*, turned so far to the right on the grip of the club that the inverted V's created by your thumbs and forefingers point to the right of your right shoulder. This will cause the clubface to *close* (aim to the left) at impact and the ball will hook. To compensate, you will have to make the clubhead follow an exaggerated in-to-out path just to keep the ball in play.

Conversely, if you have a *weak grip*, where the

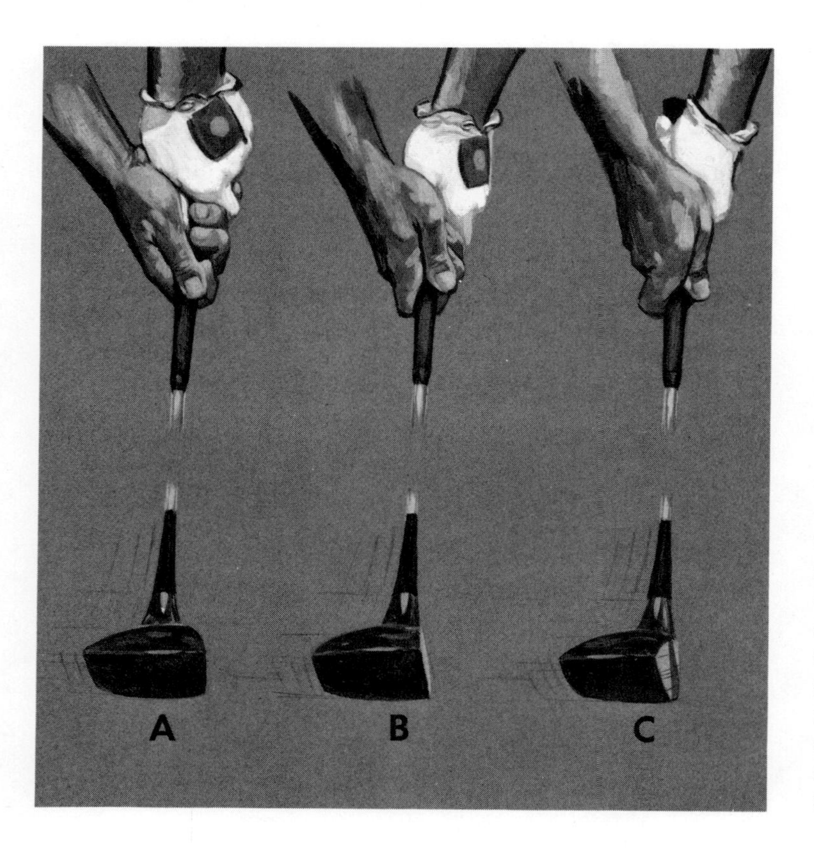

Note the marked effect the grip has on the swing For a right-handed player, if the palms are tilted to the right (A), the clubface will return to the impact area in a closed position (aimed to the left). If the palms are properly aligned (B), the hands will work correctly and return the clubface in the desirable square position. If the palms are turned to the left (C), the clubface will be returned in an open position (aimed to the right) at impact.

hands are turned to the left so that the V's point to the left shoulder, the clubface will tend to return to the ball in an *open position* (aimed to the right) and you'll slice. The compensation that you would have to make then — again, solely to keep the ball in play — would be an exaggerated out-to-in swing. Golf students who take the time to master correct positioning of their hands will be on the most direct course to improvement. Because they don't have to make compensations, they will gain a much better understanding of shot direction, and eventually will command enough control to maneuver the ball — hit it either left-to-right or right-to-left, at will.

If your grip is bad, it will be impossible for your body to function properly, because the swing is a chain reaction. The correct grip will allow your body to wind and unwind in sequence. You can't possibly play good golf with a good swing and a bad grip. However, with a good grip and a bad swing you can always improve.

POSITIONING YOUR HANDS

The grip that I advocate to my students is the *Vardon overlapping*, in which the little finger of the right hand goes over and around the knuckle of the left forefinger. This grip has proved over the years to be the most effective union of hands and club. It molds the hands together, giving a close-knit feeling, while at the same time allowing the wrists to be used freely without loss of accuracy.

Before I show you how to position your hands on the grip of a club when you pick it up, I would like to make a point without the club. Assume a normal golf stance, as though you were going to hit the ball, feet shoulder-width apart, and let your arms hang

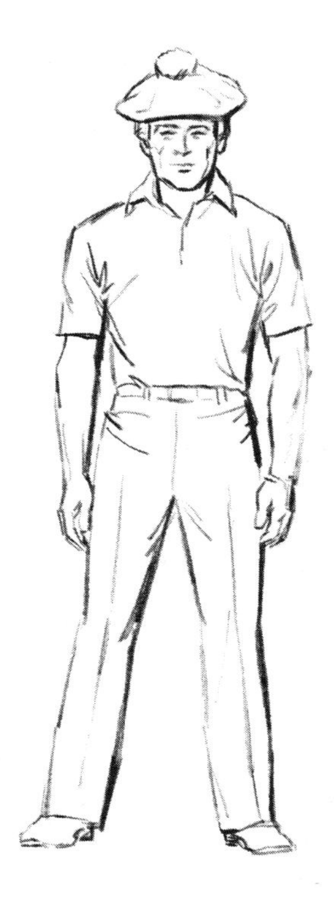

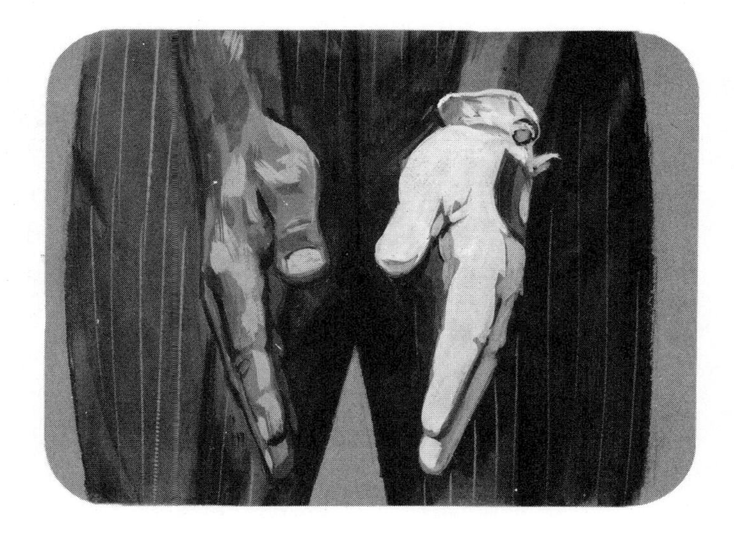

Stand with your feet shoulder-width apart and your arms hanging normally by your sides, then extend both arms until the palms of your hands are perpendicular to the target.

freely against your sides. Now extend your arms straight out, holding your hands at the same angle, palms facing one another. Once your arms are fully extended in front of you, note that the palms are perpendicular to the target line. This is the natural position they should be in once the grip is completed.

At the point of impact, the hands instinctively return to the "palms-facing" position. To get a better understanding of what I mean, extend your right arm in front of you and rotate the hand in a clockwise direction until the palm faces the sky. This position represents a "strong" grip. Were you to assume a "strong" grip (one with your hands turned to the right on the club), your right palm would be facing skyward initially but would return to impact facing the target; the clubface would be closed. The reverse is true if you rotate your palm to the left on the club:

this would represent a "weak" grip and when the palms returned to the palms-facing position, the clubface would automatically be open.

GETTING A GRIP ON THE CLUB

To insure that both hands assume the palms-facing position, first rest the club against your belly button and let your arms hang naturally at your sides. Then move your hands up, with the palms still perpendicular to the target line, so that the grip of the club is sandwiched diagonally in between. Now just wrap your fingers around the handle. Be sure not to rotate your hands.

Your hands should be placed on the grip of the club with the palms in the perpendicular (or "palms-facing") position.

Two useful checkpoints will help you grip correctly each time: (1) see that only the knuckles of

the forefinger and middle finger are visible on the left hand, and (2) see that the inverted V's created by the thumbs and forefingers point directly at the right shoulder, not to either side of it.

Most advocates of the palms-facing grip suggest that the V's should point to the chin. While this might prove a successful position for the professional or low-handicap amateur, it is not a good position for the average golfer. The average player will derive more power and significantly more control by having the V's aimed at the right shoulder. Surprisingly, this is still a palms-facing position. Unless you consciously manipulate your hands into a "weaker" position, you'll find that the V's naturally point to your right shoulder.

It is imperative that any player strive to get to a stage where he or she can position the hands purely by *feel*, without going through a one-finger-at-a-time process. This, of course, can only be accomplished through practice; there is no shortcut.

HOW HARD SHOULD YOU SQUEEZE THE CLUB?

How much energy ought it take to hold a club that weighs around fourteen ounces? About the same amount that it would take to hold an uncooked egg. Were you to grip too hard, the egg would break. If you imagine that you have an egg in each hand when you address the ball, you will have the right amount of pressure in your grip and it will be equally distributed, which is important for a smooth takeaway. Too much pressure could cause tension to spread up into the forearms and shoulder muscles, which would seriously hinder a free-flowing swing. A tense player loses the clubhead speed vital for distance and will also lose control by tending to steer the ball. It is therefore vital to be aware of grip pressure and to eliminate tension from the address. So remember: Hold the club about as hard as you would hold an uncooked egg.

Your Alignment and Setup

Every good player has his or her own method of setting up, a method that does not vary from shot to shot. A systematic setup helps you get aligned with and tuned in on your target every time you address a golf ball. It makes your address and swing more organized and positive, and you are able to keep your mind off the negative. You'll have no time to worry about the out-of-bounds markers on the left or the trees on the right because you'll be too busy making sure that you are set up correctly. Most players coming down to the wire, whether in a tournament or in a friendly nassau, tend to speed up. In their haste they forget the essentials, such as grip, stance, and alignment, and they forget where they are aiming the ball. To let your guard down for a second on the course is to invite disaster. Negative thoughts — images of the out-of-bounds markers, lakes, or trees — filter slowly into the mind. Don't allow this to happen. Keep your mind focused on positive action. Adopt a constant pattern when addressing the ball and in tight situations stick to it no matter what.

The pattern illustrated here, broken down into four steps, is the one I use, although I don't suggest that it is the only possible pattern of address; I offer it only as a model. If you prefer to develop your own specific pattern, fine.

1. I stand directly behind the ball and visualize the target line. Then I pick out a spot, a divot, a mark on the grass, or a broken tee — something that is directly on the intended line of flight and reasonably close to the ball. It is easier and just as accurate to line up the shot using an object close to the ball instead of the distant target.

2. I move diagonally to a point at a right angle to the ball, turn, and place the clubface down, aimed "through" the marker spot toward the target.

3. I step in with my right foot and set it a comfortable distance from the ball.

4. Then I set my left foot down parallel to the intended line of flight and also check to see that my shoulders are also parallel to the line. After two waggles I start my swing.

The full sequence is automatic, like "Get ready — Get set — Go!" — but you should follow your routine methodically, smoothly, unhurriedly.

2
3
4

2

The Hub—A Simple Guide to Help You Groove Your Swing

Amateur's Note

The hub *is a mental image used by Craig Shankland as a simple and effective device to focus the amateur's mind on a very crucial element in executing a sound golf stroke: a grooved, consistent swing.*

Craig often talks about the hub — basically the swing's center — as the best possible image to enable you to understand and to picture your own swing. (Most golfers, including topflight pros, are astounded to see their own swing in photographs. How we look and how we think *we look are often totally different.)*

"Put another way," Craig says, "if you are hitting bad shots — pulling, topping, or skying — you can be sure that your hub is shifting."

Why the Hub Is So Important to You

Like a large wheel, a golf swing has a center, called the *hub*. If this center were to wobble or shift, then the whole revolution, the circumference, the entire arc of the swing would be affected.

In a golf swing, the hub is principally the player's head. However, if a large enough depiction of the hub were drawn around the head, its lower half would incorporate the neck and shoulders. It is essential, then, that the head, neck, and shoulders remain perfectly centralized throughout the swing.

Other than those which result from bad grips, most bad shots occur when the hub moves from its original starting position. This excess movement can result in shanked (heeled), sclaffed, topped, fat, sliced, skied (popped up), line-drive, pulled, pushed, smothered, or totally whiffed shots, depending on how the hub shifts. If the hub moves in *any* direction, the swing circumference is affected and sound contact of the clubhead with the ball becomes unlikely.

Only when the hub remains centralized can you produce consistent shots: not only can you repeat your actions, but you can feel them taking place. Repetition is the key to consistency. Being able to repeat the same movement, shot after shot, allows you the control necessary to negotiate eighteen holes on a golf course and to avoid the wild, erratic shots that occur when you are unable to repeat your swing.

In the illustrations that follow, you will see the dramatic effect that the hub has on the swing. Note that in each case when the head, neck, and shoulders, and thus the hub, moves — to the right, to the left, up, down, or toward the ball — the fault becomes compounded on the arc circumference of the wheel.

As a teacher, I can safely say that inadvertent hub movement ranks along with a bad grip as the primary fault among average golfers. Teachers, low-handicap players, and duffers alike use many names for this movement — swaying, dipping, lifting, and so forth. Yet the fact remains that all these faults have but one cause: an unsteady hub.

A good way to implant a sound hub position into your swing is to imagine that you have a tray of teacups balanced on your head. Should the hub move in any direction, the tray would topple off your head and the cups would crash around your feet. Some teachers believe that consciously keeping the head still is inhibiting. But if you have ever watched African natives walk with giant vessels on their heads, you've seen that though their heads remained perfectly still there was absolutely no restriction in their shoulders, arms, and lower body. Those vessels wouldn't stay balanced if their heads moved, would they?

I am not suggesting that a steady hub is the only answer, or the only secret, to a sound golf swing. It is, however, a prime factor in developing a good, consistent swing, as the following pages demonstrate.

The Hub on Your Backswing

Throughout your backswing the center of the *hub* — the smaller shaded area in the illustrations — should remain perfectly steady. Your shoulders should revolve around this fixed axis, while your left arm remains perfectly straight, creating an arc radius (extending from the clubhead to your shoulder), which is necessary for control and power. This radius must create the largest possible "circular" arc around the hub.

The Hub on Your Downswing and Follow-Through

The hub should remain stationary within the arc of the swing. The body position and clubhead position at impact should almost duplicate the situation in the original address (the only difference is that your legs and hands should be slightly "ahead" of the ball laterally — closer toward target). The follow-through completes the circular arc of the swing.

Moving the Hub Up

If the hub moves upward, the lower arc of the swing moves up as well. At impact, the clubhead returns to a position above the ball; only the bottom half of the clubface makes contact. This tendency results in a topped shot or a line drive — both of which often plague the average player's game.

Moving the Hub Down

When the hub moves down during the backswing, the arc moves down with it; the clubhead is thus below the ball at impact. The result will be a fat, sclaffed, or skied shot (as described in chapter four.)

Moving the Hub Forward

If the hub moves forward, toward the ball, the club is forced to follow an unnatural arc outside of the normal path. The result: the clubhead arrives in the impact area *beyond* the ball. At impact, the neck of the club (the *hozel*) makes contact, causing a shanked (heeled) shot that goes nowhere.

Moving the Hub Right

If the hub moves to the right — away from the target — during the backswing, the rest of your body, as well as the swing arc, will move the same way. Unless you try to return the hub to its original starting position by swaying back toward the target in mid-swing, all power will be lost behind the ball. Since swaying back to the left is a compensating move that requires considerable effort to synchronize correctly, the chances of solid contact are reduced.

Moving the Hub Left

When the hub moves left — toward the target — so does the circular path of the clubhead. Thus, the arc radius behind the ball is reduced drastically, and all the extension — since the body is ahead of the ball — is wasted beyond impact. Moreover, the downswing arc will be altogether too steep, causing the clubhead to arrive at the ball in a hooded position. The result will be a smothered shot.

Shift Your Weight, Not the Hub

Unless you shift your weight from right to left — toward the target — during your downswing, you will create the effect of keeping your hub too far right and the desired arc position will be lost. There will be very little extension, plus a short arc radius

at impact and follow-through — in other words, a power loss. Furthermore, the clubhead will be forced back into the impact area while moving *upward*. The result is wasted effort: a topped shot that hardly goes anywhere. Your weight must shift — for power and accuracy — but *the hub must remain steady.*

3

Good Shots That "Warm Your Heart"

Amateur's Note

Craig's "Good-Shot Philosophy" is simple but basic: Good shots result from executing fundamental swing movements correctly.

Good shots are the result of practice after good instruction, of knowing what you are doing and why you are doing it, of making your swing consistent, of executing your movements in an unhurried, smooth, and relaxed manner.

A "good shot," says Craig, "is the result of having done everything right. There is no shortcut. You can't buy good shots for any amount of money. You and only you can perform them, and during competition on the golf course, no one can guide or assist you. You alone are the master of your golfing fate."

The Long, Straight Drive

There is nothing more exhilarating than hitting a long, straight drive. It is perhaps the most rewarding experience in golf.

A straight drive off the first tee while all your friends are watching can give you an added lift and lead to your scoring a low round. And if it's a *long*, straight drive, aside from giving you a psychological advantage over your opponent, it will long be remembered around the clubhouse. Your ego will constantly be boosted by ambassadors who'll spread the word throughout the club about your "amazing" ability to hit the long ball. In the locker room after playing, you'll hear, "Did you see Don's drive off One? — must've been three hundred yards." You may in fact have scored your worst round of the season. The long drive is remembered, the bad score quickly forgotten.

To hit a long, straight drive you must be physically qualified for the experience. You must be able to make a full, relaxed turn of your body from backswing to follow-through, without restriction. The combination of turn, arc radius, timing, and tempo gives you power and control. Brute force is not the answer. You could weigh 300 pounds and have arms like telephone poles, but all the force you could muster wouldn't send the ball very far at all. On the other hand, you could weigh 130 pounds and hit the ball anywhere from 240 to 300 yards just by harnessing your power through timing. The secret to the long ball lies as much in control of the mind as in control of the body. You can't be overanxious if you want to get the most out of your driver.

THE DRIVER SETUP

The setup plays as much a part in securing success with the driver as the swing itself. In fact, if you aren't set up correctly the odds are against your hitting the ball well.

The ball must be positioned off your left heel. You need a wide stance, your feet slightly outside shoulder-width apart. This will place most of your body weight — especially your head, which adds a large portion of the total weight — behind the ball. Your hands and the clubface should be in line with the ball.

I recommend a *square* stance when hitting with

the driver. (A "square stance" means the feet are parallel to the intended line of flight.) Any other stance, open or closed, would require you to compensate in the swing to steer the ball into the center of the fairway. With a square stance you can take a square swing and aim the ball directly at your target. With the others, if you failed to compensate you would force the ball to curve in one direction or the other.

Position the ball off your left heel, feet just outside shoulder-width apart, hands and clubface in line with the ball.

Your left arm must be comfortably straight when addressing the ball. This does not mean rigid; flexibility is a necessity. Your left arm establishes the width of arc in the swing by remaining straight until just after the ball has been struck. All you have to do then, once you have initially established your straight left-arm extension, is turn.

THE DRIVER SWING

If your left arm was straight at address, simply turn and you'll have the needed arc radius.

Your shoulders dominate the backswing turn. Simply by turning your shoulders your arms will follow. And the extension created by the straight left arm will be maintained without conscious effort for as long as the shoulders turn. I don't believe that forcing the clubhead away from the body, by pushing it low to the ground, is necessary. If your shoulders turn around a steady head position and your left arm remains reasonably straight you'll have the necessary arc radius for power and control.

Your turn should be tension-free and relaxed. Too often a player who is scared of the driver grips tightly during the address and tension spreads to the forearms and shoulders. Tension shortens arc radius; consequently, valuable motion (turning ability) is lost. The swing becomes jerky and short, powerless and without control. Don't let this happen. You should hold the club firmly but not too tightly. Be conscious of keeping tension out of your shoulder muscles. Stay loose and complete your backswing turn (windup).

You know you are fully turned when the muscles down your left side start to stretch, when your left shoulder is under your chin, or when your back is facing the hole. Out on the course, these keys can be useful to help you complete your backswing turn.

In the ideal top-of-the-swing driver position the club is nearly horizontal, with the clubshaft pointing directly at the target. Your left knee is pointed inward, to the right of the ball, and most of your body weight is on your right foot. Your head is still centered directly over the ball. From here you're in position to start the downswing.

A full turn of your shoulders is essential for a reliable swing. At the top of the backswing the clubshaft should be in nearly a horizontal position, pointing toward target.

Whereas the backswing is dominated by the shoulders, the responsibility of the downswing and follow-through is given to the lower body, specifically the knees and hips. You initiate your downswing by shifting the weight back to your left side through a *lateral* drive (a move in the direction of the target) in your knees. This starts an unwinding sequence in your upper body. Once your weight, led by your knees, is onto the left side, your hips assume the leadership role by clearing quickly out of the way. In professional terminology this is called *separation.* If there is a secret to power and consistency with the driver, separation is it. The knee and hip actions separate the lower body from the upper and create the driving power as the wrists catapult the clubhead into and through the impact area at maximum speed. The knees initiate, then the hips follow, leading ahead of the upper body, to act as the unwinding key.

To insure that you retain clubhead speed — vital for both distance and accuracy — the clubhead on

You initiate your downswing with a lateral drive made by your knees. This shifts the weight to your left side.

The clubhead is catapulted through the impact area by the wrists. Without wrist action there can be no clubhead speed.

Unwind to face toward target, and take the clubhead as far through as you are able. At the finish your hands and the clubhead should be behind you.

follow-through should be allowed to go through as far as possible. At the finish your hands and the clubhead should be behind you, and your hips and shoulders should be facing directly at your target.

The Fairway Woods

Don't underestimate the importance of fairway woods. Gary Player, one of the greatest players in the history of the game, had serious distance problems when he first came to the United States. He was used to courses where the premium was placed on accuracy rather than distance. After a few months playing on the U.S. tour, he became frustrated by his inability to reach many of the par 5s that the American pros reached easily. So he returned to South Africa and began exercising and working hard on his game, especially his fairway woods. When he returned to the United States, Player could hit the par 5s and he began winning. Today, he is one of the best fairway wood players in the game.

With all fairway woods, make a conscious effort to watch the ball until it has been hit.

Effective use of the fairway woods can do for you what it did for Player: make the long par 4s and 5s easier to cope with. If you decide to use a fairway wood, however, your choice of which one (3, 4, 5, et cetera) should not always be based on the distance to the target; consider also the type of lie you have. For example, if the ball is sitting up in lush fairway grass, you have all the options. But if it is sitting down on hard ground, unless you are an extremely capable fairway wood player, I strongly suggest you sacrifice yardage for a percentage shot and choose a more lofted wood.

As to technique, I don't recommend any drastic changes compared to the way you hit with a driver. Place the ball in line with your left heel and set your feet parallel to the target line (a square stance). Position your weight evenly between the heels and the balls of both feet. And be sure to allow the clubhead to rest with its soleplate flat on the ground. The clubface should squarely face your intended target.

If you need more height, simply hit down more.

On the backswing, be especially conscious of making a full shoulder-turn. Many bad shots occur because players make short, quick backswings. The

To gain maximum clubhead speed and control, use your hips, legs, and feet to assist in the acceleration of your arms and hands.

backswing must be full and smooth and must emphasize the shoulder-turn.

In the downswing, acceleration and a conscious effort to stay down, keeping your hub steady, will do the trick. Remember, you can't hit the ball very far using just your wrists and arms. So use your hips, legs, and feet to assist the acceleration of arms and hands for maximum clubhead speed and control.

One last word of advice: If you need additional height on the fairway wood shots, simply hit down into the ball more. The more height you need, the more you should hit down and through.

The Long Irons

To begin with, it's important to emphasize that the long irons are, compared to the rest of the clubs in the bag, a little bit harder to use because they don't have much *loft* (clubface angle) and they have longer shafts than the middle and short irons. Less loft on the clubface produces less spin on the ball, resulting in a lower trajectory. Shots hit with 5-, 6-, 7-, and 8-irons will all rise even if the ball is slightly mishit, but this isn't the case with the long irons. And because the shaft is longer, your swing's arc radius will be longer and therefore harder to control.

Though it may sound as if I'm starting off on a negative note, I'm making these points so you're aware that you can't make a haphazard swing with these clubs. But don't be afraid of long irons — the

2-, 3-, and 4-irons play a very important part in stroke-saving. They should be neither feared nor ignored.

The most common cause of bad long-iron shots is fear. Fear creates tension, which in turn leads to jerky, uncontrolled swings. So the first point I want to make with regard to technique is: relax. Your long-iron swing must be no different from any other iron swing. Don't grip too tightly, don't get tense — just relax.

To help offset the club's lack of loft and its long shaft, you should play the ball off the left heel in the address. With the ball in this position at impact, the club will not be moving down as much — the arc will be wider and more sweeping behind the ball — which will give you more height.

Other than the ball-position change (more off the left foot), most of the other fundamentals remain the same. Your weight should be evenly balanced on both feet, with your hands just slightly ahead of the ball laterally (toward target); your feet should be aligned parallel to the intended flight line. The only difference in positioning your feet for a long iron shot is that they are set slightly wider, to give you a solid base for a little bit longer swing. Now, on to the swing.

I'm asked all the time by my pupils: How should you take the club back on long-iron shots? I encourage golfers just to start the club back with the shoulders rather than worry about coordinating individual parts of the body. If the shoulders start the swing, everything else will follow naturally. The left arm will remain extended throughout the backswing for as long as the shoulders turn. If the shoulders don't turn enough on a long-iron swing, the arms and hands take over and effort is wasted. I can't empha-

I can't emphasize enough the importance of completing the shoulder-turn. Only then will the extension created by the left arm at address give you the swing arc radius necessary for success with the long irons.

Be sure that you accelerate the clubhead through to a full finish. Your hips and shoulders should be facing the target directly, your weight should be on your left side, and your hands should be high, behind your head.

size enough the importance of completing the shoulder-turn. And remember, as I said earlier, fear is a common cause of long-iron problems: it creates tension, which causes shortness in the range of motion — the distance the club is swung back. A conscious effort to relax and complete the shoulder-turn — making sure that your left shoulder arrives under your chin and that your back is to the hole at the top of the backswing — will help insure success.

Your lower body must lead the clubhead back to the ball on the downswing. If your upper body leads, you will hit the shot badly. When your lower body beats the clubhead to the ball and separates from your upper body, the clubface is prevented from closing and arrives back at the ball in a square or slightly open position — you get the trajectory that you need.

Another point on long-iron mechanics deals with the follow-through. Most high-handicap players direct too much attention at the ball when trying to achieve a high trajectory. They forget to accelerate the clubhead all the way through the swing to a full finish. The one thing you must not allow is deceleration — allowing the clubhead to slow down as it passes through the impact area. Consciously follow through to a full finish. At the end of the swing your hips and shoulders should face the target directly, your weight should be concentrated on your left side, and your right foot should be on its toe with the heel off the ground. Overall, you want to feel as if you have completed a gigantic circle, ending with the clubshaft and the clubhead behind your head and with your hands in a high position.

Finally, I want to stress the importance of good long-iron tempo and restrained force. Don't try to hit the ball any harder than you would with a middle or short iron. Swinging too hard is a major fault in most players' games. I often have my students hit five or six shots with a short iron, then hit the same number with a long iron. I consider this an excellent way of demonstrating to them that additional force is not necessary with long irons. Most golfers think that when they hit a longer, less-lofted club they must swing harder, which just is not true. The reduced loft alone will give extra distance; all that's necessary is a smooth swing. If you hit a few shots using the exercise I've just outlined, you'll see what I mean. So, when you're next faced with that crucial long-iron shot: relax, turn, start down with your lower body, and be sure to accelerate through to a full finish. And make the whole swing smooth.

The Middle Irons

The 5-, 6-, and 7-irons, also called the middle irons, are among the easiest clubs in the bag to use. Because of the amount of loft on the clubface of a middle iron it is easy to get the ball airborne. And because the middle iron's shaft is shorter than a long iron's, the clubhead arc is easier to control; there is very little chance of sending the ball too far off line.

But if you play regularly, don't make the common mistake of letting your guard down. Just because it's a middle-iron shot doesn't make it a lead-pipe cinch that you'll play the shot well. There are some key points to keep in mind.

Be sure to know how far you can hit the ball with each club. A middle iron can be used effectively by the average golfer to hit a distance of anywhere from 130 to 150 yards; with the same club, a lower-handicap player might hit the ball between 140 and 170 yards.

The middle iron's greatest attribute is its effect on ball trajectory. Because of the loft on the clubface, the ball will fly high and will stop quickly when it lands. A longer-iron shot isn't quite as predictable because it will fly lower and roll more. When a pin placement is cut close to a trap you can fly the ball right at the flag with a middle iron, whereas with a long iron, from a greater distance, you would be unable to do so.

The middle-iron ball should be played in the middle of your stance, with your weight equally divided between both feet.

The main technique difference on a middle-iron shot is that the ball is played in the center of the stance. This is the low point of the downswing arc and the place where you'll strike the ball crisply. Your weight should be equally distributed between both feet and your stance and body must be aligned parallel to the intended line of flight.

Emphasis during the swing should be placed on tempo. Of course, the only way you can have good tempo is if you coil and uncoil your body correctly. Be conscious of completing your shoulder-turn in the backswing. It is very easy to let your guard down and shorten your swing with middle irons. Don't. Complete your turn and then be very conscious of initiating your downswing with your legs and hips. Then you'll find you unwind freely and swing smoothly down and through to a full finish.

The Short Irons

THE FULL-WEDGE

The short-iron swing must be full. The most common cause of bad shots with 8-irons, sand irons, and the like is thinking that a short swing is needed because such clubs have shorter shafts and considerably more loft than all the others. Your swing must be as full as if you were playing a driver. The shorter shaft and sharper loft enable you to control the height and distance you hit the ball. The mechanics for a short shot are otherwise no different from a middle-iron shot.

The best short-iron players are able to control the *speed* of the club. Instead of concentrating on how far back they take the club on the backswing and how far they follow through, they are more concerned with how much force they put into the motion. Thus they can swing with more freedom and aren't distracted by precise mechanics. The ball, after all, responds only to the speed of the clubhead through the impact area, so the player who is able to reduce or increase the speed of the overall motion depending on the distance required is able to vary the length of shots without shortening the swing. (I'm talking now, of course, in terms of full shots. When you get very close to the green, within pitching or chipping distance — which I'll cover in the next section — the swing length must be reduced.) If, for example, you normally hit your 8-iron shot 125 yards but you are faced with a shot of only 115 yards, there's no way you can swing using full force. You're going to have to slow your tempo a little or choose a shorter club. This is a matter of feel that comes from experience. You must practice.

Practice the in-between distances that you will

encounter on the course — the shots that require a little less than maximum force. Start out by hitting full shots. Record either mentally or on paper how far you hit your 8-iron, 9-iron, pitching wedge, and sand irons with your normal swing. Then, gradually, making the same full swing, slow the tempo down. With the pitching and sand wedges, go from using full force to using minimum force. You'll be surprised to find that you're able to hit the ball only a very short distance although using a full swing. Only when you can hit the ball no shorter should you elect to shorten the swing in length.

The short-iron swing must be full, with emphasis placed on good tempo. Make the same full swing regardless of the distance you want the ball to travel. To vary distance, simply regulate the amount of force you put into the total motion.

THE HALF-WEDGE

Once you are close to the green, you should cut your swing in half. You need an action in which the club-head goes only to about hip height on both back-swing and follow-through.

The swing I advocate on these shorter shots is really only a smaller version of the big swing. I'm not a believer in fancy changes, such as sharp wrist-breaks or outside-the-line swings. You've got to keep it simple. The fewer swing-thoughts you have in your mind, the easier it is to retain a perspective on the target and the distance you need to hit the ball. It's really like tossing a wad of paper into a waste-paper basket. You see the basket and you rely on your instinct and experience to provide the necessary force and accuracy to get the paper into the can. But suppose you were conscious of even one or two movements within the throwing action — would you be able to throw as freely? Of course not. You'd clog your spontaneity.

It's the same with short shots. Your mind has to be reasonably free, not conscious of any more than one

A pitch shot is a lot like throwing a wad of paper into a wastepaper basket: you must rely on your instincts.

THE LOW-FLYING PITCHING WEDGE

You'll see the touring professionals use this shot frequently. It can be used effectively from distances up to 80 yards in situations where you are playing into the wind, to a tight pin placement — in the back or close to the sides of the green under an overhanging tree limb; or it could be used when you need to make the ball carry to the top of a tiered green and stop quickly.

The secret of this shot is the massive amount of backspin you impart with a special action. You can expect the ball to take a couple of skips when it lands and stop abruptly.

In the setup, play the ball to the right of center, toward the right foot. Set your hands well ahead of the ball laterally to reduce the effect of loft on the clubface, which should be set square. Position your weight about 70 percent on your left side, 30 percent on your right, and keep it that way throughout the swing. This will cause a steep downswing arc, to give the ball a low flight trajectory.

A conscious effort is needed to make a more upright backswing than usual; take back the clubhead outside the target line. Follow this by leading your hands through the impact area well ahead of the clubhead. Delay the *release* — the pronation, or cross-over, of your hands at impact — as long as possible. Be sure to hit *down through* the shot. These changes will give you the low flight and the backspin essential to stop the ball quickly.

Be sure to keep your hands well ahead of the clubhead, through impact. Do not allow your wrists to release until well after impact.

THE PITCH-AND-RUN

You should use this shot when there is no pressing need to put the ball in the air, as when you face no obstructions such as bunkers or heavy grass between the ball and the hole. It's a great little percentage shot.

If you find yourself just off the green with the pin tucked in the rear portion, or you have to play either uphill or to a two-tiered placement, then you should run the ball. The closer you keep the ball to the ground the easier it is to gauge distance. That's important to remember. The less green you have to work with, the more you should pitch the ball. The more green that you have to work with, the more you roll the ball.

There are two clubs that can be used effectively for the pitch-and-run: the 5- and 7-irons. The farther you are from the pin, the more you will tend to use the less-lofted 5-iron, because you'll want to roll the ball. When the pin is close to you or where you need to negotiate fringe of anywhere from, say, six to ten feet, then the 7-iron should be used for more height and a little less roll.

Play the ball in the center of your stance and choke up on the grip. Place the grip end of the club just ahead of the ball. Your feet should be placed open, angled to the left of the flag to give you better ball/target perspective.

Now to the swing: Take the club back, keeping the face square. Very little wristbreak, other than a natural break, is required. It's more of a one-piece takeaway, where everything moves off the ball together.

To set up for a low-flying wedge shot that stops quickly, play the ball well to the right of center. Set your hands well ahead of the ball laterally and position your weight solidly on the left side.

On the downswing, make a conscious effort to keep your hands moving forward toward the target and the arms straight. Consciously point the club at the target on the follow-through. As long as the hands keep going forward, the clubhead will too. *Quitting* — stopping the hands once the ball has been struck — is a common tendency. By focusing on leading the hands through to the target, there is no possible chance of a quit occurring.

Another helpful way to produce solid contact as well as consistency is to try to keep the clubhead low to the ground through impact to the finish. This will prevent any chance of lifting up and topping the shot.

Putting

There are basically two methods of putting: wrist putting and no-wrist putting. You must experiment to find which suits your game the best. Since there are both good wrist and good no-wrist putters, there is no ideal stroke. However, in careful study of a majority of the world's greatest putters, I have noticed that nearly all have very little wrist action. This is the method that I advocate and the one I use myself.

I feel that the fewer moving parts in the stroke, the less likelihood there is of error. There's too much movement in a wristy stroke. Wristy putters tend to be very streaky — one minute they hole putts from all over the place, the next they are three-putting. A no-wrist putter is generally more consistent.

Just as in the full swing, to putt well you first must have a good grip. The grip that I suggest is the *reverse-overlap*, in which the index finger of the left

I recommend a reverse-overlap grip, because it puts all the fingers of your right hand on the shaft. Your eyes should be directly over the ball.

In the putting grip that I suggest, your palms are parallel to the putter face. This grip is readily achieved by aligning your thumbs straight down the center of the clubshaft. Position the ball in line with your left foot.

hand is placed over the uppermost two fingers of the right. This locks the hands together and puts all the fingers of the right hand on the grip of the club, which is important since the fingertips of the right hand harbor all the sensitivity and feel. The left thumb points directly down the shaft. Again, I am not suggesting that this reverse-overlap grip is the best putting grip for everyone. Far from it. If you prefer to hold the putter differently, go ahead. I would caution you, though, no matter what variation of finger and hand position you use, be sure and align your thumbs down the very center of your putter grip. This will give you the palm position essential for control. If your palms are parallel to the plane of the putter face when it is correctly aligned perpendicular to the line of the putt, all you have to worry about is making sure your hands work correctly. You can putt better by concentrating on only one thing (your hands) rather than two (your hands *and* the putter blade).

Also, in the putting address you should have your eyes directly over the ball so you can strike it solidly. Rather than bending a lot from the waist, you can accomplish this by standing closer to the ball. After assuming whatever posture is most comfortable for you, be sure that your eyes are over the ball and that the putter blade is aligned properly, square to the line of the putt, before you draw back the putter blade. The ball should be played either off your left heel or toe.

The only moving parts in the putting stroke are the shoulders, arms, and hands. Everything else, especially the head, remains perfectly still. A prime cause of an inconsistent stroke when putting is movement of the head — looking up too soon to see whether the ball is heading for the hole.

Make a conscious effort to keep the palms square to the line of the putt during both the backstroke and the follow-through. Again, remember: if your palms remain square to the line of the putt throughout, then the putter blade will, too.

A useful way to consistently produce solid contact — to make the putter face strike the ball squarely in the sweet spot — is to keep the blade low to the ground during backstroke and follow-through. This is something you can practice before playing. Try to make the putter head brush the surface of the grass, back and through.

Once you have perfected your own style of putting, there are really only two things to think of when you putt: the line and the speed. No other thoughts need concern you.

READING GREENS

You should start to read the breaks in the green long before you ever reach the green itself, because you can see undulations better from a distance; you can see whether the cup is set at an angle, or if there is even a slight change in the contour of the ground. From a distance, your eyes function like a carpenter's level and you get a broad perspective of the putt facing you.

Furthermore, as you approach the green you'll be able to check to see how the grain will affect your putt. Though most golfers ignore it, the grain often affects the putt just as much as the break. In some cases the grain may even offset the break. Be wary: check for grain.

Grain is best described as the way the grass lies. If the grass leans to the left, the ball will be influenced to roll in that direction. The opposite is true if the

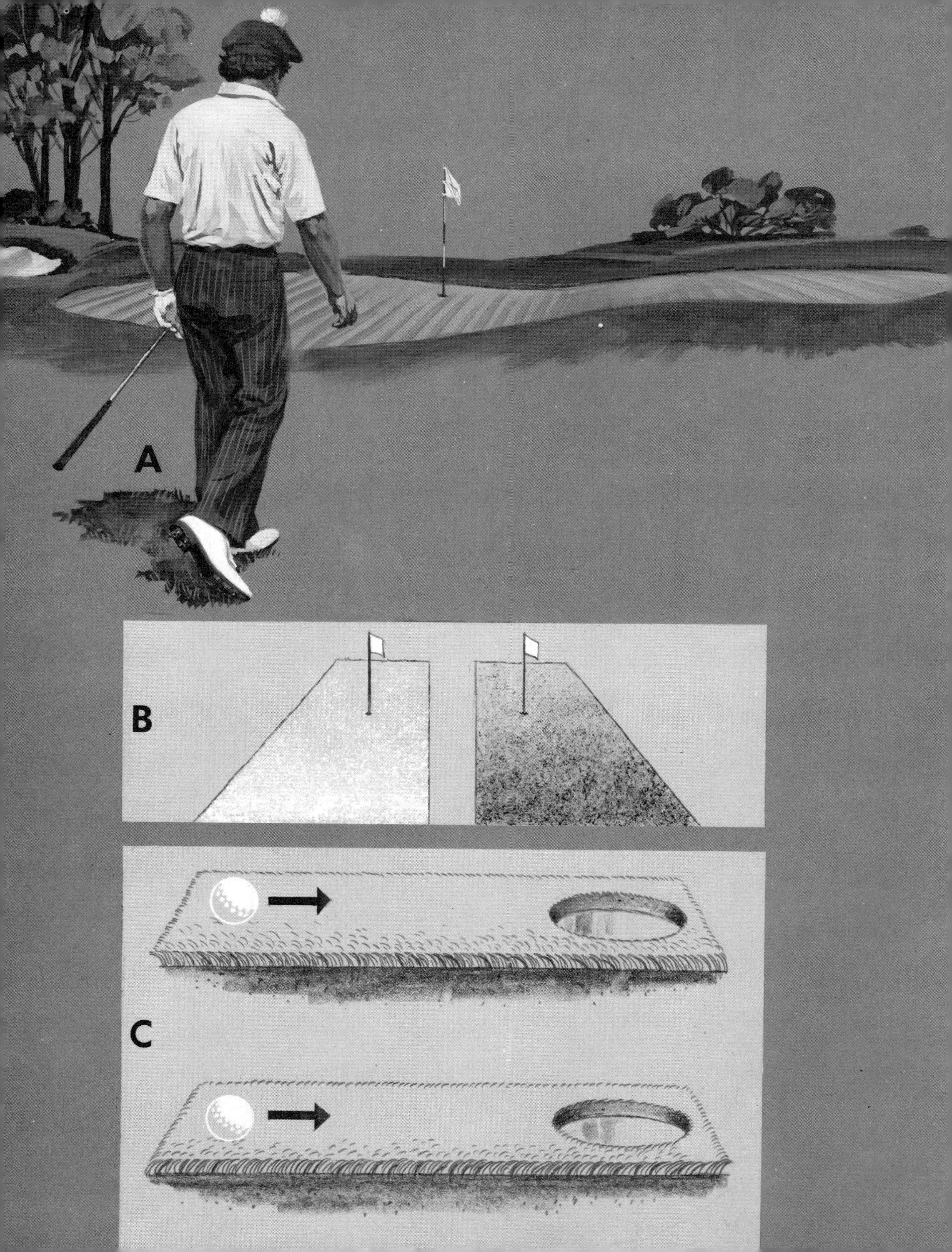
A
B
C

grass leans to the right. When the grass leans toward you, you are putting against the grain, and your putt will be considerably slower than normal. You'll have to give a little extra to get the ball to the hole. You can tell from a distance when you face a putt against the grain: the grass will appear dull, patchy, dark in color. The opposite is true — the grass will be shinier and lighter — if you are putting downgrain. The ball will roll more when the grain is with you and you don't have to hit as hard.

HOW TO DEVELOP A CONSISTENT PUTTING STROKE

(A) You should start to read the break in your putt long before you get to the green. It is much easier to see the subtleties in the terrain from a distance.

(B) If the grass shines (as at left), then the grain is with you. If it's dark and patchy (right), the grain runs against you.

(C) Remember: when the grain goes against you (top drawing), hit the putt harder. Putting downgrain (bottom drawing), stroke the ball with less force than you'd use normally.

The drill shown on page 66 will help "groove" your putting stroke or, if you have been putting badly, will cure the yips. I have used this exercise with considerable success teaching amateurs at my club and when advising professional golfers who have had putting problems. Primarily, it teaches you how to make an *uninhibited* stroke. It also teaches you how critical it is (for most good putters) to keep *wrist action* out of the stroke.

Place your left hand as close to the bottom of the club's grip as you can without putting your fingers on the shaft. You'll find the large expanse of grip above your left hand will then rest against the fleshy part of your forearm. Now clamp your right hand over both your forearm and the handle. (See the illustration to be sure you are doing this correctly.)

Stroke a few putts, keeping the grip locked solidly against your arm. Notice that your wrists are completely uninvolved in the stroke and that the putter feels like an extension of your left arm. You want the feeling that you are making this left arm/putter

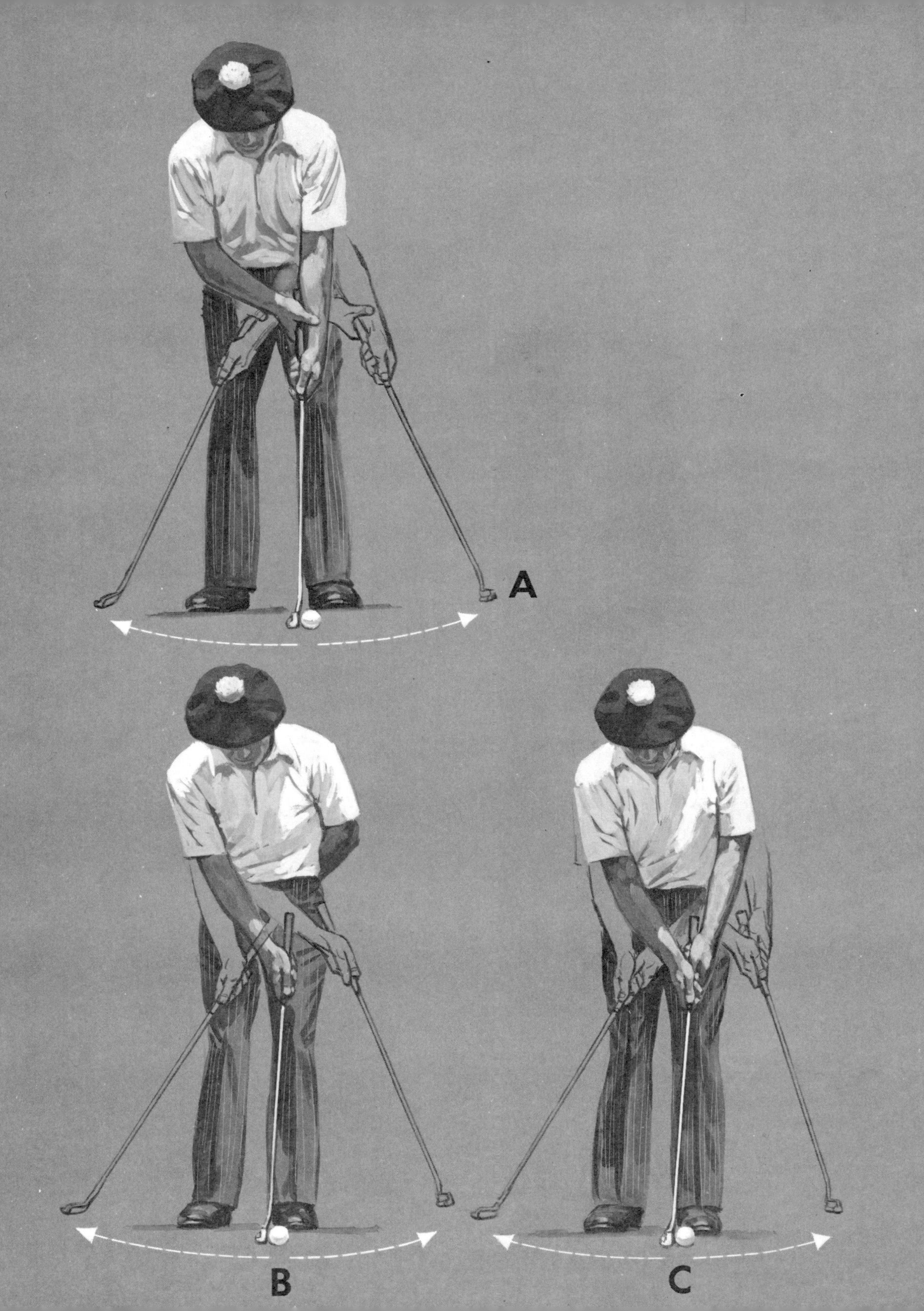
A
B
C

(A) Grasp the base of the club's grip with your left hand and clamp your right hand over the grip and your left forearm. Strike a few putts this way to get used to the feeling.

(B) Reverse the procedure. This time grasp with your right hand, but put your left hand behind you. Strike a few putts. Notice that the putter blade swings through unrestricted.

(C) Now use both hands. If there is any wristiness in the stroke, you'll notice it immediately and can correct it.

unit go through to the hole. You'll be amazed at the percentage of putts you hole from a short distance using this exercise method.

Next, to develop an unrestricted stroke, place your right hand on the handle in the same place you just had your left hand. This time, though, put your left arm behind your back. Using just your right hand, stroke a few putts. Notice that the putter blade goes through to the hole unrestricted each time; there is no left hand in the way to make it do otherwise. Use your right hand for a few minutes and you'll develop uncanny accuracy!

After practicing the left- and right-hand portions of the exercise, place both hands on the putter using your normal putting grip and stroke a few putts. You will be aware of any unwanted wristiness in the motion and can correct it; you'll also tend to follow through better, making the blade go through to the hole. Your stroke will be a lot smoother, a lot longer, and a lot less inhibited.

One last point, regarding a similar drill: Spend time putting with just the left hand (place the right behind you). This tip can be most helpful in eliminating any tendency to steer the putter blade toward the hole. Whether you practice with the right or left hand alone you'll no doubt be amazed at the putts you drop.

4

Bad Shots and How to Cure Them

Amateur's Note

No golfer plays the game without sometimes making bad shots. The exquisite, superdelicate timing, tempo, and control required for perfect shots every time can only be accomplished by a machine. No mortal can apply his or her limited physical abilities to the game — let alone confront the devilish effects of of golf's mental *strains — and seriously expect errorless execution on every shot.*

One of the most frustrating aspects of the game is to repeat a basic error — a hook, a slice, a shank, et cetera — and feel helpless and inadequate in searching for the necessary correction. We all flounder, experiment, overcompensate, grasp at straws . . . and often accept the inevitable. "OK," we righthanders say, "if I'm doomed to slice, I'll just aim each shot well to the left and let nature take its course."

Nature does *take its course — resulting in the "banana-ball flight." But you needn't fight the laws of physics. (In fact, the more doggedly you compensate for error instead of correcting your technique, the more grievous and harder it will be to change your swing.) Our suggestion: refer in this chapter to the bad shot that most often plagues you and, next time out, try to apply the cure. Then, as others from the eleven categories of bad shots described here begin to threaten your game, you can develop confidence by knowing the truth, which will enable you to attempt to apply the right correction rather than meekly accept the bad shot.*

Craig's advice is simple and to the point:

"Know the cause, then apply the cure.

"Don't be fooled into thinking that a misplayed

shot is a solitary happening. Your off-key swing, if you'll understand the whys and wherefores, has a message for you.

"Don't let bad shots terrorize you, and don't let bad breaks destroy your confidence or optimism. Instead of dwelling moodily on bad shots, you should analyze your swing for possible error. The next shot, then, can contain corrective measures rather than despair over the last poor shot.

"Obviously, you should absorb, analyze, and try to reason why the shot was mishit. But don't overreact or overcompensate. If you think positively, you'll be surprised at how your natural correction reactions — smooth, calm, unhurried — will result in that next shot being to your liking."

Slicing

A *slice* results when the clubhead crosses the target line from out to in, with the clubface in an open position at impact. This action causes a large amount of clockwise ball spin, resulting in a curve to the right.

The player who slices usually has two visible faults in his or her address position: (1) a "weak" grip — one with the hands turned too far to the left on the handle; and (2) a poorly aligned body, aimed well to the left of the intended target.

During the swing, a slicing tendency can be caused by moving over the top of the ball with the right shoulder; instead of the proper rotation under the

(A) A slice results when the clubhead moves across the target line from out to in, with the clubface in an open position at impact.

(B) Making a grip change can have a drastic effect on the path the clubhead follows. With a proper grip the clubhead will approach the ball along the correct path and meet the ball squarely.

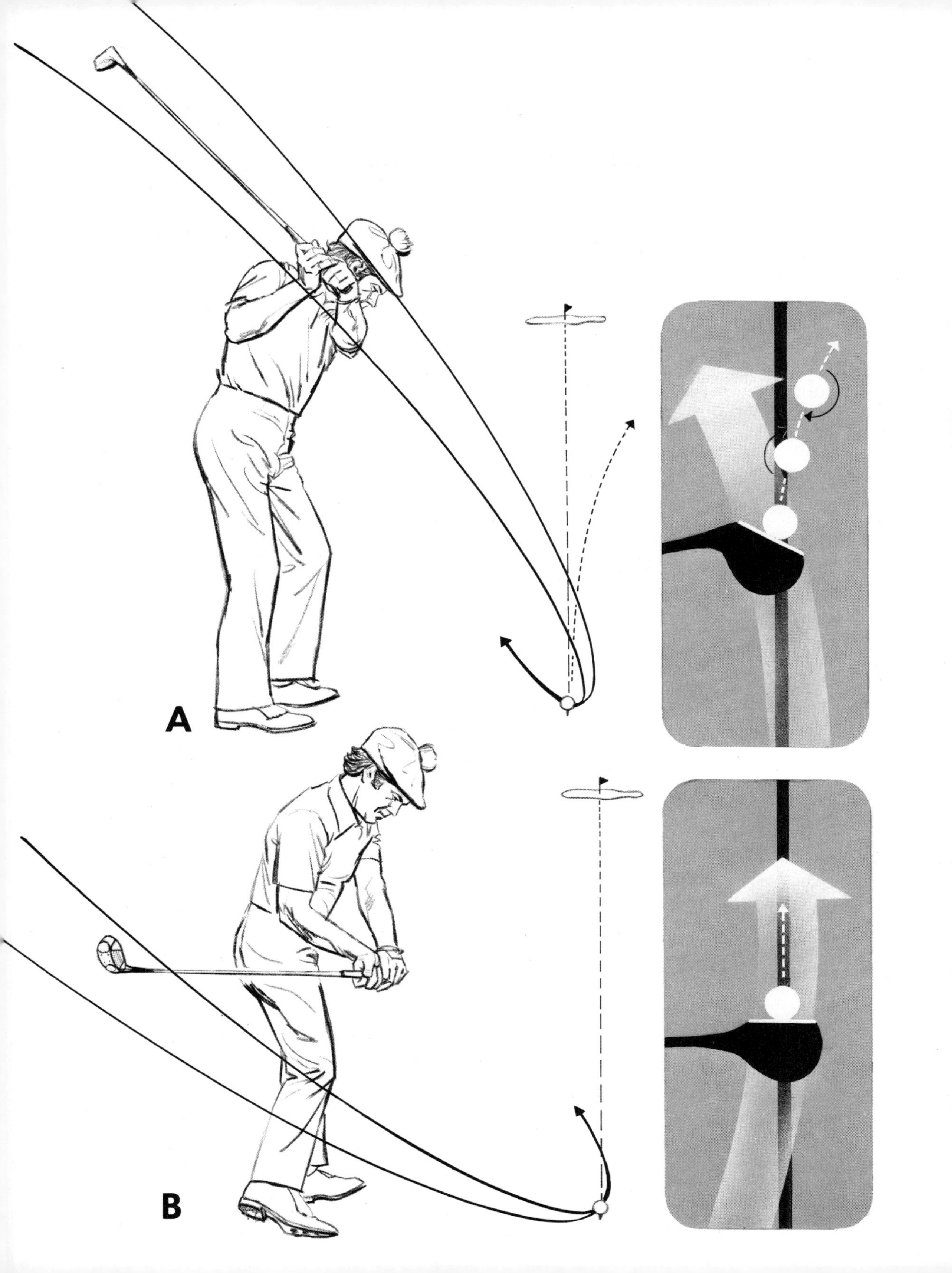
A
B

chin, the right shoulder turns into the follow-through on a more horizontal plane. Another common cause of slicing is failing to release — to pronate the hands through the impact area. If the right hand doesn't turn over the left, the clubface will remain in an open position. It's also possible that the clubface could be open at address, causing a slice upon impact.

I have found that a slicing tendency usually stems from a "weak" grip, which causes the clubface to open more than it should during the swing. Since the clubface will be an open position at impact if the hands are turned too far left on the club's grip, the player must eventually compensate by aiming to the left and using his or her right side to prevent a massive banana ball. Of course, a right-sided swing with open alignment only compounds the fault by forcing the clubhead even farther outside the line and turning the clubface into an even more open position.

If you slice, remember that the ball reacts to the face of the club, to its position at the point of impact. Logically, to cure a slice you first must look to the part of your body that directly controls the clubface: your hands.

I have eliminated slicing with tremendous success by making players who slice change from their "weak" grip to a "strong" one and then gradually back to an orthodox position. Slicers trying a strong grip immediately see the influence hand position has on the pattern of their shots; most of the time they abruptly cease slicing and start to hook consistently. Then, as they get used to seeing the ball travel to the left, I gradually move their hands back into a more orthodox position (see pages 13–19 for a full description of the standard grip) and shots begin to straighten out.

KEYS TO CORRECT SLICING

1. Check your grip; if it is "weak," correct it.
2. Hold the club lightly.
3. Check alignment. Be sure you're square to target.
4. Remember to release your wrists.
5. Swing to target.

If you're trying to correct a slice, I encourage you to try a grip change first. Once you have established the correct grip, there will no longer be any need for alignment compensations: your stance and the clubface can be aimed square to your target. Having used an open position for so long, a change to square alignment will at first feel strange. But as you consistently hit straight shots you'll gain more confidence.

If you have a good grip and find you still slice, then the fault obviously must be in your swing. Once you have set yourself up at address properly, the fastest way to eliminate a slice is to consciously make your right hand turn over your left (release) through the hitting area. If you force your hands to pronate, the clubface will close passing through the impact area, resulting in counterclockwise spin and a shot that if anything will hook rather than slice. Making a conscious effort to release, you may even find you pull the first few shots you hit. Just allow this to happen. Because of the increased understanding you'll have of the function that your hands perform in the swing, it won't be long before your swing begins to follow the correct path.

Hooking

A *hook* is caused by the clubhead crossing the target line from in to out, with the clubface in a closed position at impact. This causes counterclockwise spin on the ball and results in a sharp curve to the left. The ball reacts both to the direction in which

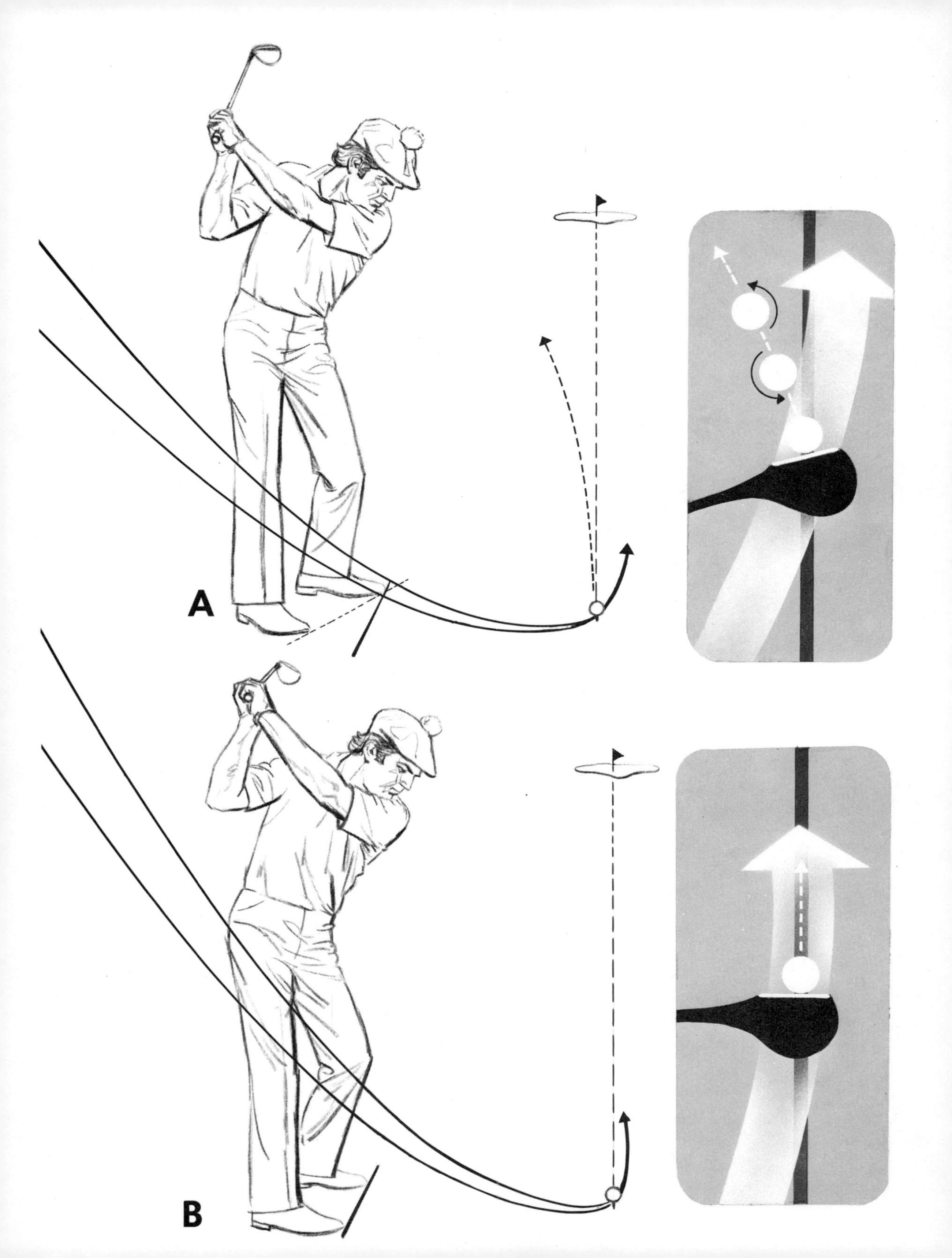
A
B

the clubhead is traveling and to the angled position of the clubface at impact.

Most players react to a hooking tendency by aiming farther to the right of the target. As the hook becomes more pronounced, such players aim farther to the right. This forces them to take the club back even farther to the inside and to use their right side to close the clubface more, just to get the ball back in play. Of course, the more the clubhead approaches the ball from the inside with the face in a closed position, the greater the counterclockwise spin and the more the ball will hook. Eventually, the problem becomes so serious the golfer must start fighting to prevent a *duck hook* — a short, diving hook.

To eliminate a hook, delve to the root of the fault: the grip. Then concentrate on other sound fundamentals that will help you return the clubface to the ball in a square position. But you must first realize that the hooking habit took a long time to become ingrained and will take a long time to correct.

The most common cause of hooking is too "strong" a grip — one where the hands are turned too far to the right on the handle of the club. The left hand, instead of showing two knuckles beyond the left wrist, shows three or four, and the inverted V's formed by the fingers and thumbs point to the right of the player's right shoulder. Unfortunately, the player's swing, from address through finish, will build around this one fault in trying to compensate for it.

Changing from a "strong" grip to an orthodox position will feel uncomfortable and "weak" at first. You will undoubtedly have to suffer through a few bad shots until your muscle memory absorbs the new feeling. However, once this is accomplished you will

(A) A hook is caused by the clubhead moving in an exaggerated inside-to-outside arc across the target line, resulting in a closed clubface at impact. The follow-through arc then fails to continue on line to the target.

(B) A grip correction and a conscious effort to swing the clubhead along the target line will help to eliminate the hook.

agree that the sacrifice was worth it. (Refer to pages 13–19 for a thorough description of the proper grip.)

At address, be sure that the clubhead sits flat on the ground with the clubface square to the target. If the toe of the clubhead is in the air, the heel will catch the ground first, forcing the clubface to twist closed on impact. Be sure that your shoulders are aligned parallel to the target line, since they influence the path the clubhead follows. If they were closed, angled to the right of the target, you would be forced to use your right side to compensate and would hook the ball. Your toes should also be parallel to the target line; in all respects, address the ball squarely.

In the takeaway, allow the clubhead to follow the natural turn of your shoulders. And in the downswing, swing the clubhead through toward, not away from, the target. If the clubhead travels down the target line for as long as possible, the ball will not deviate off line much, even if the face of the club is slightly open or closed.

Since the hook is a right-side dominated fault, you must insure that the left side remains the controlling factor throughout the downswing. This is readily accomplished by clearing your left side out of the way first to trigger the downswing. Then the clubhead and your hands will be following your lower body through the impact area and will not get ahead of it. "Beat the club, don't let it beat you."

KEYS TO CORRECT HOOKING

1. Check your grip. Is it too "strong"? Correct it.
2. Be sure your alignment is square.
3. Swing to target.
4. Develop more left-side control on the downswing.

Topping

When the clubhead travels through the impact area on the upswing and strikes the top half of the ball, the shot will be *topped.* Instead of contacting the ball at the low point of the downswing, the clubhead is moving up as it strikes the ball. The result: the ball is struck with either the leading edge or the sole-plate of the clubhead and it never fully compresses on the clubface.

If this is your problem, your mistake could be:

- Looking at the target before hitting the ball.
- Jerking the club back from the ball in the backswing.
- Tensing up in the address position and thus overcontrolling the club during the swing.
- Moving your hub (head, neck, and shoulders) upward from its original address position.
- Staying back on your right side, so that you have too much weight on your right foot at impact (see pages 35–36).
- Positioning the ball too far left in the address.

If you are consistently topping the ball but can't isolate your particular fault, I can almost guarantee that your problem lies in the address. Tension in the forearms, wrists, and hands will cause overcontrol to set in. The tension will prevent the clubhead from swinging freely in its natural arc, and the swing will in effect become a totally right-handed motion. Be sure not to grip the club too tightly, since this is the principal cause of tension, and keep your knees flexed, not stiff.

Focus on good balance in the address position and on smoothness throughout the entire swing. There is a routine that I suggest to my students to help ac-

KEYS TO CORRECT TOPPING

1. Don't be too tense; relax.
2. Avoid too much weight on your left side at the top of the backswing.
3. Avoid too much weight on your right side at impact.
4. Guard against bad posture; flex your knees.
5. Don't overreach.
6. Insure extension; keep your left arm straight.
7. Don't swing too quickly; be smooth.

complish natural movement: from the time you select the club from the bag until the finish of your swing, make your movements smooth and deliberate. Don't hurry. In aligning your feet and looking from the target or target-line marker spot back to the ball, move with rhythm and smoothness.

During the swing itself, be sure to keep your head still. This is the most basic and undoubtedly the best way to cure a topping problem. If you continually raise your head or move it to the right, sooner or later you will top some shots. Keep your head still and allow your shoulders to turn.

Another precaution you can take in the swing is to make a conscious effort to pull the club down with the left hand leading. If you keep your left hand in

Don't be tense in your address. Having your knees rigid or allowing tension in your upper body can lead to a fast, jerky swing.

Keep your knees flexed and your arms and hands tension-free.

mind, you'll prevent your right hand and right side from dominating. Check your ball position, keep a steady head position and a smooth, unhurried swing — and you'll quickly kiss your topping problem good-bye.

Shanking

A *shank* is undoubtedly the most feared shot in golf. Once you have hit one you are always wary that you'll hit another. Unfortunately, the more you fear a shank, the more likely it is to happen, which is one reason why many players have a stretch of several shanked shots.

You shank when the ball is struck by the hozel, the round part where the shaft is joined with the club-head. The result is a shot that shoots off at a sharp angle to the right.

A shank will occur more often around the green than on longer shots, because on short shots you may tend to try *too* hard to get the ball close to the hole. Instead of swinging freely, you become tense and try to *steer* the clubhead toward the hole. This tension and inhibited swing result in a failure to release your hands — they remain well ahead of the clubhead, which arrives at the point of impact with the face wide open.

I consider tension and steering the primary causes of shanking. Both can force the clubhead out of its natural arc. In other words, while the clubface will start in the ideal position, with the ball in the center

KEYS TO CORRECT SHANKING

1. Eliminate tension; grip the club lightly.
2. Balance yourself properly; be sure your weight is on the balls of your feet.
3. Swing the club; don't steer it.
4. Don't stand too close to ball at address.
5. Release your hands freely at ball impact; don't block the shot.
6. Pull your hands through toward your belt buckle.

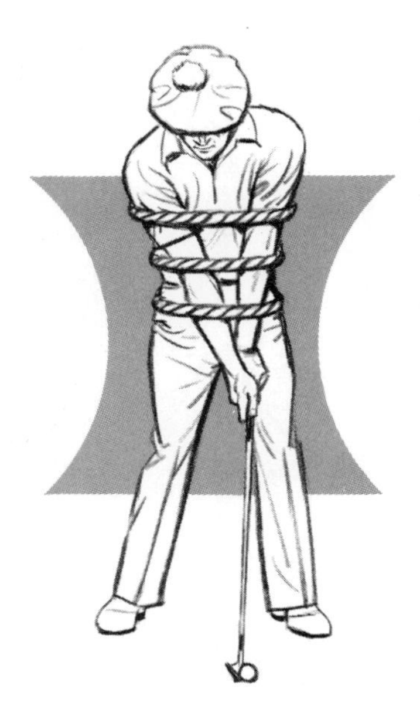

Make sure that you aren't bound with tension in your address.

of the face at address, at impact the clubhead will have returned with the face outside the ball. This is because the club was taken back on a reasonably sound path but then, either because of tension or an attempt to steer the ball, it was forced to make a big loop outside of its natural arc.

Though the most common cause of shanking is looping to the outside, you can also shank if the clubhead moves into the hitting area from a sharp inside path. (This isn't quite as common, although it also stems from tension or steering.) Other causes include standing too close to the ball at address, gripping the club too tightly, turning the clubface wide open in the backswing so that you are unable to close it in the downswing, or shifting too much weight to your toes while swinging through the impact area.

Before I discuss the many possible cures, I should point out that some will work for one player and not for another. I encourage you to experiment until you find the one that works consistently for you.

To correct a shank, the first step is to quiet your mind. Forecast a positive result. Picture clearly a smooth tempo, a solid strike, and the ball landing by the hole. Positive thought breeds positive action. This done, focus on your address position.

Relax and don't crowd the ball: stand farther away than normal. If you have been hitting the ball on the hozel, the most logical way to contact the ball squarely on the clubface is to stand back. In extreme shanking cases, I even go so far as to instruct a student to stand farther away from the ball and attempt to hit it off the toe of the clubhead. I realize that this is going from one extreme to the other, but it's the fastest way to stop shanking, and it makes the player conscious of what he or she has to do to make solid

The most common cause of shanking is looping the clubhead outside the target line. You can see here, both from an overhead and rear view, what happens to the clubhead in the backswing and downswing. The insets show why the ball leaves the clubhead at a sharp angle to the right.

contact: make the downswing path almost duplicate the backswing path.

Position the ball in the center of the clubface and don't grip too tightly. Your weight should rest on your heels and remain there throughout the swing. If your weight starts on your toes, or shifts forward when the swing is in motion, then the path of your downswing will also move forward (see chapter two), bringing the hozel of the club into play.

You can prevent the clubface from *spreading*, becoming too open in the takeaway, by envisioning an imaginary straight line between the target and the ball. Just make the clubhead stay on the line, with the clubface at right angles to it. This will insure a square position.

Relaxing grip pressure and standing farther away from the ball will help alleviate the danger of shanking.

Overall, the swing should be smooth. Don't be afraid to release your hands. Remember, once you have hit the ball you can't do a thing about it. Don't try to steer, or overcontrol, the clubhead; let it swing naturally.

I'm not a great believer in gimmicks, but in the case of a serious and frustrating fault like shanking, I do use one or two tricks to eliminate the problem. For example, I'll often place a block of wood or a second golf ball approximately one inch from the ball to be hit, outside the target line, and have pupils try a shot. Players who have been shanking will usually hit the wood or the marker ball first, since their downswing arcs approach sharply either from the outside or from the inside. The shock of impact quickly makes them realize their fault. Then, I ask that they imagine that they are pulling their hands in toward their belt buckle through impact. When they are able to miss the wooden block or the marker ball and strike the shot solidly, I remove the ob-

Place a block of wood about an inch from the ball, outside the target line, and try hitting. When the clubhead misses the wood, there's no way you can shank a shot. A second golf ball, placed one inch from the ball to be hit, can substitute for the wood.

stacle and make them repeat the shot. Most of the time, any tendency to shank disappears.

Skulling, Thinning, or Hitting the Line Drive

If I were to rank the most frequently hit bad shots, *skulling, thinning, or hitting the line drive* would follow right after shanking. These three shots — low, screaming, ground-huggers — are joined under one heading because all have the same cause.

There you are, sitting pretty either just in front of the green or in good shape to play your second shot in, and what happens? Instead of that nice, floating trajectory that you had hoped for, followed by the ball landing softly on the green, you get a low screamer that barely gets off the ground.

Why does the ball assume such a low trajectory? What happened that caused it to fly over the green? Your clubhead contacted the ball above the center and as it was moving up. (A "skulled" shot goes much farther and lower than planned; a "topped" shot, which has a similar cause, is a dribbler that gets no distance.)

In most cases this fault is caused by lifting the head (hub) up as the clubhead swings through the impact area. When your hub lifts, the low point of your swing moves up also (see chapter two). Thus, it is the leading edge of the clubhead rather than the clubface that makes contact with the ball. The clubface can only make proper contact if the leading edge of the club strikes the bottom half of the ball

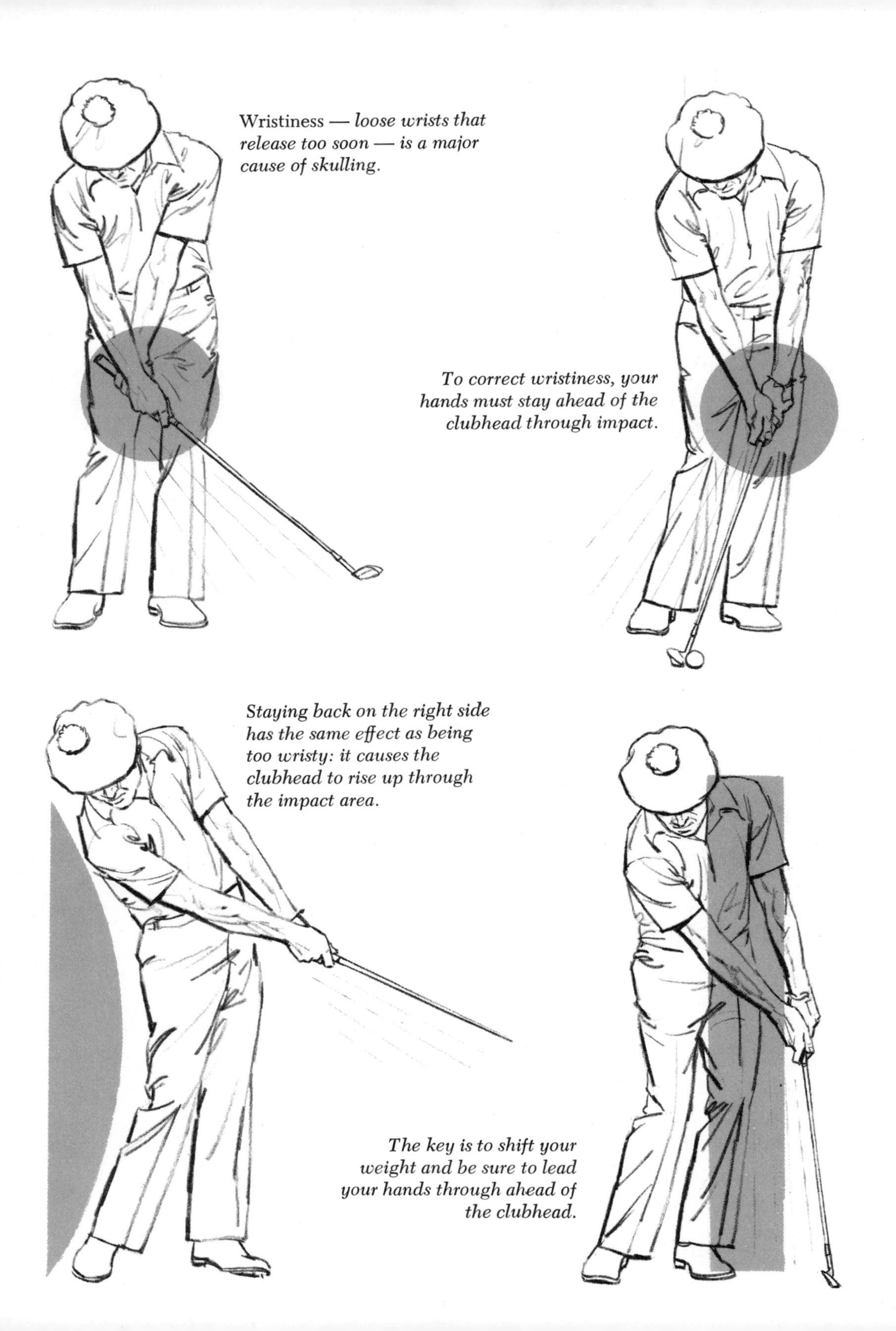

Wristiness — *loose wrists that release too soon — is a major cause of skulling.*

To correct wristiness, your hands must stay ahead of the clubhead through impact.

Staying back on the right side has the same effect as being too wristy: it causes the clubhead to rise up through the impact area.

The key is to shift your weight and be sure to lead your hands through ahead of the clubhead.

at the point of impact. The ball then spins up the face and gains height.

The only way to insure solid contact is to keep your head/hub still throughout the swing, especially during impact. To help yourself "stay down," so to speak, keep your eyes focused on the ball's ID number or on the manufacturer's name. You can work on this a lot in practice. Set the ball so its imprint faces away from the target and is just within sight during address; then keep your eyes focused on the writing until the ball is airborne.

Another cause of these low-flying shots is swinging too fast, especially under pressure. Be conscious of your tempo and try for smoothness, not speed. With a steady head and a smooth swing, you'll be able to feel that the clubhead is still descending until the ball is airborne. If you are too "wristy" or fail to shift your weight, you're inviting a skulled shot.

One of the best ways to ingrain the feeling of solid contact when hitting irons is to practice *punch shots.* On the practice tee, practice "hitting down" and abbreviating your follow-through to about waist height. This will train you to hit down, not up.

Finally, when you are on the course playing a match, be sure to pick a club that will give you the distance you require. Don't *ever* force a club. To force a club you must speed up your swing — and I've already outlined the problems that will create. Rather than force a club, it is better to select a lower-numbered one and slow down the overall speed of your swing.

KEYS TO CORRECT SKULLING, THINNING, OR HITTING THE LINE DRIVE

1. Don't be loose and overly wristy; keep your hands ahead of the clubhead through impact.
2. Don't straighten up before impact; keep your hub steady.
3. Remember tempo; make your overall swing smooth.
4. Hit down and finish low.
5. Be sure to shift your weight to the left side.

Pulling

A *pulled* shot — one that travels to the left without curving — results when the clubhead travels along a line that points to the left of the intended target, with the clubface aimed squarely in that same direction. This fault can happen with any club and on all shots, even short pitches, chips, and putts, and does not necessarily result from a bad swing. In fact, if the swing on a pulled shot is reasonably good and the ball is struck solidly, the only missing ingredient is the right direction.

Pulled shots can be caused by:

- Standing too far away from the ball.
- Playing the ball too far forward, with the shoulders misaligned toward the left of the target.
- Failing to complete the shoulder turn on the backswing.
- Allowing the clubhead to approach the ball from too far outside the target line.
- Omitting leg action in the swing.
- Rushing the overall tempo of the swing.

In the address, check to see that you aren't overreaching. Your arms should be comfortably extended, but not rigid and too straight. Keep the upper half of your arms resting lightly against your sides.

Be sure also that the ball isn't too far forward, to the left of your left heel. This causes the shoulders to misalign to the left. Your shoulders have the greatest influence on the path of the clubhead through the impact area.

Throughout the backswing be especially conscious of completing your shoulder-turn. Although incorrect, it is very easy, especially in a crucial situation, to shorten your backswing. Your left shoulder should

KEYS TO CORRECT PULLING

1. Don't overreach; stand closer to the ball.
2. Align yourself properly; be sure your shoulders are parallel to the target line.
3. Check ball position: Is it too far forward?
4. Check your shoulders at impact: Are they in a square position?

A primary cause of pulling is standing too far away from the ball.
Be sure that you aren't overreaching. Your arms should be comfortably extended.
Failing to turn the shoulders on the backswing is another common cause of pulling.
At the top of your backswing, your left shoulder should be under your chin and your back should be facing the target.

be under your chin and your back should face the target at the top of the backswing. A good backswing shoulder-turn sets up the proper stroke plane and the correct downswing path. The clubhead will be inclined to follow more of an inside than an outside arc into the ball.

In the downswing, the lower body must lead the hands. If the knees are used properly, moving toward the target laterally, you will block out any chance of an early release of the hands that would force the clubhead out of the correct path and cause the clubface to close. For the same reason, be especially conscious of your overall tempo; if it is too fast, the clubhead will be thrown out of line by your wrists and will arrive at the ball ahead of your lower body, in a closed position.

One final note: During practice, check your shoulder position at impact by swinging the club to the top of your backswing, then down, and freeze at the point of impact. Your shoulders should be perfectly square, parallel to the target line. If not, keep practicing until you arrive at the ball in a square-shoulders position. When you accomplish this, try hitting the ball. You'll find that you return instinctively to the square-shoulders position, and the pulling tendency will diminish.

Pushing

A *pushed shot* — one that travels to the right without curving — results from the clubhead in the follow-through swinging out to the right of the target, with the clubface aimed squarely in that direction. Like a pulled shot, the swing is not necessarily bad — the ball can be struck solidly and travel far — it just lacks proper direction.

If the swing is indeed correct, an obvious cause of pushing could be misalignment — for example, when the shoulders are aligned aiming directly *at* the target, instead of *parallel* to the ball's imaginary target line. Also, positioning the ball too far back in the stance can result in a push.

You can easily check to see if your shoulder alignment is at fault. Assume your address position, then freeze. Take the club and run the shaft across your shoulder blades. If you find the club points either directly toward or to the right of the target, simply pull your left shoulder back slightly until your shoulders are parallel to the intended flight path (target line) of the ball.

One other common cause of a push is the lower body getting too far ahead of the hands in the downswing. This is largely the result of bad tempo — failure to synchronize the movement of the upper and lower body — and can be cured by a slower, more controlled takeaway.

My final point, and undoubtedly the golden key to eliminating the push, is to concentrate on making the clubhead move out along the target line after the ball has been struck. Remember: swing the clubhead along the target line and through to the target.

KEYS TO CORRECT PUSHING

1. Check alignment; your shoulders should be parallel to the ball's target line, not aimed *at* target.
2. Check ball position: Is it too far back?
3. Don't rush or jerk the downswing hip-turn.
4. Swing to target.

Skying, or Popping Up

A shot that is *skied*, or *popped up*, generally lands short: it virtually goes nowhere except up. This is a frustrating dilemma common to wood shots, from the tee or fairway. In either case, the fault is caused by an extreme downward, chopping-type blow that contacts the ball not with the clubface, but with the polished surface of the top of the clubhead. The player who consistently skies the ball can easily be recognized by the clubheads of his woods, which are freckled with white marks.

Let's take a look at how those white marks get there. The following are possible causes:

- Gripping the club too tightly.
- Shifting too much weight to your left side at the top of your backswing.
- Using your right hand excessively during the swing.
- Moving your head and dipping the hub downward.
- Bringing the club down into the impact area too steeply, from outside the target line.

When using a driver from the tee, a player's first reaction to a skied shot is to tee the ball lower. While this serves as a psychological aid, it usually does not cure the fault. A pop-up is usually not caused by a high tee, but rather by a steep downswing arc — the clubhead descends toward the ball at a sharp angle. A player who consistently skies his tee shots will almost certainly sky his fairway wood shots. The cure, then, must be to eliminate the faults which lead to this steep downswing arc. A review of the basics is necessary.

First: position the ball off your left heel on all

Two causes of skying are having the ball too far back toward your right foot in the address and shifting your weight too quickly to your left side during the downswing. Each results in the clubhead approaching the ball at too steep an angle.

Play the ball off your left heel, and make a conscious effort to sweep the clubhead through the impact area on a level plane.

KEYS TO CORRECT SKYING, OR POPPING UP

1. Eliminate tension in your address; relax!
2. Keep your weight equally balanced at the start.
3. Avoid an abrupt pickup; keep the club low in your takeaway.
4. Keep your head still; watch out for a dipping hub.
5. Sweep the ball; don't chop at it.
6. Play the ball more off your left heel at address.
7. Use less right-hand force during the swing.

wood shots; extend your left arm to provide maximum width of arc, which in turn will result in the essential sweeping action. Second: hold the club as if there were eggs in both your hands — firmly but not tightly — and position your hands slightly ahead of the ball laterally at address. (Players who grip too tightly or position their hands behind the ball at address will be inclined to pick up the club in a jerky fashion with the right hand dominating the backswing.) Distribute your weight equally between both feet.

Once again, I cannot stress enough the importance of a steady head during the swing. Don't allow your head to shift, wobble, or turn. Imagine that you are balancing a tray of cups on your head throughout the backswing and downswing. But most important of all, be sure that at the top of your backswing the bulk of your weight is on your right side. If your weight is on the left, then you will be forced to use your right hand in the downswing and the result will be another skied shot.

Overall, try to imagine that you are about to *sweep* the ball off the tee or the ground. I observe many of my pupils on the first tee practicing swinging with their drivers and taking huge divots. This is not only bad for the tee area — it ingrains a fault into their swings.

The key is to avoid hitting down with the woods and to sweep instead. To convey the importance of this to my students, especially those who are skying the ball, I tee up a ball *extra* high for them. Then I ask that they try hitting the ball several times while attempting to leave the tee in the ground. This quickly alleviates the tendency to hit down and, to their amazement, the skying problem disappears.

If skying is your problem, ask yourself: What's the

opposite of chopping? The answer is, of course, sweeping — it will stop popping up.

Smothering is caused by an overdominant right side that forces the clubhead to close and to cross the target line moving toward the inside on the follow-through.

Smothering

A *smothered* shot is best described as a shot that barely leaves the ground and veers to the left. This often occurs when a player is under pressure to win a match, is on a tight hole, or needs a par on the last hole to score the best round of his life.

The cause of smothering is an overdominant right side, which forces the clubhead to close and to cross the target line from outside to inside at impact. The right side dominates in pressure situations because the player is so tense he tends to steer the ball instead of allowing the club to swing freely, and he shifts too much weight to the left side too early in the swing. As a result, the player leans toward the target and is unable to clear his left side effectively without overusing his right side.

To cure this problem — as with any major fault in the swing — you must first check to see that your setup is correct. Your first consideration must be the grip. Be sure that you aren't using too "strong" a hold on the club. The V's should be pointing to your right shoulder, not to the right of it.

Next, be sure that the clubface is aimed square to the target, not closed. The soleplate of the club should be flat on the ground. If the toe of the club is in the air — if there is a gap between the toe and the ground — the heel will catch the turf first and cause the clubface to close. Position the ball off your

A full shoulder-turn will prevent your right shoulder from going out over the top of the ball. Be sure to swing the clubhead toward the target on the follow-through.

KEYS TO CORRECT SMOTHERING

1. Check grip: Is your right-hand too tight? Grip lightly.
2. Keep the clubface square, not hooded.
3. Make a good shoulder-turn.
4. Remember target awareness; swing the clubhead toward the target on follow-through.

left heel when hitting woods and long irons, and in the middle of your stance when hitting other clubs. Having the ball too far back can cause a smothered shot, because the clubhead approaches the impact area at a steep angle of descent. (The smothered shot results from the clubhead coming *down on* the ball; a "skied" shot results from the club coming *down under* the ball.) Lifting the club by breaking the wrists too quickly in the takeaway will have the same effect as positioning the ball too far back.

A conscious effort to make a good shoulder-turn will insure that the clubhead *sweeps* back away from the ball and is not "picked up." Besides the shoulder-turn, a good extension of the arms throughout the backswing will maintain a wide, sweeping arc.

To eliminate a smothering tendency, I make my students very target conscious, from the minute they address the ball. If your mind is not aware of where the target is, it will fail to *tell* your body how to guide the swing. Make yourself aware of where the target is, then attempt to swing the clubhead toward the target in the follow-through. Remember: the basic cause of a smothered shot is swinging the clubhead leftward rather than directly at the target.

KEYS TO CORRECT SCLAFFING

1. Shift your weight from right foot to left before impact.
2. Avoid too much right hand; be smooth.

Sclaffing

The term *sclaffing*, which originated in Great Britain, means hitting too far behind the ball — although not in the same sense as on the *fat* shot. When you hit a fat shot, the clubface hits ground behind the ball (laterally) but doesn't contact the ball at all: the loosened turf lifts the ball into the air. A sclaff is almost a good shot because the face of the club does make contact; unfortunately, impact occurs *after* the clubhead has struck the ground. When this happens clubhead speed is reduced, resulting in loss of distance.

Sclaffing stems simply from failing to shift your weight during the downswing. Instead of moving your weight from right to left, you leave it on your right side. This causes your upper body to dominate, your hands to release early — and a sclaff.

Fortunately, the cure is as simple as the cause: just consciously move your knees laterally to start the downswing. This will make your lower body the leader throughout the downswing and will eliminate any chance of your upper body dominating. Also, be sure to swing smoothly and keep your right hand relaxed.

When my students have a sclaffing problem, I make them hit shots and "walk after" the ball — literally step forward with the right foot on the follow-through. The only way you can walk after a shot is to shift your weight correctly; the sclaffing problem is gone with the first step.

Failing to shift your weight to your left side and staying back on your right side will cause the clubhead to strike the ground first, resulting in a sclaffed shot.

Hitting the Fat Chip or Pitch

There is nothing more frustrating to a golfer than hitting a *fat* pitch or chip shot — one that catches too much turf before the ball, preventing clubface contact.

Use your knees to shift your weight laterally to the left, to be sure you hit the ball first.

The fat chip can result from having your hands behind the ball laterally in the address and from having too much weight on your right side.

Make sure that your hands are well ahead of the ball initially and that your weight is on the left side.

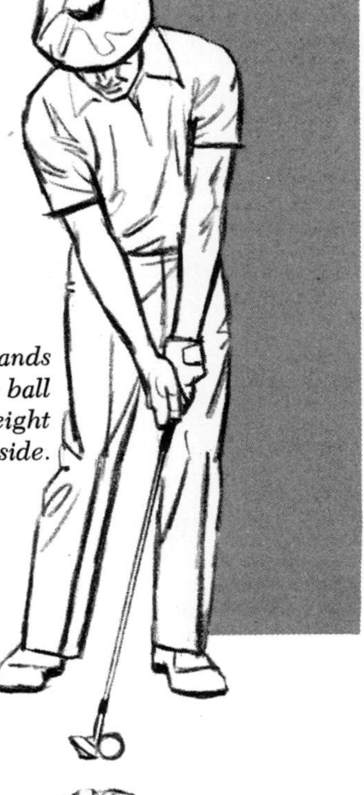

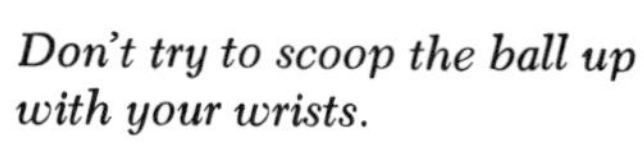

Don't try to scoop the ball up with your wrists.

It is vital to keep your hands moving through to the target. If your hands stop, the club will too.

Fat shots can have several causes. Fear of playing a short shot off hard ground, for example, creates tension, which can cause overcontrol to set in — the clubhead is not allowed to swing freely. Other causes are:

- Taking a quick, jerky backswing.
- Scooping at the ball with your wrists.
- Using your arms only, without any lower body action.
- Having too much weight on your right foot at impact.
- Lifting your head up.
- Forgetting to stay conscious of where the target is located.

The address position is the key to overcoming fat shots. If you feel you are set up correctly, and you have the target and the type of shot you want to play clearly in mind, you will give no thought to mishitting the ball. Your stance should be slightly open, to give you a better ball-target perspective than the normal square stance provides. Play the ball in the center of your stance and set your weight to favor your left side. Place your hands well ahead of the ball laterally for a smooth takeaway.

Be sure not to grip the club too tightly or tension will spread into your arms; the buildup of tension destroys your natural tempo. A relaxed hold on the club will serve to calm you down and keep the overall motion smooth.

Most of the backswing movement should be controlled by your shoulders, arms, and hands, in that order. Keep your lower body relatively still.

KEYS TO CORRECT THE FAT CHIP OR PITCH

1. Correct your address; balance your weight on your left side.
2. Position your hands ahead of the ball at address.
3. Keep your arms, hands, and club moving through to target.

5

Basic Trouble Shots—Bunkers, Wind, Water, Rough—and How to Master Them

Amateur's Note

As a particularly pleasant part of the research for this book, I had the opportunity to play some of Scotland's finest courses — among them, Saint Andrews, Carnoustie, Gleneagles, Troon, and Turnbery — as a "partner/pupil" of Craig Shankland, our teaching pro. It was not just the advantage of playing eleven rounds in eight days — with dozens of hours of concentrated, on-the-course instruction from this outstanding teacher — that was so instructive; I also came to realize that the Scottish attitude toward the game is so pure and uplifting that we Americans might well reflect upon and borrow from it in our own approach to golf.

I mention this as we come to the chapter "Trouble Shots and How to Master Them" (one of the most valuable chapters in the book, in my opinion), because the healthy Scottish approach to trouble shots especially deserves our admiration and imitation. The rough-and-tumble courses in Scotland bear little resemblance to our manicured greens and pampered fairways. Scottish golfers eagerly accept troublesome aspects such as wind, rain, wild rough, and cavernous bunkers, as basic elements of the game. They revel in the "trouble" rough weather and tough terrain offer and rejoice in the opportunity to execute new and unexpected shots.

For the golfers of Scotland there are no winter rules or improved lies. I sometimes think that too many of us in the United States are spoiled to the point that we take it as a personal affront, a dastardly trick of fate, when we don't end up with a perfect lie, or when we get a less-than-kindly kick, or when we hit a tree and, instead of bouncing into the fairway, veer into the deep rough. Who would really like a golf course where you always drive downwind and downhill, where there are no trees, bunkers, or rough to impede your progress, and where all greens are funnel-shaped, so that any shot to the vicinity of the flag rolls unerringly into the cup?

As for trouble shots, Craig prefers to call them challenge or recovery shots. I agree, and hope you do, too. When your prospects look bleakest you should rise to the challenge, knowing that you can recover; your mind should tell you that all is not lost — that your swing can propel the ball to the target because you know the essence, theory, and technique of the shot. As soon as we accept the truism that in any round of golf we will inevitably find trouble and face challenging shots, we realize that these seemingly negative aspects of the game are really what give us the greatest positive feelings of accomplishment. When we conquer the trouble, meet the challenge, solve the problem and recover — that's when we deservedly experience the thrill of achievement.

In tough situations you combine your mental preparation for a golfing round with your physical approach to individual on-the-course shots. If you know that trouble is inevitable, it's not such a brutal shock when it arrives. Remember: as surely as you will mishit a number of easy shots, you'll also invariably find your share of trouble shots on and off the fairway. You will, at times, land in the rough, confront precarious fairway lies, settle behind a tree, lodge in a hazard, bury in a bunker.

So this chapter on basic trouble shots and the chapter that follows on related problems are, we hope, "worth the price of admission." Use these chapters before you play to review and bone up on the situations that cause you the greatest headaches.

And also use the pointers here after *your round, to determine what you might have done to solve a recurrent problem. Next time out you will do better.*

Here are further thoughts for you from Craig:

"Mere hope or an accidental swing can never be your salvation when you are faced with a difficult trouble shot or a formidable recovery situation. Some people take the easy way out: they put the ball in their pocket — pick up and, really, give up. Nothing could be more alien to the game's philosophy than a belief that all hope on a particular hole or on a particular shot is lost.

"Play it. Try it. Make the attempt. And, at worst, play the shot to a safe position and hope that your next *shot will put you in position for a one-putt. This involves* planning ahead. *Visualize the next shot, and the one after that. Always have a target to shoot at, even when playing safe. Know what you want to do and where you want to go even before you hit that safe shot.*

"And remember that there is no drastic mechanical swing change for even the most challenging trouble or recovery shots. Tempo, visualization, an unhurried attitude and swing — those are what add up to success."

Bunkers

The Basic Bunker Shot

The swing you use with a sand iron in the bunker is the same swing you would use with any other club. The length of the swing should not change (you use a full backswing) even though the distance the ball travels and the force that is used might. There are no drastic swing-plane changes in mid-swing. Fundamental changes in the address will, however, produce a cutting action — a natural swing in which the clubface remains slightly open and cuts through the sand on an out-to-in path. A complete knowledge of the necessary fundamentals will assist you in keeping your bunker swing rhythmic, smooth, and simple.

Set your feet in an open stance, shoulder-width apart. (An open stance is achieved by pulling your left foot back from the target line, so that a line drawn across your toes would intersect the target line at approximately a 45-degree angle.) Form a firm foundation for your swing by digging your feet in, wiggling them from side to side, until the sand feels solid beneath your heels. Just as a building would crumble if its foundations were not laid correctly, so will your swing if it doesn't have a solid base. As a result of digging in you will be lower in relation to the ball, so compensate by *choking up*

(A) On basic sand shots, always be sure to aim two inches behind the ball. Imagine that you are tossing the ball to a specific target on the green.

(B) Use an open stance for all standard bunker shots.

(C) On a long shot, try to take just a saucerful of sand beneath the ball.

(D) For a little less distance, take enough sand to fill a soup bowl.

(E) For a very short shot, take enough sand to fill a mixing bowl.

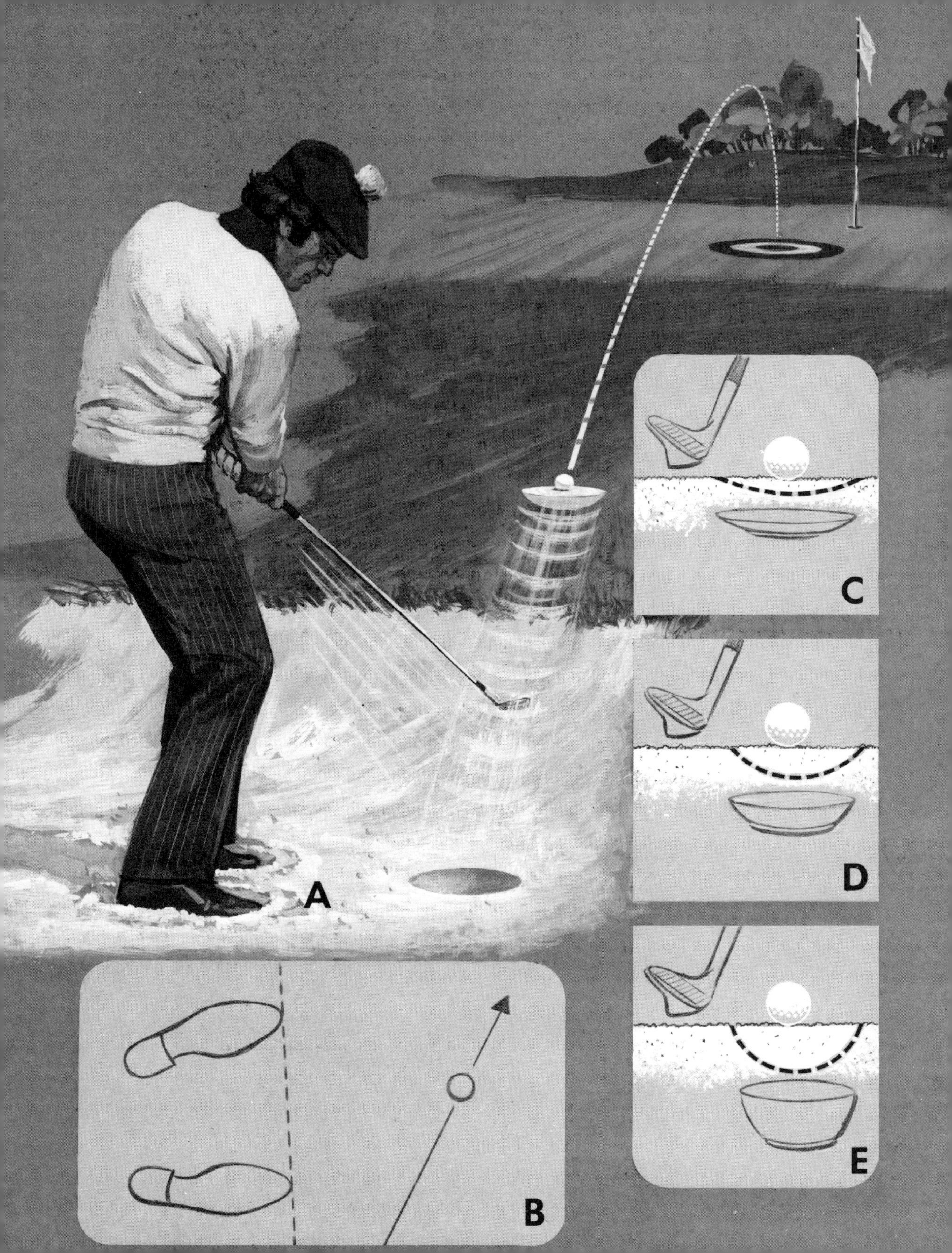
A
B
C
D
E

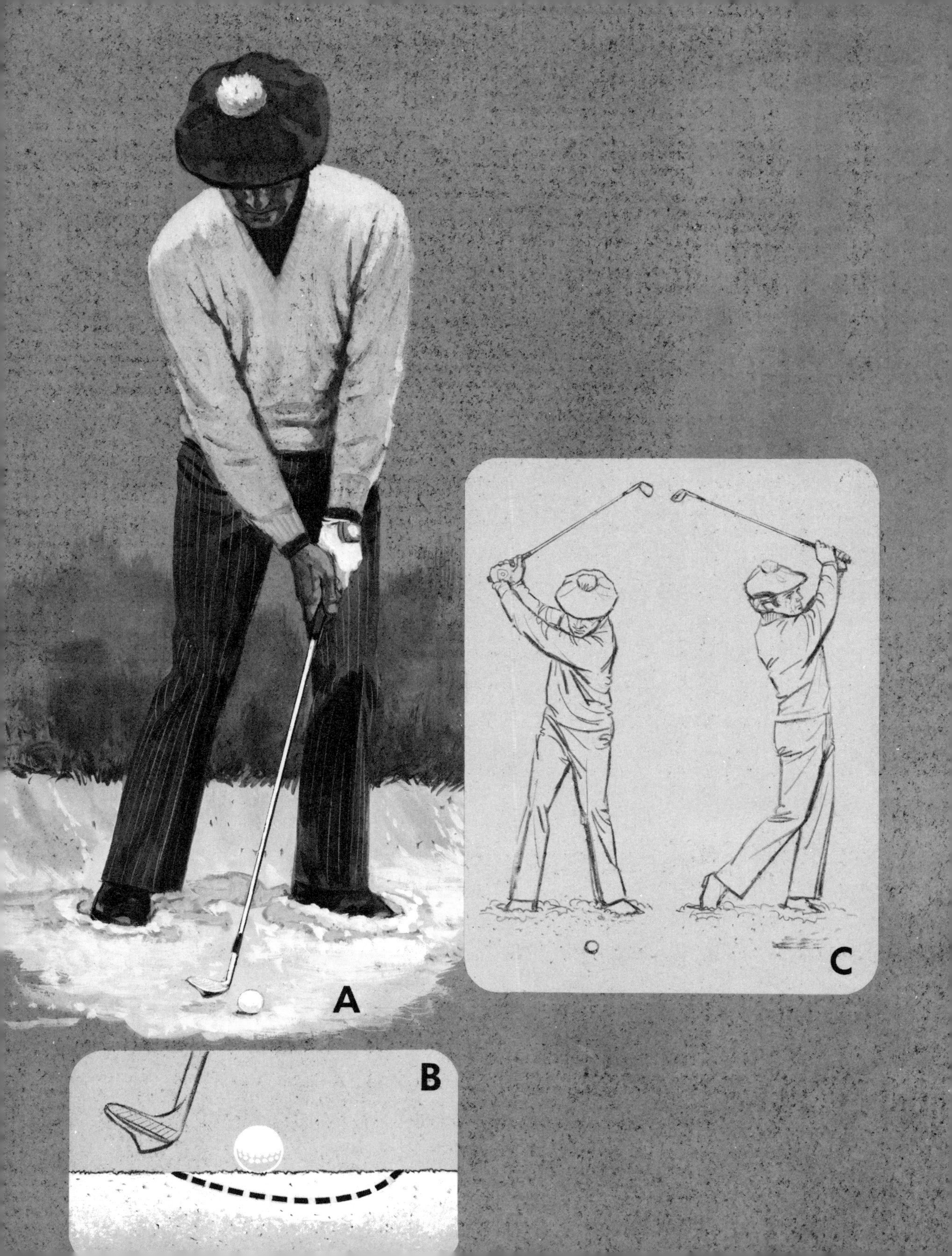
A
B
C

on the handle of the club: grip farther down the shaft. Position yourself so that the ball is in the center of your stance. Open the clubface and set your hands slightly ahead of the ball laterally. Having your hands forward will encourage a smoother, more controlled takeaway.

I have already mentioned that the length of swing should not change, regardless of the distance the ball must travel. What then enables you to control distance correctly? The answer: force within the swing and the amount of sand you make the clubface take under (not behind) the ball. Don't make the common mistake of changing the amount of sand taken *behind* the ball. Aim the clubhead at a spot two inches behind the ball, and vary the height and length of shots by the controlling amount of sand you take *under* the ball. If you need a long shot, hit shallow — imagine you are taking enough sand beneath the ball to fill a saucer. For a little less distance, hit deeper — take enough sand to fill a soup bowl. For a very short shot, hit deeper still — take enough sand to fill a mixing bowl. But in each case use the same length swing. A simple key: think *shallow for longer* shots and think *deep for shorter* distances. A conscious effort to make a full backswing is essential. The best bunker players in the world all make a full shoulder-turn, so that the club is a little short of the horizontal position at the top of the backswing.

The downswing with the sand iron, as with any other club, should be initiated by your legs (specifically your knees), which supply the drive to get the clubhead down through the sand. Move your knees laterally.

To avoid the common tendency to *scoop* — that is, to hit the ball first, rather than the sand — be sure

(A) Set the clubface in an open position on sand iron shots.

(B) Your objective is to slice a portion of sand from under *the ball to lift it.*

(C) A full backswing and follow-through are essential on all bunker shots.

to keep your eyes focused on the spot two inches behind the ball and keep your hands well ahead of the clubhead through impact. You want to feel that the clubhead is still descending even after the ball has left the sand.

The length of the follow-through, like the backswing, should be full. Your hands must finish high to insure that you don't *quit* (stop after impact).

The two things to fear the most on bunker shots are leaving the ball in the sand and hitting it beyond the green. Leaving the ball in the sand is usually caused by hitting too far behind the ball as a result of overusing arms and hands and underusing the lower body, hips, legs, and feet. Hitting the ball over the green is caused by taking too little sand behind the ball as a result of swinging too hard, using too much right hand, or focusing your eyes on the ball instead of the sand. A helpful tip for avoiding such problems: make a *complete* golf swing, both back and through.

DRY, SOFT SAND OR HARD, WET SAND

The first step when hitting out of dry, soft bunker sand is to open the face of the sand wedge in the address. If the clubface were not open it would dig deeply into the soft sand, causing the shot to come up short.

As on the basic bunker shot, use an open stance and keep your eyes focused on a spot two inches behind the ball. Place the clubhead at that spot at which the clubhead should enter the sand. Your objective is to cut a thin slice of sand from under the ball, so a full swing is again important. In soft sand you can expect the club to sweep through without obstruction, so no extra force is necessary.

It is quite common with soft sand to find the ball buried, in which case you should apply the technique outlined on pages 112–114.

Hard sand is in many cases wet sand and the technique for both situations is the same. If the lie is good, if the bunker lip isn't too high, and if you have a reasonably long carry to the flag (more than thirty feet), choose a pitching wedge instead of a sand wedge. A pitching wedge has no flange to skid or bounce off the surface of hard, wet sand, so you'll be less likely to skull the shot, a common occurrence in this situation. As on a normal pitch shot, position the ball in the center of your stance with your hands slightly ahead of it laterally, keep your stance and clubface square, and balance your weight to favor your left side.

Use a smooth, upright swing and try to pick the ball cleanly off the sand's surface. Don't hit down! If you swing properly, you can expect a low shot that bites quickly.

If the ball is partly buried, if you are faced with a high lip, or if you have a short distance to the flag, then use the sand wedge. In this case you must hit the sand, so aim at a spot two inches behind the ball. Square the clubface, to eliminate the flange and get the advantage of the leading edge's cutting power. Also, square your stance, choke up on the club, and keep your weight on your left side.

Now, make a full, smooth swing: take the club straight back along the target line, and with emphasis on good leg action hit down through the spot two inches behind the ball. The ball will come out on a low trajectory, bounce, and roll.

THE BURIED LIE

In most cases, a buried lie results when a high shot lands in soft sand. The ball is left sitting in a depression, half encased in sand, looking somewhat like a fried egg. Don't be alarmed: the shot really isn't as tough as it looks. It just requires a few fundamental changes and some understanding.

There are three changes to make in your address: First, rotate the grip of the club in your hands until the clubface is closed. This will eliminate the bounce effect caused when the part of the sand wedge that protrudes beneath the leading edge contacts the sand first, with a closed face, the leading edge acts like a knife and easily cuts down under the depression that surrounds the ball. Second, to encourage a steeper downswing arc, position yourself with the ball farther back in your stance than usual. Having the ball back will also set your hands farther forward, which helps you cut through the sand without stopping. Third, open your stance less than you normally would in a bunker, and position 60 percent of your weight on your left side to insure that you don't raise the clubhead at impact.

Surprisingly, very little force is required to hit from a buried lie. Having the clubface closed and the ball farther back in your stance creates a low-trajectory shot that runs like a hare being chased by the hounds. There will be no backspin because the club never actually touches the ball: it's the sand that lifts the ball into the air. Your swing should be as long and smooth as possible — not hard

On your downswing, aim at the outer rim of the depression. Expect your follow-through to be somewhat restricted by the depth the club travels under the ball. Make a conscious effort to lead your hands as far into your follow-through as the limitations of

(A) On buried lies, set the clubface slightly closed and on the downswing aim for the spot where you want to hit down into the sand.

(B) A stance slightly less open than for a normal bunker shot is needed.

(C) A closed clubface will give you the cutting power to get under the ball. The sand will lift the ball out.

A
B
C

the lie allow. Remember: you need a full swing, not a hard swing, to play this shot successfully.

The Very Short Sand Shot

There are two ways of playing a short bunker shot, where the pin is close to you. The first method is to *cut* the ball out — play a lob shot that stops quickly: Set the clubface wide open in the address. Then, make a short, soft, upright swing and skim through the sand two inches behind the ball. You can expect the ball to stop dead owing to a massive amount of backspin imparted by the shallow cut.

The alternative method is to open the clubface and use a full swing, but this time take a lot of sand underneath the ball. By taking more sand you slow the clubhead speed down, which guarantees that you don't hit the ball too far.

The short swing is best used for fast greens, where you don't want the ball to roll too much. The full swing serves best for a slow green or a slight uphill situation, where you want the ball to roll.

However, I should caution you that the short swing is dangerous in a pressure situation for anyone but a well-practiced bunker artist. If you lack confidence and swing too short, the clubhead and the ball might get stuck in the sand. When you swing fully you can be confident that at least the ball will get out.

(A) On short sand shots, align yourself in an open position in relation to the flag.

(B) To stop the ball quickly, set the clubface wide open and try to skim through the sand.

(C) Using the short-swing method, make a smooth, upright swing and try to cut *the ball out.*

A
45°
B
C

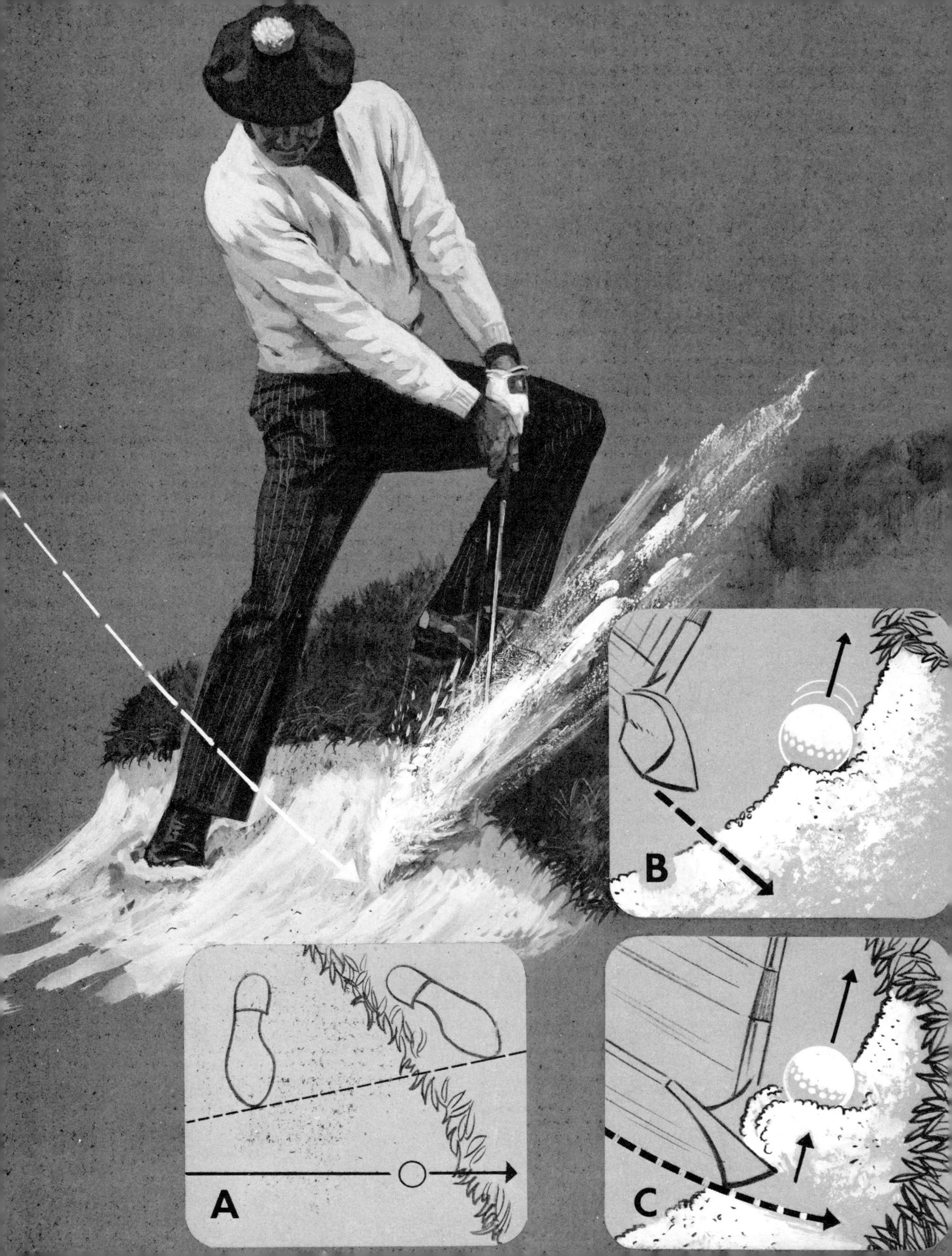
B
A
C

(A) When hitting a ball buried under a bunker lip, set your feet slightly open, and be sure they are solidly planted.

(B) Aim to hit down into a spot three *inches behind the ball.*

(C) With the clubface square you'll have the cutting power to dig down beneath the ball. The angled clubface hitting the slope will force the sand to lift the ball out of the bunker.

Ball Buried under the Front Lip

First, when facing a bunker shot, you must be realistic. If the ball is directly under the front lip or really buried, you have no chance of getting out, so take a drop and a penalty. This will save you strokes in the long run.

If you face a shot that's possible, build yourself a solid platform by grinding your feet down into the sand. Flex or bend your left leg as much as necessary to offset any slope. The ball must be positioned in the center of your stance.

Now here's the trick: the clubface must be square. You'll undoubtedly say "How can he tell me to square the clubface when the ball is buried under the lip?" Easy. The squared clubface will give you cutting power, to get down under the sand; the sand will lift the ball out. All you have to do is swing fully and hit down into a spot *three* inches behind the ball. But be sure to use a lot of force — hit hard — in the downswing to make up for the mass of sand that will restrict your follow-through to just after impact. And allow for the shock of impact by gripping a little firmer than usual in the address.

Ball against the Back Edge

For even the most competent golfer, a ball against the back edge of a bunker presents a dangerous situation. Not only do you have an obstruction to your swing but also, in many cases, you have a downhill lie to contend with. The player must be realistic: regardless of whether it's a flat or downhill lie, it sometimes pays to take a penalty stroke or to wedge out sideways if the ball is too close to the lip. You must have room to hit the sand behind the ball; the danger on this shot is that you'll contact the ball first, and send it screaming across the green.

The first step, then, is to insure that you have sufficient room to hit a spot approximately two inches behind the ball. As you address the ball, keep your eyes focused on that spot. Square the clubface: set it perpendicular to the target line. Set your weight almost totally on your left side and flex your knees to help you stay down through impact.

In the takeaway and throughout the backswing you want the feeling that you're picking the clubhead straight up, because a sharp wristbreak is essential to avoid the lip. You should, prior to playing the shot, take a few practice swings outside the trap to feel how much wristbreak is needed to avoid catching the bunker lip.

In the downswing, lead your hands down ahead of the clubhead, maintaining the cocked-wrist position you established in the takeaway until after impact.

Most importantly, be sure both to hit down into the sand, following its contour, and to swing through to the target. Feel that the clubhead is still going down after impact.

When hitting from a bunker's back edge, aim for a spot two inches behind the ball. Break your wrists smoothly but sharply and make it your objective to hit down through the spot. Make the clubhead follow the contour of the sand.

Ball below Feet

In a bunker, when the ball is below your feet a warning alarm should sound in your head: there is danger. Because you literally have to reach for the ball and are forced into an awkward address position, it is very easy to hit the ball rather than the

In a bunker when the ball is below your feet, your swing plane will be more upright than usual, causing the ball to travel to the right — so aim yourself slightly left of target.

sand first and send the shot out of control over the green.

Despite this danger, take the time to think out what changes must be made to cope with the situation. If you do, and then play this shot well, you'll derive sufficient satisfaction so that any momentum that might have been lost will be back on your side.

In this situation, the ball will tend to go to the right, so aim yourself slightly to the left. To help you get down under the ball, grip at the very end of the club handle, stand as close to the ball as possible, grind your feet down, and flex your knees into a crouching position. Be careful not to cause a minor landslide that would disturb the ball and cost you a penalty.

In the takeaway, break your wrists quickly. This will provide you with a steeper downswing arc. Throughout the swing keep your head steady and your eyes focused on the sand rather than the ball. A steady head, a smooth tempo, and a conscious effort to hit down through the impact area will prevent any chance of mishitting. Keep your head down and your knees fully bent until the ball has left the trap. Because of the downslope, you feel somewhat restricted. The use of your legs and wrists will enable you to play the shot successfully.

Ball above Feet

As far as technique is concerned, the ball-above-feet situation in sand is similar to the same shot on the fair-

When the ball is above your feet your swing plane will be "flatter" and the ball will travel to the left, so aim a bit toward the right.

way or near the green (see pages 181–183). Remember, the ball is going to go to the left because of its low elevation at address. Compensate for this by aiming at a secondary target farther to the right than the actual one. Pick out a tree or bush located in the background a yard or so to the right of the pin and square the clubface to face this marker. Choke up on the grip of the club and shuffle your feet down into the sand. Unless you have solid footing, you could slip and find yourself pulling away from the ball at impact, which would be disastrous.

Position the ball in the center of your stance. Flex your knees slightly and equally distribute your weight on both feet, to help maintain balance throughout the stroke.

In the takeaway and throughout the backswing the club should follow the turning of your shoulders. There is no need for a wristbreak: this would cause the clubhead to dig deeply into the sand.

In the downswing the clubhead should be aimed at a spot two inches behind the ball. I must emphasize that the use of your hips and legs on this shot is important to drive the clubhead through the sand to a full follow-through. Force on this shot is not necessary. Swing smoothly and be sure to follow-through.

The Uphill Lie in Sand

This is one of the easiest bunker shots to play because the ball rests on a launching pad — the only way it can go is up. Start by burrowing your feet down for solid footing. Next, for good balance, flex your left knee. Play the ball in the center of your stance, with your feet aimed only slightly left of your target. The face of the club should be aimed square to the target to eliminate some of the additional height that will be created by the upslope. Aim to hit a spot two inches behind the ball.

With a full swing and emphasis on hip and leg

action in the downswing, hit through the spot in the sand. Make the clubhead follow the contour of the slope — up — as much as possible. You want the feeling that you are swinging *up*, not down, through the sand. Sweep, don't dig. Expect your follow-through to be somewhat restricted.

The ball will fly much higher than usual; consequently, you will lose distance, so don't be afraid to use a lot more force to get that ball to the hole.

On the uphill lie in sand, flex your left knee. Play the ball in the center of your stance and aim at a spot two inches behind the ball. Try to hit up *the slope.*

In fact, try to imagine a second target beyond the pin. If you try to get the ball past the hole, you rarely will! On long shots use a stronger club than is normal (for instance, instead of a sand wedge, use a pitching wedge to hit your usual distance).

The Downhill Lie in Sand

With a downhill lie in a bunker, the main danger is that you could take too much sand behind the ball and never get the shot out or not hit the sand at all and skull the ball. The following precautions can prevent these errors.

In the address, position the ball in the center of your stance and turn the clubface open slightly. Because of the downslope, even with the clubface open, you should expect the shot to fly low, so you must allow for this and consider the bunker lip in front of you. If the front of the bunker is high, then I suggest that you choose the safest course to get the ball onto the green. In extreme cases this could mean wedging out sideways.

Be sure to get as comfortable as possible. If you feel awkward at first standing over the ball, readdress it. If you don't feel good starting out, it's unlikely that you will play a good shot.

Take aim at the spot two inches behind the ball and keep your eyes focused on it throughout the backswing and downswing. Take the club back smoothly, cocking your wrists early in the takeaway. An early wrist-cock is essential in this situation, to

On the downhill bunker lie, get as comfortable as possible. Position the ball in the center of your stance with the clubface slightly open. Aim two inches behind the ball and consciously hit down the slope.

give you a downswing arc that parallels the slope, plus a little extra height on the shot. The backswing should be as full as the limitation of the downslope allows.

On the downswing, hit down into the spot two inches behind the ball and make the clubhead follow the contour of the sand through the impact area. To help do this you should be sure to use your knees:

drive them laterally. The legs are the sole agent to keep the club driving *low*. Even when the ball is on its way, feel that the club is still moving down the slope.

The overall swing should feel as though you're picking the club straight up and leading it straight down with your hands. Remember to allow for a low shot and for the ball to roll more than normal.

Ball Inside/Feet Outside

This bunker shot is an extreme ball-below-feet situation. The key is to adopt a posture that will enable you to hit down through the sand behind the ball.

Square the clubface to the target, grip at the very end of the handle, and bend your knees to assume an exaggerated crouching position. How much you bend your knees depends on how far the ball is below you. In some cases you may even want to kneel on your left knee and put your right leg inside the trap, or vice versa. Get into the most comfortable position that will allow you to execute the shot effectively. Balance, gained through address posture, is vital in this situation.

During the swing, be sure not to straighten your knees any more than they were at address. If you rise up, you'll hit the ball rather than the sand first. Stay down until after the ball has left the trap. Swing full, be sure to make your tempo smooth, and don't

When hitting a sand shot from outside a bunker, make a reasonably full swing and be sure not to straighten your legs any more than they were at address.

Choke up on the grip of the club and get as comfortable as possible when you're in the bunker and the ball isn't.

try for distance. Just try to get the ball out and onto the green.

Ball Outside/Feet Inside

This shot requires that you more or less invent a way of playing the shot. There is no set technique. Although extreme, this situation is like a normal ball-above-feet lie (the only difference is that you have to contend with the sand beneath your feet); most of the fundamentals outlined on pages 121–123 apply here.

Try various stances and select the one that feels the most comfortable. Get good footing: burrow your feet down in the sand. Grip far down the shaft. The more elevated the ball at address, the shorter you should grip the club. In some cases, this may mean you will be forced to grip the steel shaft itself.

You should remember that the ball's high elevation at impact will cause the shot to fly to the left. Allow for this when setting up. Try for the longest swing radius possible, but whatever its length, keep a smooth swing and a constant arc. And don't try for distance, but merely for improved position.

Above all, try for solid contact. It is very easy to scuff this shot. Aim to sweep the ball off the turf with a smooth motion, keeping the grip ahead of the clubhead laterally through the impact area.

The Putter Shot from Sand

Many players believe that to play anything but an explosion shot from a bunker is a cop-out. But the best shot to play is a high-percentage shot. Sometimes you'll be playing the percentages to your best advantage if you use a putter.

If the sand is firm, if the lip of the bunker is shallow, and if the ball is reasonably close to the front of the trap, your putter becomes an immediate option. However, it is not advisable to putt on soft sand, because the ball tends to burrow as it travels. Putting across a large expanse of sand, unless it is hard-packed and smooth, is also dangerous. You also have to consider these elements:

- The distance from the pin. If it is far, a putter will be difficult to gauge and control.
- The width and length of grass on the apron. Obviously, if the grass is long or the apron is wide, a putter is risky.
- The type of undulation and the speed of the green. If it's a downhill shot or a slick green, you'll be better off playing a sand wedge, because you'll get the ball to bite quickly.

If you decide to use the putter, grip far down the shaft — choke up — to insure that the putterhead remains above the sand throughout the stroke. Position the ball off your left heel. Hit slightly harder than you would normally hit a putt of the same distance on a green. Be conscious of making a smooth, well-timed stroke. Don't be in a hurry — you could top the ball and barely get out of the bunker, or worse.

Aim to hit the center of the ball as the putterhead is starting the upswing. This will produce the neces-

(A) Choose to play the putter-from-sand shot only if the lip of the bunker is shallow, as in the YES *illustration.*

(B) Try to hit just below the center of the ball as the putter head is starting the upswing. This will give you forward spin.

(C) Be sure the surface of the sand is smooth. Use your normal putting grip.

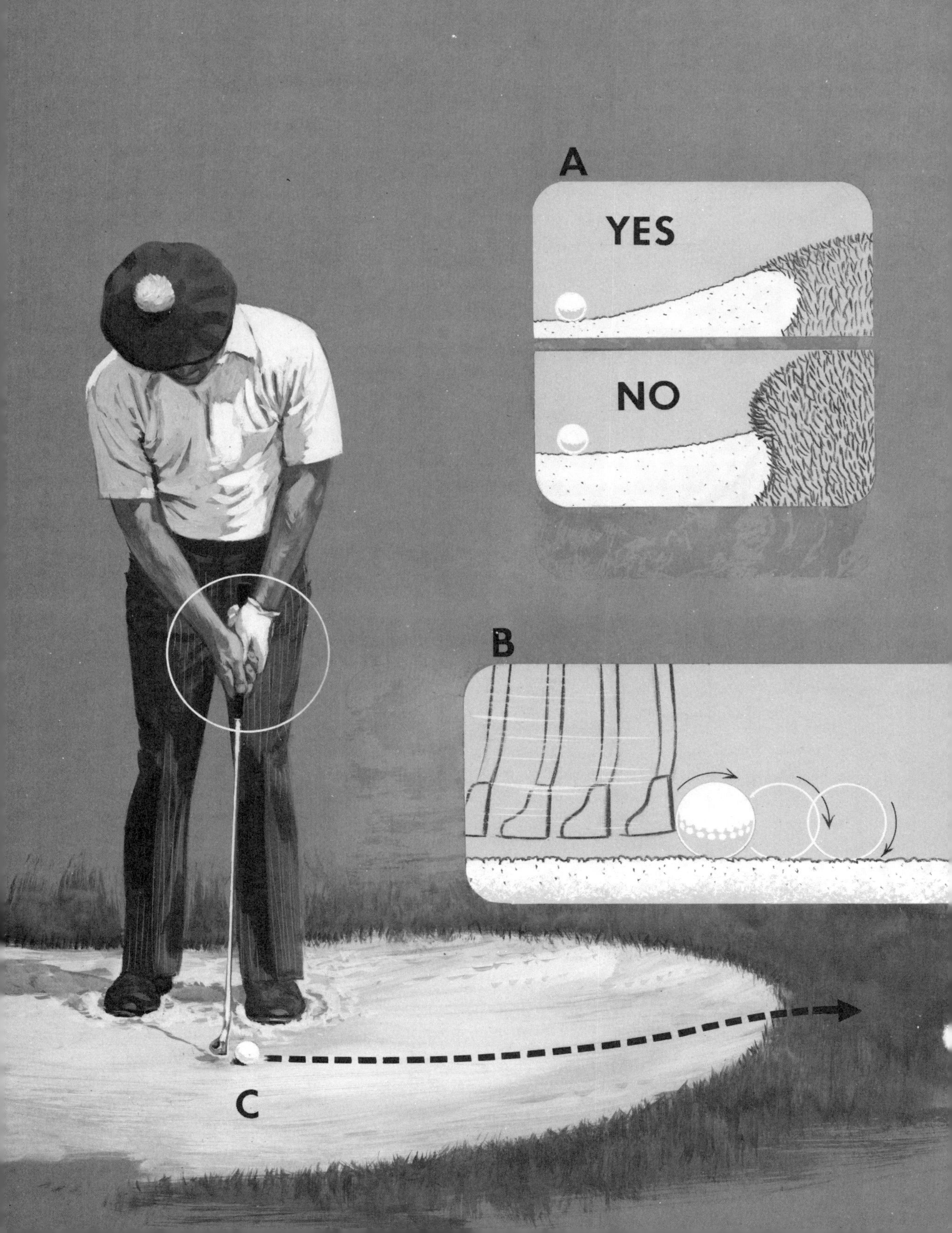

A
YES
NO
B
C

sary forward spin to assist you in negotiating any undulation. Exaggerate your follow-through to be sure that you don't stop the putterhead immediately after the ball is struck.

The Run-Up Shot from a Bunker

When the pin is all the way at the back of a long green and the lip of the trap is cut low and the ball is sitting on top of the sand, I suggest you run the ball up with a 7- or 8-iron instead of blasting out with a sand wedge. The run-up is a higher percentage shot because you will achieve a lower, easier-to-control trajectory; the long explosion shot is one of the most difficult bunker shots to play because you can never be totally sure how much sand to take. At least with a run-up the sand is not a factor: you just play the shot as if it were a normal near-the-green chip.

You need make no fancy changes: Address the ball as you would a chip shot. Position the ball in the center of your stance, choke up on the club slightly, favor the left side with your weight, and keep your hands well ahead of the clubhead laterally. The clubface should be set to face the pin squarely.

The key to the successful execution of this shot lies in hitting the ball before the sand. To accomplish this I suggest that you focus on a spot two inches in front of the ball, toward the green. This will help make you strike the sand *after* the ball.

From the start, be especially conscious of a smooth,

(A) When the pin is set back, the lip is low, and your lie is good, you can play a run-up shot from a trap. Simply imagine that you're playing a normal chip from grass.

(B) The YES *inset shows a favorable lie; in the* NO *situation you would have to blast out.*

well-timed stroke. Should you swing too fast or jerk the club back away from the ball, it's likely that you'll miss the shot. Keep your eyes focused throughout on that spot in front of the ball. If you don't, you will hit the sand and lose any possible overspin. You'll want to use a little wrist action in the swing also, to help you pick the ball cleanly off the surface of the sand. Keep your hands well ahead of the clubhead laterally through impact.

The Deep Trap

Average golfers often have two inclinations when they get into a deep trap near the green. They mistakenly think (1) that they need to scoop the ball up (it's almost as if they don't trust the club's loft to do the job, so they use wrists and body to try to help the ball into the air); and (2) that they need brute force to get the ball out. Actually, technique is the requisite, not brute force. Don't try for distance: let it happen as a result of the fundamental changes you make. Let the clubface do the work.

First, since you are obviously going to need a high trajectory, turn the clubface wide open. It should face the sky and be as flat as a frying pan parallel to the ground. Position the ball off your left heel and use a stance that's more open than normal. The more open your stance, the more the clubhead will cross the target line moving from the outside to the inside. This cross-cutting action, along with the wide-open clubface, will provide you with additional ball height. Also, break your wrists sharply in the takeaway. Then focus on making a *full*, upright backswing.

Taking a shallow amount of sand, attempt to simply "splash" the ball out. Make sure the clubface stays open by leading with your left hand; keep the grip end of the club ahead of the face, and don't allow the right hand to roll. Be sure to keep your eyes focused on the spot two inches behind the ball where the club enters the sand, and follow through to a full finish.

In a deep fairway trap, follow the same procedure; use a more lofted club, trust its loft, and don't try for distance.

(A) Hitting from a deep trap, an early wristbreak is essential.

(B) Set your stance wide open.

(C) The clubface should be wide open also, and as flat as a frying pan.

A
B
C

C
A
B
D

The Fairway Bunker

The swing for a fairway bunker shot should be no different from your normal fairway swing, and you should try to hit the ball, not the sand, first. For the most part, the lie determines the club you select. If the lip is low and you have a good lie, you can actually hit a fairway wood (anything from a 4-wood up); the choice is up to you. A basic change in the fundamental address is that the ball should be placed off your left heel. Use a slightly open stance and select a club that will give you the most distance. If the lie isn't too good or the lip is high, it's better to sacrifice yardage and go to a more lofted club.

As I said, the key is to hit the ball first, and for this reason, there are a few changes to make in the address. Most importantly, grind your feet down into the sand to get a solid base. If you slip while making the full swing that's needed on this shot, it could be disastrous. Choke up on the grip; this will make the low point of your swing slightly higher than usual. Place the ball in the center of your stance and rest your weight on your left side.

(A) On all iron shots from a fairway bunker, choke up on the grip of the club and play the ball nearer to the center of your stance.

(B) Set your feet slightly open and place the ball off your left heel.

(C) Aim the clubhead through the ball.

(D) The lie inevitably determines what club you use. With a good lie, your 4-wood can be quite effective. Be sure to aim at a spot in front of the ball so you don't hit the sand first.

Now here's the real key: aim at a spot approximately one inch *in front of* the ball (laterally, toward the target). Remember: the object is to hit the ball, not the sand behind it. Keep your eyes focused on the spot ahead of the ball and try to aim the clubhead through the ball. You'll be surprised to find that the ball will be struck first, and solidly; the sand won't be touched by the clubhead until the ball is in the air.

There should be no mechanical changes in your swing. However, it is even more vital than usual to maintain a smooth tempo. Don't jerk the club back or try to hit the ball hard. Swing smoothly.

The ball will tend to fade when hit from a fairway bunker, so you should aim slightly left of your target when you align the shot. Also, use a club one gradation stronger than you would normally, because the massive amount of backspin imparted by "clean contact" will cause the ball to fly much shorter.

Ball in a Footprint

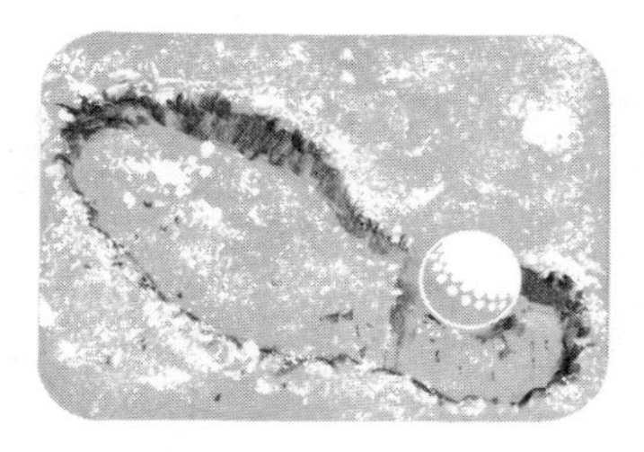

It is very hard to anticipate what the ball will do from this type of lie, so look for the easiest way out. Don't try to go for the pin or you may find yourself back in the footprint, where you started.

The key to successful execution of this shot, as on a buried lie, is the clubface position: the face must be closed. This will bring the leading edge into play and give you the cutting power necessary to dig the ball out. Assume a slightly open stance and grind your feet down to get a solid base for what will be a reasonably full swing. Position the ball in the center of your stance to give you a steeper downswing arc, and balance your weight so that 60 percent favors the left side. At the start, pick a spot in the sand approximately three inches behind the ball, and keep your eyes focused on the spot throughout the backswing and downswing.

In the takeaway, break your wrists sharply. This, and a full shoulder-turn, will give you the leverage to pull down through the sand. In the downswing, the feeling you want is that you are driving the clubhead down into the footprint — literally trying to explode the ball *and the footprint* out. But be aware that, because of the closed clubface, the clubhead will dig down deeper than normal. So that you don't stop (quit) once the ball is struck, be sure to use your lower body. Effective use of the hips and knees will keep the clubhead moving through the sand. You can expect your follow-through to be somewhat restricted because of the depth the clubhead travels under the ball. The result will be a low shot that rolls a lot.

One last word of caution: if the sand is extremely gritty or hard, or if the ball is well down into the footprint, it is sometimes better to take a penalty to insure you don't get into more trouble. Remember the percentages!

Wind

Hitting against the Wind

FROM THE TEE

Most players are intimidated by the wind when it's blowing against them. Instead of accepting the fact that they will lose distance, they try to hit the ball as far as they would normally by swinging harder and faster. The result is a disastrous pop-up, a slice, or a hook.

First, remember: even the 300-yard boomer has to accept the fact that distance will be lost hitting into the wind. Second: you must swing as if there is no wind at all. Think smoothness. From start to finish, don't accelerate beyond your normal calm, easy pace. Try to hit a low shot — one that will stay under the wind and give you extra roll. A high shot will always stop dead in wind and is therefore undesirable.

Position the ball between the center of your stance and you left heel, and choke up on the grip. These changes will give you a shorter, more controllable arc, as well as help insure that the ball is struck as the club is still descending, which is necessary for a low shot.

Some players have the impression that the answer to driving into the wind is to tee the ball lower. This is not the answer! If you tee the ball too low you are forced to hit down rather than sweep the ball off the tee. If you hit down too much you can easily catch the ground in front of the ball and sky the shot. Tee the ball at normal height, make the basic changes I have outlined, and try to *sweep* the ball off the tee.

Heavy emphasis must be placed on tempo. If the overall speed of your swing quickens, your right side could overpower your left, causing the clubface to arrive at the ball ahead of your hands — offering maximum rather than minimum loft to the ball, which results in a high shot. It is vital to keep your hands ahead of the clubhead through impact.

TO THE GREEN

When playing irons into the wind, you should change the ball position at address. When hitting your long irons, play the ball to the right of the normal ball position, almost at the center of your stance (see the illustration on page 170, for standard ball-position information). For middle and short irons, play the ball just to the right of center. This change will reduce the effect of the clubface loft by placing your hands farther ahead of the ball at address, thus providing you with a lower trajectory. The lower you want the ball to fly, the farther to the right you should place the ball.

At address, set your weight on your left side and keep it there throughout the swing. This will prevent you from swaying to the right, and will keep your head centered over the ball. Don't let the clubhead pass ahead of your hands laterally; you want the face to remain in a hooded position at impact. Try to finish low, with the clubhead just above waist height. This will give you a punched-type shot that has very little spin on it.

When driving into the wind, position the ball between the center of your stance and your left heel. Tee the ball at normal height and choke up on the club's grip.

A 1-iron is an excellent club to have in your armory in windy conditions. It has only 14 degrees of loft, so using it with the fundamental changes I've just outlined produces an extra-low shot.

Hitting with the Wind

FROM THE TEE

When the wind is behind you on a tee shot, don't make the mistake that so many players do and try to knock the cover off the ball. True, the wind is going to give you a few extra yards if you execute the shot correctly, but if you make a bad swing it will also give you a few extra yards sideways. Brute force could mean the difference between being in the woods and being in the rough.

If you are looking for extra distance, tee the ball a little higher and position the ball farther forward laterally than you normally would — in other words, more opposite your left foot. Having done this, just concentrate on making a smooth, rhythmic swing. Don't jerk and don't use brute force. Just try to sweep the ball off the top of the tee, and make your overall tempo smooth.

Consider also that a 3-wood shot will often travel farther, with the wind at your back, than a driver shot; the 3-wood has more loft and gets the ball up into the maximum velocity area of the wind faster, and the higher the ball flies, the longer the wind has to push it forward.

Driving with the wind at your back, position the ball farther to the left than you normally would.

TO THE GREEN

If you have a strong wind behind you when you face a shot to the green, make yourself aware of possible trouble before you select your club. Obviously, if there is a lot of trouble, such as a lake or out-of-bounds markers behind the green, then you want to be sure to select a club that will not carry the ball over. Depending on how hard the wind is blowing, this could even mean using a higher-numbered club than you would normally hit.

After selecting the conservative club, just swing normally. Don't try to slow your swing down, or you could decelerate and mishit the shot.

The Left-to-Right Crosswind

A left-to-right crosswind can be most helpful to the average player, providing it is used correctly. The most important lession in playing a crosswind: don't fight it, use it to your advantage.

When a crosswind blows from left to right, pick a secondary target to the left of your intended target. Then try to hit the ball straight to the secondary target.

For example, don't try to hit the ball straight at the target; you could find yourself in serious trouble — out-of-bounds, in the woods, or in heavy rough to the right of the green. First, visualize the shot in your mind. Take into account the wind factor as you picture the shot. Next, select a secondary target to line up with — a tree, bush, trap, or bare spot in the rough, to the left of the primary target. Then just go ahead and swing through to that secondary target. The ball will start for where you are aimed; then, when it loses spin, it will blow in toward the target. That's all there is to it. *A crosswind does not require*

In a right-to-left crosswind, pick a secondary target to the right of your intended target. Aim to hit the ball straight to your secondary target.

any mechanical change, only an alignment adjustment.

For the player who has the ability to maneuver the ball at will, a left-to-right crosswind offers the opportunity for more distance. Simply align left and let the ball fade from left to right. The clockwise spin will be amplified by the wind, and when the ball lands it will roll twice the normal distance.

If you tend to hook the ball, you should feel comfortable in a strong left-to-right wind without compensating. Aim straight for the target. You see, the wind acts like a wall. You can't possibly hit the shot too far left, because all the hook-spin is knocked off the ball. In fact, a hook will often straighten out in this form of wind: the ball hits the wall and often seems to bounce back.

A word of caution to the player who regularly slices the ball: Since the wind will cause an exaggerated amount of clockwise spin, which will compound the results of your fault, I strongly recommend that you align yourself much farther to the left than normal.

The Right-to-Left Crosswind

In a right-to-left crosswind, align toward a secondary target at the *right* of your main objective. This secondary target could be a tree, bush, bunker, or even a spot in the rough. Once you have selected your target, after visualizing the shot and calculating how much the wind will affect it, hit toward that target.

Don't try to hit the ball straight at the main target or you might find yourself out of bounds to the left, in a bunker, in the woods, or Lord knows where. Use the wind's direction to your advantage and aim to the right. This rule, which applies if you hit the ball relatively straight, is especially applicable if you often hook sharply or make the ball draw slightly. You see, the wind in this case will accelerate counter-clockwise spin on the ball and will cause the shot to curve a lot more. A fader or slicer should be a lot more at home in this kind of crosswind, because he or she can aim straight at the target without fear that the ball will land to the right. With slices, the wind acts like a wall pushing the ball back to the left.

In summary, then, assuming you usually hit straight shots, treat a crosswind like a long-breaking putt: you have to allow for the slope, or the ball will fall below the hole; you have to allow for the wind, or the ball will be blown off-target.

Water

Whoops — you've landed in the water! When you get to the ball you see that it is close to the edge of the hazard, so there is a possibility for recovery. Can you play it? Let's see.

If any part of the ball is showing above the surface, you have an excellent chance of getting it out. However, if the ball is totally submerged, even if it's just half an inch below the surface, forget it. Take a penalty and drop out.

In technique, the water shot is similar to a sand shot. Instead of blasting out of sand you will be blasting out of water, so be prepared to get wet. If you have any rain gear, put it on: it will help prevent you from worrying about getting your best golf wear wet — that fear might cause you to pull up and away from the ball at impact.

The club to select is a sand wedge, unless the ball is resting well above the water surface, in which case you could hit a pitching wedge or 9-iron. Use nothing with less loft, though. A sand wedge is ideal because of the weight, the loft, and the flange, all of which enable you to get down under the ball.

Get as comfortable as possible. Use an open stance, with the ball in the center and the clubface slightly open. Aim to hit a spot approximately one inch behind the ball. But don't touch the water as you address the ball; that would cost you a stroke penalty.

(A) A water recovery shot should only be attempted if the ball is above the surface.

(B) Even if the ball is mostly covered by water, you still have an excellent chance of recovering.

(C) If the ball is below the surface totally, forget it!

A
YES
B
YES
C
NO

Make a full and upright backswing. In the downswing, move your knees laterally and hit down into the spot. Stay down. Whatever you do, don't pull away in an attempt to save yourself from getting wet.

Rough

Deep Rough

LONG SHOTS

The critical factor in hitting long shots from deep rough is always club selection. Pick a club that has enough loft to get the ball clear of the long grass. The longer the grass, the more loft you need.

Unless you are extremely strong, the 2- and 3-irons are never a good choice — the grass creates too much resistance. Faced with a long shot, you are better off choosing a 5- or 6-iron, or a lofted fairway wood. These are percentage clubs. The fairway woods, from the 4 through the 7, are ideal. They have small heads and a sleek design, which enables you to scythe easily through the grass.

An exception to the general rule regarding club selection is wet grass. In this case you should choose a much more lofted club and just aim to get the ball back into play. If necessary, use a pitching or sand wedge. The loft and weight will give you the elevation and the cutting power essential for getting out.

The key in terms of technique is to get as little grass between the clubface and the ball as possible. To accomplish this you must start by holding the clubhead off the ground; then it won't get caught on the takeaway and throw your swing out of kilter.

An upright swing is also essential. The closer the clubhead stays to the target line (as it will with an upright swing), the more direct will be its course of attack on the ball; the clubhead will approach at a much steeper angle and will avoid the tall grass. Although you try to keep the clubhead close to the target line, a conscious effort to take the club back slightly *outside* the target line in the takeaway will help you actually do so and thus adopt an upright swing.

Because long grass has a pronounced effect on the path of the clubhead through the impact area, and on the clubface at the point of impact, there are some additional precautions that must be taken to prevent mishitting the shot. Grip the club firmly, to prevent it from spinning open as a result of the grass grabbing and twisting the head. The force of impact, regardless of how hard you grip the club, will cause the head to turn. If the face was square at address, inevitably it will be forced into an open position at impact, causing the ball to fly to the right of your target. To guard against this, close the clubface slightly at address. Then, at impact, the clubface will be forced into a square position. Even so, the overriding tendency will be to hit the shot to the right. Accordingly, you should allow for this when you align the shot.

One last, very important point: *Don't* use extra force — you don't need it. Swinging too hard is the worst mistake of all because it will make you hit well behind the ball and will only get you into more trouble. Swing smoothly!

In rough, hitting with the grain, the ball will fly lower than usual and will run when it lands.

In rough, hitting against the grain, the ball will go higher and shorter.

Hitting from a "flying lie" (when the ball is resting on tall grass, high off the ground), sweep the ball — don't dig the clubface into the rough.

SHORT WEDGE SHOTS

Average players dread a wedge shot from deep rough around the green. They just don't know which club to use or what changes to make to get the ball onto the green. Often, through trying to hit the ball softly, they find that the clubhead gets stuck in the grass and the ball travels only a few feet. (*Caution:* be sure your grip is firm.) The sand wedge is often the best club to use in this situation. It is heavy and has sufficient loft to lift the ball over the tall grass.

Since this is just going to be a full swing in miniature, nearly all the fundamentals outlined for a long shot from deep rough apply. This time, however, instead of closing the clubface, you'll want to open it slightly. Position the ball in the center of your stance, and to compensate for the ball moving to the right, use an open stance. An upright and fairly full swing is essential. On the downswing, consciously lead the grip end of the club through to the target. Don't allow your hands or the clubhead to stop at impact. Stay down on the shot and swing through to a reasonably full finish just above waist height.

Expect the ball to roll a lot.

When hitting a short wedge shot from rough, don't allow the clubhead to stop at impact. Allow for more roll than usual because of the heavy grass.

PUTTER SHOTS

When I first showed this shot to one of my pupils he was absolutely astounded! You will be too. Who would ever consider that a putter could be an option on short shots from deep rough around the green? Surprisingly, it is a good percentage shot.

Because a putter has almost zero loft, it makes solid contact easily with a ball resting in long grass. Solid contact with a pitching or sand wedge is more chancy than with a putter, because the leading edge juts out in front of the clubface.

This shot is pure simplicity. Your object is to make

(A) Take the putter up sharply with the wrists. Drop the head right onto the ball. No follow-through is needed to bounce the ball out of the rough.

(B) Only firm ground works.

A

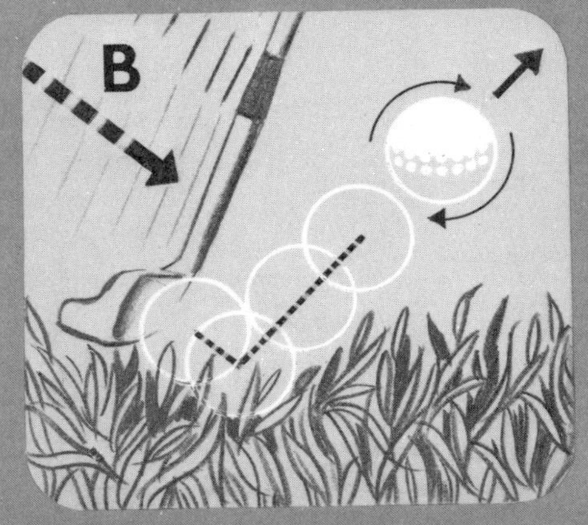
B

the ball bounce out of the grass! Simply align the ball in line with your right heel, and place your weight on your left side. Move your hands well ahead of the clubhead laterally. These changes, in combination with a sharp cocking of the wrists, will produce a steep downswing arc. Drop the putterhead directly onto the ball. No follow-through is necessary; just be sure to use enough force to make the ball bounce out of the rough. You can expect a high hop and a lot of roll. With practice you can learn to control this unusual shot as easily as any other. It's a great shot to have in the bag!

I caution you not to select this shot when the grass is overly wet or when the pin is less than ten feet away. Attempt it only when you have a lot of green to work with and when the ground under the grass is firm.

Shallow Rough

LONG SHOTS

The first thing to remember when hitting long shots from shallow rough is that the ball is going to travel farther than normal because two or three inches of grass will get trapped between the ball and the clubface. This prevents the grooves on the face of the club from making contact, so, instead of backspin, your shot has very little in-flight spin of any kind. This causes what is commonly called a "flier": the ball travels as though hit by a club one or two gradations stronger than the one used, and rolls a lot upon landing.

The best precaution is to select a weaker club. For example, if you think it's a 4-iron shot, use a 5-iron, et cetera. There is no need for mechanical changes in your swing. Just be aware of the extra distance the ball will fly and adjust the force within your swing accordingly.

You can choose any club you would use in a normal fairway situation. But be cautious with your club selection. Remember: take less club.

SHORT SHOTS

As on a long shot, when playing a short pitch from shallow rough, you must anticipate extra roll. You won't be able to stop the ball — there will be no backspin — because grass will get caught between clubface and ball.

Select a sand wedge to give you a high trajectory, which can reduce the roll. Simply open the face of the club and your stance. Just swing normally, but allow for the ball to travel to the right because of the cutting action created by the open stance.

Above all else, remember: the ball is going to run, so swing a little easier and use less club.

Sandy Rough/Loose Impediments

Your ball has come to rest in sandy rough, or on pine needles, twigs, gravel, or cut grass. What do you do?

A

B

(A) When you address a ball that's lying on pine needles, don't ground the clubhead — that might move the ball and cost you a penalty stroke.

(B) In sandy rough, sweep *the ball into the air.*

Tread lightly! In moving any loose impediments from behind the ball, be careful not to disturb it; if the ball is displaced by more than half a turn, it will cost you a penalty stroke. In the same vein, don't ground the club during the address; hold the clubhead off the ground.

The objective here is to sweep the ball airborne without catching the clubhead in the impediment, so choke up on the grip of the club an inch or two. Place your weight on your left side and make an upright backswing. This will make your downswing a little steeper — so that you won't catch any debris in front of the ball. Play the ball in the center of your stance.

In the execution, be very careful not to rush the swing. It's a nerve-wracking situation, but it can be handled if you stay calm. Make your swing smooth and keep your head still and the shot will come off as planned.

6

Recovery and Challenge Shots— and How to Execute Them

Amateur's Note

In the preceding chapter, we covered many different trouble shots from the arsenal you need when you are confronted with a golf course's fundamental hazards — bunkers, the rough, water, and wind. In this chapter, we face similar challenge and recovery shots, involving other situations that you naturally consider to be troublesome too. Actually, though, they help give the game of golf its never-ending variety of man-made and natural problems to be solved (and solve them you can).

Your golf course would be dull indeed if it did not have such challenges as uphill, downhill, and sidehill lies. You would be the rarest of rare golfers if you did not at times inadvertently put yourself in a position requiring a shot that is essentially "abnormal," — an intentional hook or slice; a high shot over trees; a low shot under trees; a downhill pitch; a cut shot requiring a fast stop; a shot from a nasty lie in a divot, entailing an obstructed stance, or involving dozens of other challenges that the practice tee cannot in any way duplicate.

Do you panic? Throw up your hands and admit defeat? Never! You have the will and there is a way. Recognize the situations and heed the advice that Craig gives you in this chapter. Your enjoyment of the game will go up as your score goes down.

The Intentional Slice

Sometimes you will want to hit an intentional slice — in situations where you need to bend the ball sharply to the right around trees or other obstructions. Before you can do so, you must understand what causes the ball to slice. A slice is caused by the clubhead moving across the target line through the impact area from out to in, and by the clubface contacting the ball in an open position. The more pronounced the out-to-in swing arc, and the more open the clubface, the more the ball will slice. It's that simple.

Before the address, look toward the target from behind the ball and visualize the amount of slice you'll need on the shot. If you see the shot clearly in your own mind, you'll be able to make the necessary physical adjustments. In other words, since you obviously have to align yourself aiming well to the left of the target to allow for the slice, through visualization you'll be able to gauge the exact alignment adjustment required. Then simply pick a tree or bush as a secondary target and align your feet and body to it.

Having done this, set the clubface open (aligned square to the primary target), and at the same time, "weaken" your grip: rotate your hands to the left on the handle so that the V's formed by your index fingers and thumbs point directly to your left shoulder (this is insurance that the clubhead will return to an *open* position at impact and remain open).

KEYS FOR HITTING THE INTENTIONAL SLICE

1. Visualize the ball in flight before your address.
2. Align toward a secondary target to the left.
3. Set the clubface square to the primary target.
4. "Weaken" your grip: point V's to your left shoulder.
5. Start the club back outside the target line.
6. Keep the clubface open by preventing your wrists from rolling.

(A) On the intentional slice, align toward, and swing through to, a secondary target well to the left of the actual target.

(B) Position the clubface slightly open, aimed at the primary target.

(C) Use a "weak" grip and be sure that your hands lead the clubhead through the impact area.

A

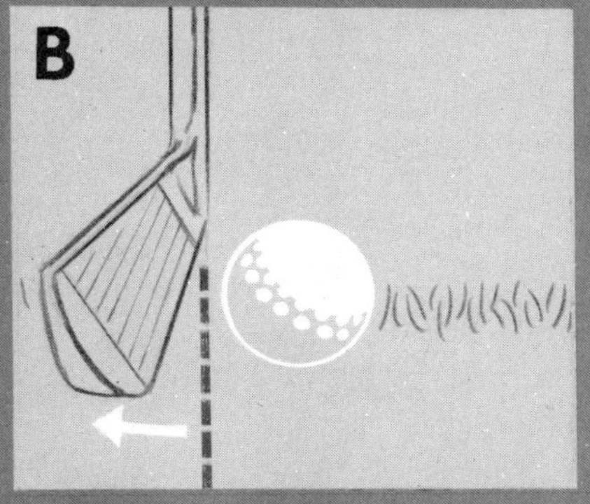
B

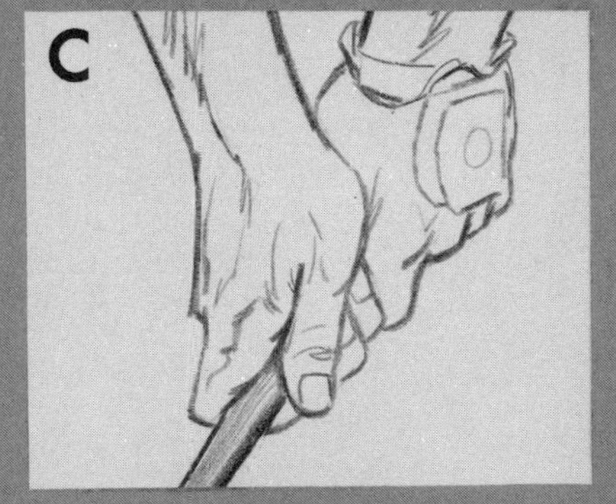
C

A
B
C

The Intentional Hook

KEYS FOR HITTING THE INTENTIONAL HOOK

1. Use a strong grip: point V's beyond your right shoulder.
2. Pick a secondary target to the right of the green and line up toward it.
3. Close the clubface so it aims squarely toward the main target.
4. Hit through with your right side.
5. Swing smoothly.
6. Insure that your right hand rolls over your left hand.

An intentional hook is a requisite in any recovery shot armory. Provided that you have a reasonably consistent golf swing, it is also an easy shot to play. There's no trick to it.

Start by "strengthening" your grip position and closing the clubface slightly. This means both V's in your grip should be rotated to point to the right of your right shoulder. This will immediately force the clubhead to follow more of an in-to-out path — a basic requirement for a hook or a draw (which has a less-pronounced curve). You'll note that after impact your right hand, because of the strong grip, will naturally tend to roll over the left more than normal, thus closing the clubface; the result will be a hook.

Your alignment determines the severity of the hook. You should pick a secondary target, a tree or bush to the right of your intended target. Once you have it chosen, close the clubface so it aims squarely toward the main target. In some cases, where you have to bend the shot around a bush or some trees, you may be unable to see the primary target, so you will have to estimate the degree of hook required and the amount the clubface should be closed. Once you have established your secondary target and have aligned your stance and clubface, simply swing normally toward that point. The ball will start off in the direction that your feet are aligned, then will hook back in. All other fundamentals — ball position, width of stance, and so forth — remain standard for the club you are using. Additional force is not necessary provided that you have applied all the fundamentals I have outlined.

Here's a special hint: To insure that your right

(A) When hooking intentionally, align toward a secondary target well to the right of your intended target.

(B) Position the clubface closed, aimed directly at the primary target.

(C) Use a "strong" grip and make your right hand roll over your left more than it normally does.

hand does roll over the left, I advocate making a concerted effort to drive your right shoulder under your chin. The more right-side power you apply, the more the ball will hook.

Controlling Trajectory

THE CLUBFACE AND BALL SPIN

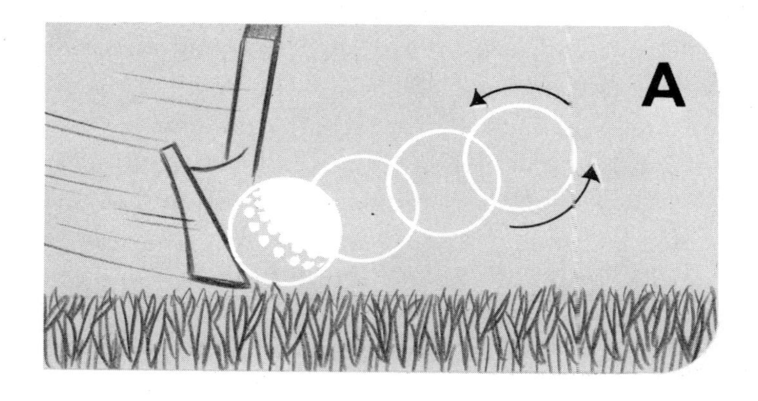

(A) When you keep the clubface square, you get a shot with perfect backspin.

(B) When hit with an open clubface, the ball spins across the face from heel to toe, causing clockwise spin and a shot that curves to the right.

(C) If the clubface is closed, *the ball spins from toe to heel, causing counterclockwise spin and a shot that curves to the left.*

(D) A hooded *clubface prevents the ball from gaining height; you get a low shot.*

BALL POSITION AND LOFT CHANGE

By simply changing the position of the ball in your address you can change the loft on the clubface, and thus the trajectory of your shots. To hit the ball low, move the ball anywhere to the right of center. The lower you want the ball to go, the farther to the right you should play it. A standard trajectory (medium height for short and middle irons, low for long irons) will result when you play the ball in the center of your stance. A high trajectory (with short and middle irons) or a medium trajectory (with the long irons) results when the ball is positioned opposite the left heel. Playing the ball still farther to

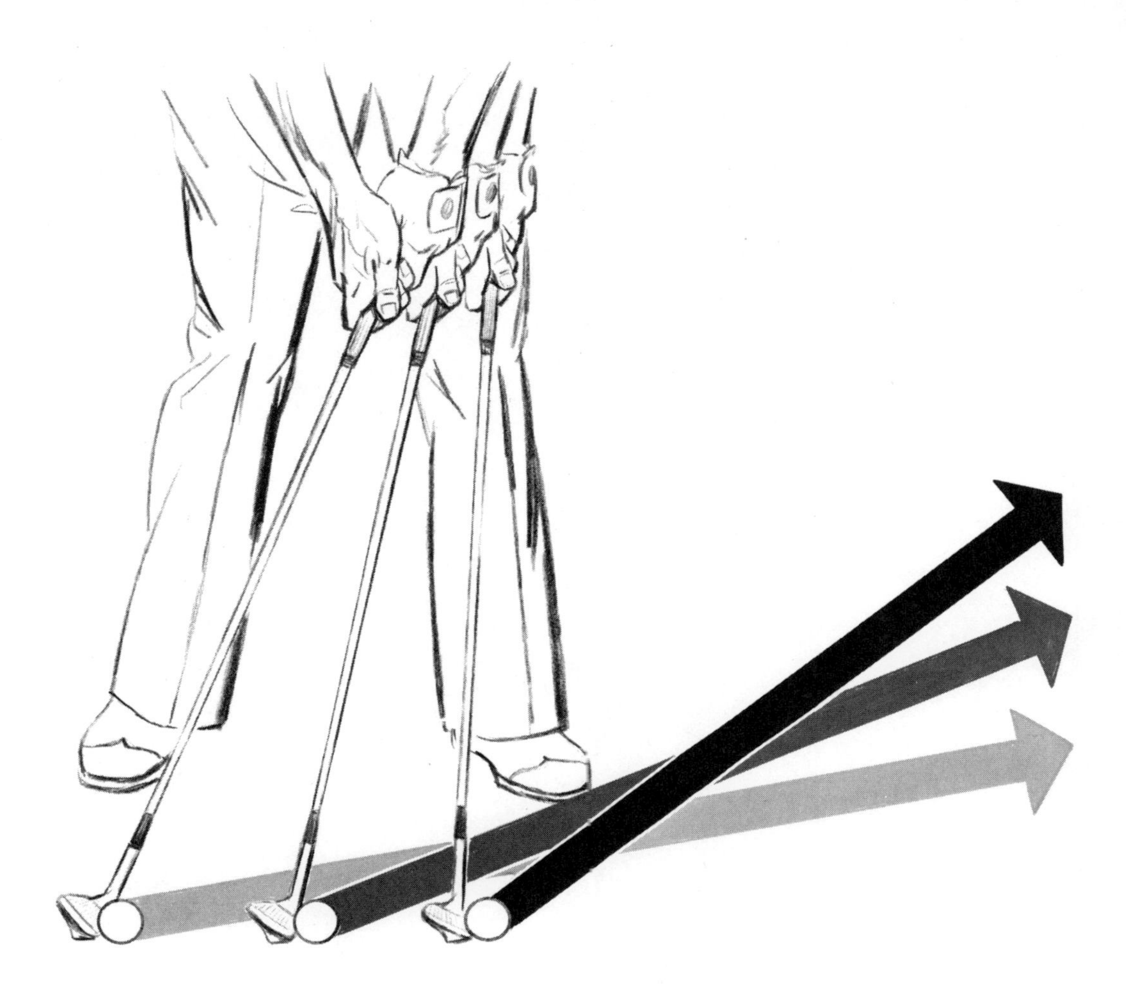

the left, with any of these clubs, will result in a still higher trajectory.

You can see from the illustration that the farther in front of the ball you set your hands, the more the loft on the face will be reduced. The more you keep your hands behind the ball, the greater the loft that will appear on the clubface. This loft principle is a simple basic that can be applied to both your address and swing.

The trajectory of the ball is directly related to its position at address. For a normal trajectory, position the ball in the center of your stance at address; play it off your right foot for a low trajectory, off your left foot for a high one.

Low Shots under Trees

KEYS FOR HITTING LOW UNDER TREES

1. Select a driver, or 2-, 3-, or 4-iron.
2. Choke up on the club.
3. Keep your weight on your left side through to finish.
4. Use a three-quarters swing.
5. Keep your hands ahead of the clubhead in the downswing.
6. Hold the grip end ahead of the clubhead end through the impact area.
7. Finish low — waist high.

When you are faced with a situation that demands a low shot, such as under tree limbs, the first consideration must be club selection. This is where the 2-, 3-, and 4-irons will prove helpful. The lower the branches, the lower the club number you'll want. In some cases, where distance is required, you also have the option of using a driver. That's right, a driver! It has so little loft that the shot will invariably stay low. However, opting for a driver depends solely on the way the ball is lying. Don't use a driver to hit from a lie in heavy grass; but if the ball is lying well, or it's on hard ground, a driver is fine.

For any low shot, choke up on the grip. By gripping farther on down the shaft toward the clubhead, you'll be shortening the width of your swing arc — which will give you more control, to keep the ball down. Position the ball in the center of your stance with your hands slightly ahead of it laterally and your weight resting on your left side. Keep in mind that *your weight must remain on your left side throughout the swing.* A three-quarters swing is all that is needed.

On the downswing and into the follow-through, the clubhead must not be allowed to pass the hands. Try to lead the club's grip through the impact area ahead of the clubhead; if your hands remain ahead of the clubhead, the clubface will contact the ball in a hooded position, the loft will be reduced, and you'll hit a low shot. If the clubhead passes ahead of your hands, the clubface will return in an open position and you'll hit a high shot — just what you don't want!

A
B
C

(A) To hit low under branches, choke up on the club's grip and position the ball in the center of your stance, with your hands slightly ahead laterally.

(B) Keep your weight on your left side throughout the swing, don't let the clubhead pass your hands through the impact area, and finish low.

(C) A driver can be very effective for a low shot if the lie is right.

Up and over the Trees

Visualization plays a major part in this situation. When you are facing a shot over trees, you must first picture the shot in your mind and then base your club selection on the height and distance you have visualized. When you are close to the trees, club selection should be your major concern: be certain that you choose a club that is lofted enough. If the trees are far away, your emphasis should shift from club selection to technique. You can make any shot go higher, even with the less lofted clubs, simply by making a few basic changes. Here's how:

Set up with a slightly open stance and the clubface open too. Position the ball forward, off your left heel. Your weight should be distributed evenly between both feet. Now you are in position to make the swing.

The backswing should emphasize an upright swing. Start the club back straight along the target line. After making a full backswing-turn, unwind so that your right shoulder works it way *under* your chin. Seek the overall feeling that you are staying well behind and under the ball, not out and over it. Finish with your hands and arms high. Often, average players become intimidated by trees and, in desperation, hit down and finish low. The result, of course, is a low shot right into the tree. Sweep upward and finish high!

If you first visualize the shot — imagine it going up into the air as high as possible — then make the above changes, you'll program your muscles to give you the height you need.

To get up and over trees, use a slightly open stance, an open clubface (see inset), and play the ball farther forward than usual. Emphasis should be placed on an upright swing, and a conscious effort should be made to unwind so that the right shoulder works its way under the chin.

A "Window" Out of Trouble

In thick trees or in what may seem to be an impossible situation, don't rush up and hit the ball "hoping" that you'll get out. Hustling-hitting-and-hoping will get you nowhere. Take your time and consider your options.

Try to imagine a window frame through which the ball can escape. Often, when in trouble, because of the number of trees and branches that surround you, it is possible that you won't immediately see all the openings; thus, you eliminate certain options. Only when you have considered *all* possibilities should you execute the shot. This window-frame concept will help bring *all* the openings to your attention.

Once you have spotted all the openings — windows — high or low, visualize the club that will provide the trajectory to get the ball through each. Then single out the best window; wherever possible, favor a club that you know you hit the straightest. In other words, if there is a window at 7-iron height, another of equal size at 5-iron height, and you know that you hit the 7 the straightest — you know what to select. The most important thing is to get the ball back in play safely. Remember: open a few windows to get fresh air.

A
B

The Uphill Lie

In this situation, choose window A if you are better at fading the ball than making it draw, and use a low-numbered club (for a lower trajectory) to avoid the branches. Use window B if you are better at drawing the ball, and use a more lofted club to make the ball rise quickly. The center circle is really not a "window" — it represents an almost impossible shot and the percentages would be heavily against you.

The uphill lie presents you with two problems:

First, the upslope acts like a launching pad, increasing the loft of the club and causing an extremely high trajectory; much distance will be lost to height. The ball, upon landing, is going to stop dead. To compensate you'll have to select a club one gradation stronger than normal (if you would normally hit a 5-iron, use a 4, for example). Be sure to select enough club to carry the ball to your target.

Second, you are presented with a balance problem. Your address position, because of the gravitational pull of the slope, is going to feel awkward. You must counter the tendency of having your weight forced to your right side in the address, by bending your left leg (how much you bend the leg will be determined by the degree of upslope). This will help to distribute your weight evenly between both feet, a necessity for balance.

Balance in this situation is vital. Setting your weight on your right side is asking for trouble. You'd tend to hit up on the ball too much, causing it to fly even higher and shorter than you want.

Regardless of which club you're using, position the ball in the center of your stance. Playing it any farther to the left will add even more height to the shot. And be sure that both of your knees are flexed rather than straight. The upslope has a tendency to deaden and stiffen your knees. Flexibility in the knees is vital to supply the drive in the downswing needed to hit through the ball.

In the swing, good rhythm is important. Many players who are intimidated by an uphill lie try to kill the shot — hit it too hard. This mistake most

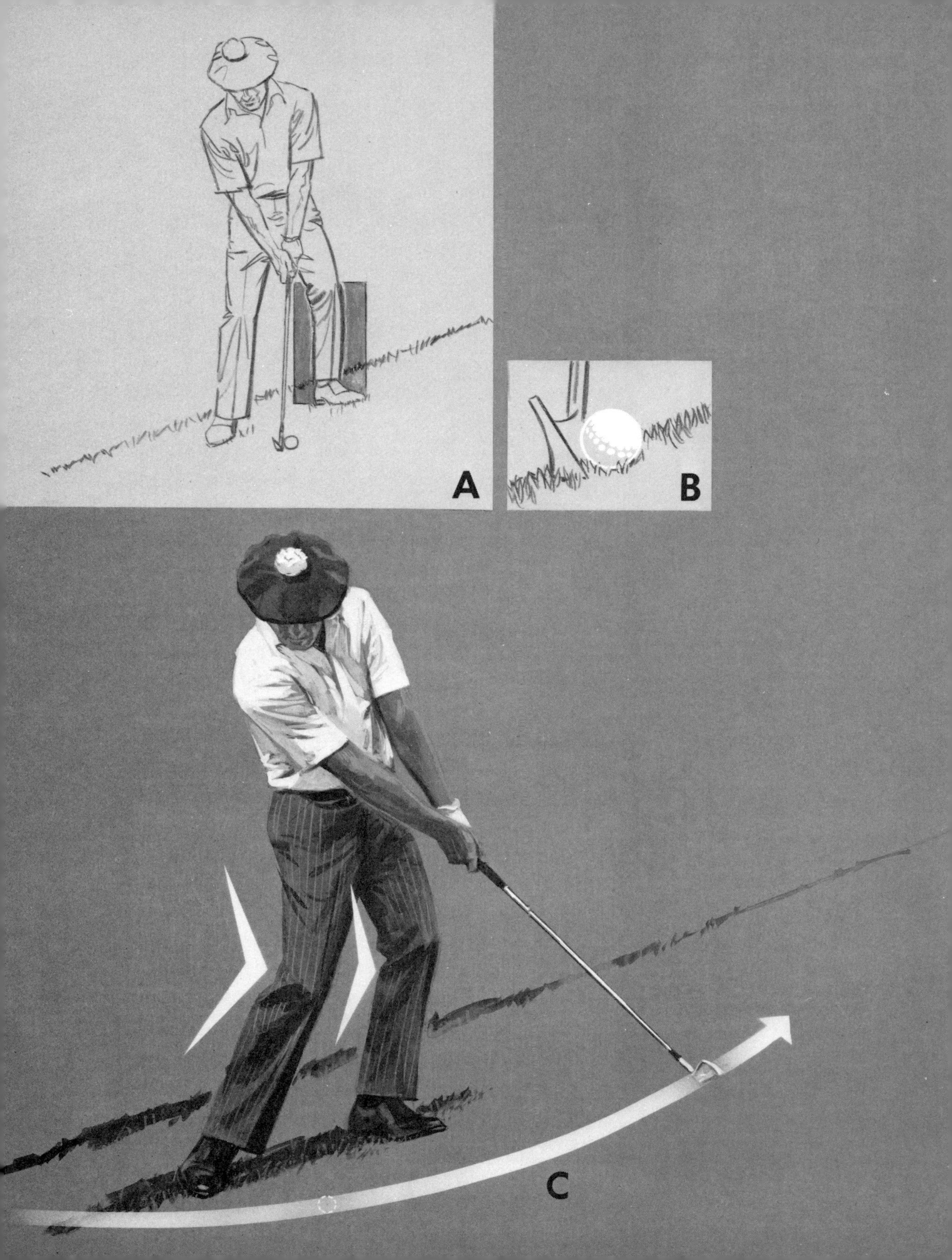
A
B
C

(A) On an uphill lie, bend your uphill leg, to offset the slope.

(B) Hit a club one numerical gradation lower than normal (a club with less loft).

(C) Try to make the clubhead follow the contour of the slope, and keep your knees moving through impact.

often causes a snap hook. Be tempo-conscious and swing smoothly throughout.

Since balance is a problem that you must face in the swing, too, you must be sure that your weight doesn't stay on your right side on the downswing — that would cause the clubhead to be rising up toward the ball at impact. Use your knees to shift your weight to the left side in the downswing. Then, through impact and into the follow-through, try to make the clubhead follow the contour of the slope by moving your weight forward, up the hill. Avoid falling backward at all costs.

Also, allow for the ball to draw somewhat, because you'll tend to release your hands more than usual and thus will close the clubface slightly on an uphill lie.

The Downhill Lie

A downhill lie is one of the hardest shots in golf. Because of the downslope, the loft of the club you select will be greatly reduced. This causes the shot to fly lower and run farther than normal. Thus, if your position would normally call for a 5-iron to the green, you should opt to hit a 6-iron. I must add that the less-lofted clubs, such as 2- or 3-irons, are extremely difficult to get airborne in this situation, so I advocate anything from a 4-iron up.

The address is critical on downhill lies. Align yourself slightly left — place your feet in an open stance — to allow for the ball's tendency to fade. Also, to help to prevent a pulled shot (another com-

A
B

(A) On a downhill lie, set the clubface slightly open and put more weight on your left side. Select a club with more loft than is normally required for the same distance.

(B) On the downswing, lead with your legs — specifically your knees — for good balance, and to enable the clubhead to follow the contour of the slope.

mon tendency), and to encourage a higher trajectory, I suggest setting the clubface slightly open in the address. The ball should be placed in the middle of your stance to make your downswing arc steeper. If the ball were played farther forward, off your left foot, the club might rise up through the impact area and you'd skull the shot.

On the backswing, because of the downslope, it becomes difficult to turn the shoulders fully. Don't fight this. A three-quarters swing will do nicely. However, try and make the plane of your swing more upright — to insure that you hit the ball, not the ground, first. Scuffing is common with a downhill lie.

On the downswing, use of the legs, specifically the knees, is essential for good balance, and it enables the clubhead to follow the contour of the slope. Emphasis should therefore be placed on a lateral movement of the knees to start the downstroke. Finally, through the impact area, be sure that the clubhead follows the contour of the slope for as long as possible.

The Sidehill Lie

BALL ABOVE FEET

With a sidehill lie, having the ball above your feet requires some fundamental changes in your address position and alignment. The most important thing to realize is that the ball is going to travel to the left. The higher the ball is above your feet, the more it will travel to the left. It's easy to understand that this kind of lie causes your swing plane to become "flatter" than normal — rather like a baseball player's near-horizontal swing. This plane causes the clubhead to leave the target line, to the left, faster than normal. The result is a hook. You can allow for the ball curving left by picking a secondary target to the right of the green. Again, how far right should be dictated by the degree to which the ball is elevated.

On a sidehill lie when the ball's above your feet, stand slightly taller, choke up on the grip, and allow for the ball curving to the left by aiming at a secondary target to the right of the original target. The upslope is going to cause your swing plane to be more horizontal, which in turn will cause the ball to hook.

I cannot overstress the importance of a sound address position in this sidehill situation. I suggest choking up on the grip to offset the ball's being closer to you. Also, in this respect, I advocate standing taller — with a little less flex in your knees. These changes will help make your swing plane match the contour of the slope.

Since balance is a critical factor, be sure to place your weight toward the balls of your feet; otherwise the natural tendency could be to fall back during the swing. Finally, be very conscious of making a smooth swing. Try, as much as the limitations of the slope will allow, to swing normally.

BALL BELOW FEET

One of the most awkward lies you can encounter is when the ball rests below your feet on a hillside. There is an ever-present danger of skulling the shot because of the awkward, restrictive stance required by the low ball position. But, with the correct fundamentals and a tight rein on your emotions, you can approach this situation with confidence.

As with other trouble shots, most of the changes called for involve the address. First, you must realize that the ball will travel to the right, because the downslope forces you to have a more upright swing plane. Allow for the ball's slice: pick a secondary target — a tree or bush to the left of the original

target — and aim toward it. How far left you set up is governed by how far the ball is below your feet; the steeper the slope, the farther left you align. There is no need consciously to hit toward your secondary target. Simply allow this to happen naturally.

The club must be gripped at the very end of the handle and your knees should be flexed more than normal. These two points will help you "get down" to the ball and hit it solidly. Also, so that you can maintain your balance throughout the swing, place your weight back on your heels.

A good point to remember is that your backswing will be somewhat restricted because of the ball position and the downslope. Don't fight this. Just take the club back to a point where you feel you can control it. A shorter, more compact backswing is desirable.

On the downswing and follow-through, be especially conscious of staying down — keep your head down (your hub steady) until the ball is long on its way. If you rise up, you might skull the shot.

(A) When the ball's below your feet on a hillside, grip the club at the very end of the shaft and flex your knees more than you do normally.

(B) Pick a secondary target to the left *of your original target. The downslope will cause your swing plane to be more upright than usual, resulting in a curve to the right.*

The Extreme Cut Shot

Many times you'll see a professional who's faced with a shot of some 20 to 30 yards over a really high bunker or who's playing over a bank to a tight pin placement use a sand wedge and cut the ball high into the air. When the ball lands it stops dead. This shot is rarely used by the average player.

I've shown the technique for the extreme cut shot

A
B

to many of my pupils, but for some reason they rarely practice it and are seemingly afraid to put it into use. Don't you be. This shot is an invaluable addition to your trouble-shot armory. All you have to do is practice it.

Hold the club lightly. Set your feet open. Align aiming well to the left of your intended target. The clubface should be turned wide open (as flat as a frying pan). Play the ball off your left heel. These changes alone will give you a lot more height than normal.

Make a *full* backswing-turn, taking the club straight back and up. On the downswing, try to make the swing arc parallel the foot line (an imaginary line that runs across your toes). Be conscious of leading your hands ahead of the clubhead through the impact area, and hold the clubface in the open position so that you slice under the ball. Were the clubface to overtake your hands, the face would tend to close and you'd lose the high trajectory.

Since the ball is going to fly very high, you can use a little more force than for a normal short shot of the same distance. There is very little chance — because the ball flies higher rather than longer — that you'll carry too far past the flag. Swing the club through to a full finish. In other words, you will use a full swing back and through.

One word of caution though: you should use this option only when you have a good lie. To attempt the extreme cut shot when the ball is on hard or bare ground could be disastrous. The rounded sole of the sand wedge could bounce off the earth into the ball and send it screaming over the green.

A final note: do not attempt to lift or "scoop" the ball up high. Rely on the loft of your clubhead and its downward path to do the job.

(A) A properly executed extreme cut shot will result in a high trajectory — the ball will land softly on the green.

(B) Remember to make a full swing, and try to keep the clubface open through impact.

(C) Set your feet in an open stance when you address the ball.

(D) Also, be sure to set up with the clubface wide open.

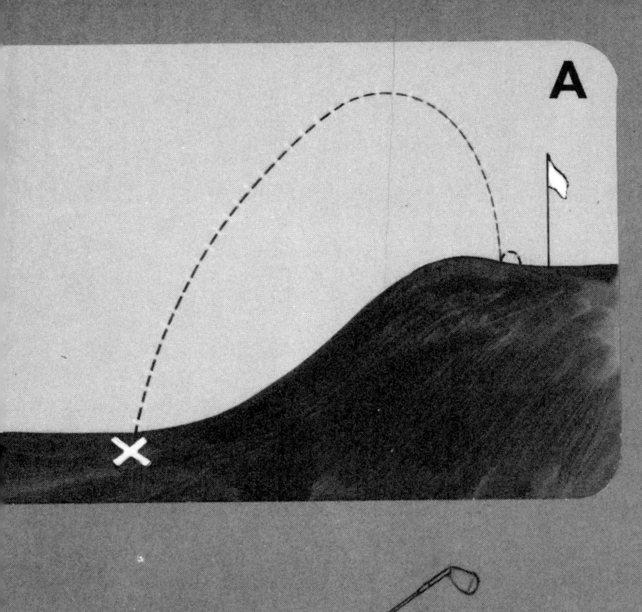
A

B

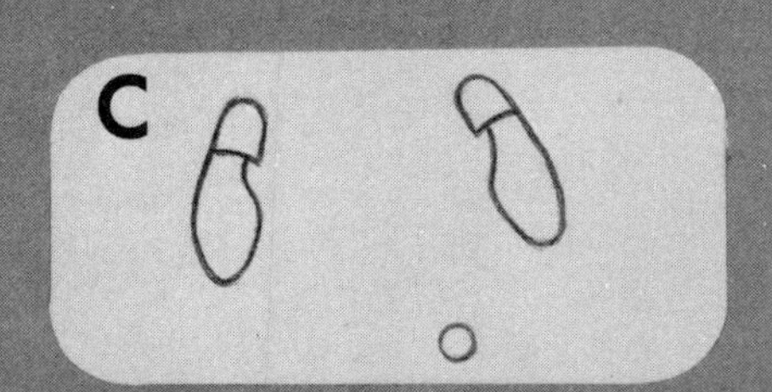
C

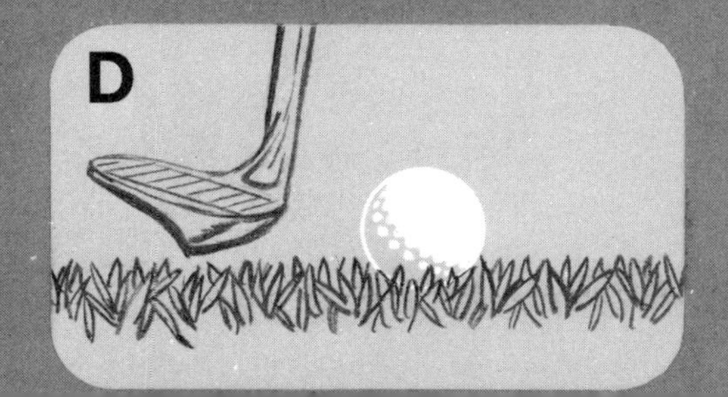
D

The Downhill Pitch

Whenever you are faced with a downhill, near-the-green situation, the basic rule is: use a lofted club. The steeper the downslope, the more loft you need. A lofted club will give you the maximum available backspin necessary to stop the ball quickly. Since lesser-lofted clubs like the 5- and 7-irons put forward spin on the ball, they are much harder to gauge and thus harder to control on a downhill slope.

If you have a reasonable amount of green to work with and the downhill grade is not too steep, select a spot just barely on the green and try to land the ball there. If, however, the pin is cut close to the near edge, use the fringe as a cup brake — pitch the ball short of the green and let it check and roll down to the hole.

(A) In any downhill, near-the-green situation, use an extremely lofted club.

(B) Pick a spot on which to land the ball. If the pin is set close to the edge of the green, use the fringe as a brake.

Choke up on the club slightly, place your weight on your left side, position the ball in the center of your stance, and keep your hands slightly ahead of the clubhead.

On the takeaway, break your wrists early. This will give you a steeper downswing arc and will provide you with height and backspin on the shot. On the downswing, make a slight lateral move with your knees; the knees help you to adjust to the slope and to stay well down through the impact area.

With any pitch from a downhill lie, make the clubhead follow the contour of the downslope — exaggerate the feeling of keeping the clubhead low to the ground. Keep the clubhead down low, right through to the finish. To prevent a skulled shot, which too often results from this situation, a smooth swing action is necessary.

The Left-Handed, Upside-Down-Clubhead Shot

There are times when a right-handed golfer wishes that he had a left-handed club in the bag, such as when the ball comes to rest close to a wall or some other obstacle that prevents a normal right-handed stance. You may not realize it, but there *is* a left-handed club in the bag!

All you have to do is turn a right-handed club upside down, so that the toe points downward. Then just reverse your fundamentals so that you're set up as a southpaw would be. The major change, of course,

If you're right-handed but can't address the ball normally from the right side, turn the clubhead upside down, and reverse your fundamentals so that you are set up just as a southpaw would be.

On a one-handed shot, turn your back to the target, with the ball a comfortable distance from your right foot. Pick the club up sharply but smoothly, and swing the clubhead through to the target.

is in the grip: your left hand is placed below your right.

The club I suggest using is a 7-iron, because it offers the largest clubface area and a reasonable amount of loft for height and distance.

To execute the shot, I suggest keeping the swing as simple as possible. Your object should be to produce solid contact, not to try for distance. You will be surprised at how much distance you can achieve by catching the ball solidly. Next time you are on the practice tee, be sure to practice this shot. Someday it could save a match for you.

The One-Handed, Back-to-Target Shot

Your ball is close to a tree, leaving you almost without option — seemingly with no shot selection. But there is no need to take a drop and a stroke penalty. You can delve into your shot repertoire and pull out the "one-handed shot."

Turn your back to the target, with the ball a comfortable distance from your right foot. Keep your eyes focused on the ball, pick the club up sharply but smoothly, and swing the clubhead through to the target. But remember: not designed to produce distance, this shot is solely for the purpose of getting the ball back into play to avoid a penalty. So, focus primarily on making solid contact and on using the natural weight of the club to propel the ball out.

Ball against Fence

Suppose that you were in a situation where your ball had ended up almost touching a wall or fence, permitting a right-handed shot but preventing you from taking your normal address position. Instead, the only way you can stand to the ball is with your back to the target. Have you got a shot? You have!

Provided that you can fit the clubhead between the ball and the obstacle, you're in business. Simply set up with the ball placed about four inches to the outside of your left foot and address the ball with your stance as open as the limitations of the obstruction will allow. Your back then, is almost facing the target. Now here's the trick: close the clubface until it is facing directly at your target — in other words, until it is totally closed.

All you do now is make a normal swing going back and through, holding that clubface in a closed position. Amazingly, the ball will fly in the direction the clubface is aimed.

This is just one more option that you can work on, and it's certainly one that will save you strokes in the long run. Be sure to consider it!

Under Trees on Your Knees

Some situations that may arise during a round of golf require that you employ a novel method of recovery. For instance, say the ball is resting under

Hitting right-handed, up against a fence, close the clubface so that it will be aimed directly at the target, and open your stance. Take the normal backswing and keep the clubface closed throughout.

Under a tree on your knees, keep your eyes on the ball and allow for a swinging action that incorporates a very "flat" (horizontal) plane.

the overhanging limbs of a tree and you are prevented from standing. There is still a way to advance the ball toward your target without taking a penalty: just get down on your knees!

Select a 7-iron. This club is ideal because of its broad face. Obviously, there will be no way you'll be able to sole the club (to rest the bottom of the club on the ground), so don't fight this. Once you are on your knees, try to get as comfortable as possible. Choking up on the grip of the club will help accomplish this.

Since solid contact is your primary objective, you must be very, very conscious of keeping your head still and your eyes directly on the ball. If your eyes remain on the ball throughout the backswing and downswing, you should not have any problem making solid contact. Before you start the swing, remember that you are not about to try for distance. Focus on smoothness. Because you're on your knees your swing plane is going to be very flat, so don't be alarmed when the club goes back sharply to the inside on the backswing.

Your main thought as you go into the downswing is to lead your hands in a way that will allow you to sweep the ball off the ground. Keep your hands leading the clubhead through to a follow-through position just above waist height. If you hit down, the club might get stuck and the ball will go nowhere.

Ball in a Divot

Many times you will hit a long, straight tee shot down the middle of the fairway only to find that the ball has come to rest in someone's unreplaced divot. Don't get upset — the shot is not as hard as you think. Consider that it was a club that made the divot in the first place and also that the dirt that the ball sits on is usually soft. This makes it easy for you to dig the ball out.

Unless the ball is in an exceptionally deep mark, requiring a lofted club, you can hit a fairway wood when you have a fair distance to your target. The 4- and 5-woods are ideal in this situation, because they have contoured soles *and* the loft necessary to get the ball up into the air quickly.

There should be no change in your address position. Address the ball as you would on any normal fairway shot. In the swing, though, you must be more upright — start the club back away from the ball slightly outside the target line. This will give you a more upright backswing and a steeper downswing arc, to cut the ball out. Also, on the downswing, be very conscious of making a strong lateral drive with your legs. This will keep the clubhead moving down and through to the target after impact. A hand/arm swing, with no leg action, is useless.

A mental image that I have used with considerable success is that I'm trying to make a divot within the divot. This makes me stay down and prevents me from mishitting the shot. The divot image is especially useful when using a lofted iron close to the green — when you *must* hit with accuracy to insure a successful result. No matter where the divot is, be

When hitting out of a divot, use a steeper downswing arc.

sure to allow for the ball's tendency to fly to the right by compensating when you set up.

The "Bump and Run"

You watched in disgust as your tee or second shot bounced on the back of the green and rolled over down a steep embankment. Now you are left with a shot back to a tight pin placement on a green that slopes from back to front. You realize that to select a sand wedge and to attempt to loft the ball softly to the top of the bank is risky: the ball might catch the top of the slope and roll back down to your feet, or, if you land on the green, it will roll all the way to the front, leaving you a long putt. There is only one other option: the "bump and run." Simply pick a spot on the hill and bounce the ball onto the green!

Select a club with very little loft. A 5- or 7-iron is perfect. Anything more lofted will produce too much height on the shot, causing you to miss the slope completely and fly over the green.

Hood the face of the club by moving your hands well ahead of the ball laterally. Play the ball in the center of your stance. Set your weight on the left side. Having your weight on the left and your hands well ahead of the ball will help give you the low trajectory you need.

Aim for a spot halfway up the bank. Now make a smooth half-swing. Be sure that as you swing through, your hands stay well ahead of the clubhead; then the clubhead will return to the ball with the face still in

(A) The objective on a "bump and run" is a low trajectory with limited roll.

(B) Pick a spot halfway up the hill and make a smooth half-swing. Be sure that as you swing through, your hands stay well ahead of the clubhead.

(C) In the address, hood the clubface by moving your hands ahead of the ball laterally.

A
B
C

a hooded position, trapping the ball on the lower half of the club and preventing it from gaining too much height. Use a little more force than you would for an unobstructed shot of the same distance. You can plan on the ball hitting hard into the bank, and, because the spin is knocked off with the first bounce, it will skip softly up onto the green.

The bump and run will be less of a gamble if you try it in practice first. The simple key to remember is: "short backswing, low finish."

The Running Chip through Sand

When the pin is cut close to the edge of a trap or the overhanging limbs of a tree prevent you from pitching the ball to the flag, the shot to play is a running chip "through" the sand, if the bunker has a shallow lip and the sand isn't too soft. If the trap has either a steep lip or the sand is soft, you will have to pitch the ball onto the green in spite of the hazards or pin placement. But if the conditions are in your favor, there is an excellent chance that you can go for the flag by running through the sand, and can make an excellent recovery from what at first appeared to be a rotten situation.

Select a 5-iron. Position the ball in the center of your stance and your hands well ahead of it. This will hood the clubface to provide you with the low trajectory you need to run the ball over the sand. Choke up on the handle for control and use a light grip pressure to make sure you don't quit on the shot.

(A) To run a chip through sand, choke up on the handle and use your normal chipping technique. A nice, smooth action is needed to roll the ball across the sand.

(B) Select a 5-iron and place your hands ahead of the ball to hood the clubface.

A
B

Now use your normal chipping action, but make a conscious effort to roll your right hand over your left through the impact area. This action will cause the clubface to close at impact and impart a small amount of counterclockwise spin on the ball, which will also help it negotiate the sand. No extra force is necessary. A nice smooth action is mandatory.

The Sand Wedge to a Difficult Pin Position

The sand wedge is one of the most versatile clubs in the bag. It is effective not only for escaping from sand, but for all shots that require the ball to stop quickly, such as a shot over a water hazard or bunker to a pin placement that is cut close to the edge of the green. These are situations in which you want a great deal of height and backspin — you must toss the ball right at the flag and expect it to stop.

An exception to this height-and-backspin objective occurs when you're playing to a downhill placement, but even then the sand wedge is the ideal choice. Its 55 degrees of loft and its unique contoured sole will provide you with maximum stopping power to negotiate the downslope. Of course, you'll have to land the ball well short of the flag, but you can count on the spin to put the brakes on: the ball will roll gently down the slope to the hole. It's difficult, even hitting downhill, to roll the ball too far beyond the hole with a sand wedge — that's important to remember.

An additional advantage of the sand-wedge shot is

The sand wedge is especially effective when you have a shot over water and need to stop the ball quickly (A), when you have a short shot over a bunker and the pin is cut close to the edge of the green (B), or when you face a downhill pin placement (C). Your sand wedge provides you with maximum height and backspin.

C
B
A

that you can swing fully, both on backswing and follow-through, without fear of hitting the ball too far. On a full swing, the club's loft will give you more height, but not more distance. Thus, even the most competent of players can only hit the ball around 95 yards with a sand wedge. In playing a sand-wedge shot, be sure to focus on making a full finish. The technique is otherwise no different from the one used when hitting a pitching wedge.

7

How to Think Your Way to Better Golf

Amateur's Note

Your mind's eye, when properly used, can be an amazing stroke-saver. When improperly used, it can cause you spectacular woe.

In this final chapter, about positive thinking habits, you will see a number of references to "imitation" and "visualization," which both relate to your mental approach to golf. These two functions have osmotic qualities — they seep into your unconscious; they should be used to advantage.

Imitation *means simply calling upon your stored mental pictures of the good golf swings you've seen demonstrated by your pro, exhibited on TV, used in tournaments, performed by better players in your foursome, or illustrated in such books as this one.*

Visualization *is something that you — and only you — can control for yourself. "See the shot before you hit it," Craig advises, "but be sure to* see it as a good shot, not a poor one."

As you have perhaps discovered, your muscles will often follow the bidding of your mind, even though you are not conscious of the connection. If your outlook is negative, it has a capacity for creating rampant disaster for your golf, and with unbelievable speed. If, a split second before you swing, you visualize a shot mishit into the bunker (surely buried), then shudder at the thought of missing one or more shots from the sand, and expect with certainty to follow with a three-putt green, that's probably what will happen. Why not visualize positively? As you line up that shot with the bunker between you and the flag, see the ball sailing high and true to nestle near the pin with an excellent chance for a one-putt.

Shakespeare said it perfectly: "There is nothing

either good or bad, but thinking makes it so." It's not really such a long way from the drama of the Elizabethan stage to the dollar-bet drama you face on the eighteenth hole — that challenging 9-iron shot over a yawning trap between you and the flag: the result, good or bad, is usually governed by your thoughts.

Which choice will your mind's eye take? Think about it.

Mind over Matter

There are basically two requisites for developing a sound golf game: (1) the physical aspect — sound basics and a fundamentally correct swing, and (2) the mental process — the ability to program your mind for positive action.

Throughout this chapter I will refer to the physical aspect as the "mechanics" of the swing. The *mechanics* are the individual components that make up the swing as a whole. The *mental process* is the sum of the individual thoughts you use to refine your swing or make it work. I contend that in the past golf instructors and technicians have spent too much time focusing on the physical aspects and almost no time on the thought process. After all, it is the mental process that makes good and bad shots happen.

I have seen players with terrible-looking swings produce some of the finest shots and score some of the lowest rounds. The power of positive thought, the ability to forecast a successful result, offsets their many physical deficiencies. Conversely, I have seen players with good-looking swings hit horrendous shots. The power of negative thought, the tendency to project failure, offsets the physical attributes of their swings.

In this chapter I shall focus on the key areas of the positive thought process as they relate to your golf swing and to your thinking on the golf course. My primary purpose is to make you aware of the mental changes needed to improve both your golf swing and your scoring ability. You will be amazed and gratified at the progress you'll make if you properly program yourself.

Program Your Mind to Improve Your Swing

I am convinced that in the future teachers will give much greater emphasis to the use of visual aids and imitation than to verbal instruction when teaching their students how to swing. I have found in my own teaching that verbally outlining the mechanics of the swing often presents a distorted image of what good positioning looks and feels like. I have much more success when I make a player imitate me, or place a pupil in the correct position. There is a lesson to be learned from this: your mind relates easily to pictures and to new feelings.

Take youngsters to a baseball game and it's almost guaranteed that when they get home and throw a ball in the backyard they'll have adopted the same technique and even some of the mannerisms of the pitchers that they watched earlier. Why? Because each child has a full-color sequence indelibly printed in his or her memory bank.

If you're a tennis player, you may have had a similar experience after watching a tournament on TV. You go out afterward to play one or two sets and serve and volley beautifully.

It's the same with golf. You go to a pro golf tournament and see the world's best players in action, then go back to your club and often play the best golf you have all year.

In each case, like the child, you are imitating the pros from pictures in your memory bank. Those pictures are so clear in your mind that they are easily transformed into physical feelings, different positions — better positions. Unfortunately, the images and feelings fade. But you can call on your powers of visualization to reinforce the images. An excellent method of so doing is to examine still photographs or movies. Have photos taken of your swing and compare them to a sequence showing a professional's swing. If, for example, you see that your backswing position is bad, simply imitate the professional at the corresponding stage of his or her swing. A full-length mirror is excellent for reinforcing images while you practice your swing. If you imitate diligently, until you have a clear mental picture and the feeling of what the good position feels like, eventually the proper swing will be etched into your subconscious.

I should add that any changes must be made with the realization that it takes time for the mind, consciously and unconsciously, to accept them. Your mind literally has to reprogram itself. Your muscles, too, must be redirected and allowed time to adjust to the new patterning.

Don't "Think Mechanics" on the Course

The mechanics of golf must be kept simple. A golf swing must be as spontaneous as crossing the street in traffic. It would be very difficult to walk freely if you were concentrating on the various joints in your legs. It's immensely difficult to swing a golf club with any freedom while consciously focusing on the various elements that make up the overall motion. You have enough problems to solve. "Overthinking" tends to make you look like an automaton — preprogrammed, yet clumsy.

A great quarterback or third baseman doesn't consciously move the joints in his arm during a pass or a throw. He sees his target and fires the ball. His reflexes, primed through many years of practice, tell him how hard and where to throw.

Conscious thoughts about mechanics should be almost nonexistent on the course and should be kept to the bare minimum in practice — one or two thoughts at most. And if you focus on such a mechanical element, you must change the thought into a *picture* of what you are trying to accomplish. Then you must incorporate it into a clear image of the swing as a *whole*. Consciously focusing on one area of the swing, if you're not careful, can disjoint the natural movement, make your swing jerky.

Sometimes a club member will come into my pro shop after playing a bad round, desperate for help, and I'll suggest a lesson. On the way to the range all I'll hear is how badly the player was hitting the ball and how he had been trying this move and that move to recover.

When we get to the range he hits every shot very well. "Why couldn't I do that on the course?" he asks. The answer is simple: After hitting his first bad shot on the course, the player started to experiment with conscious swing changes in an attempt to find the cause. After two or three bad shots, his mind started to race. He panicked. Pretty soon his mental computer was feeding him stored information from all the lessons he had taken and from all the golf books and magazines he had read in the past. The result of this machine-gunning of the conscious mind was that his swing fell to pieces. His body couldn't handle the commands that his mind was spitting out. Instead of *trusting* his swing, he became too judgmental and *blamed* the swing.

The time for mechanical analysis is not on the course. You must trust your swing. Never go on a "physical" rampage and dissect your swing during a round — this will spell disaster. Your mind will be so preoccupied with mechanics that you will lose sight of your primary objectives: your target and swinging to it.

Project Your Target

A great percentage of bad shots stem from a lack of conscious awareness of where the target is. Too many players are so concerned with hitting the ball, with getting it airborne and striking it well, that they forget where they want the shot to go. If your mind doesn't have a clear picture of the target, it can't direct the body muscles effectively.

Before hitting the shot, mentally program a positive result. How many times have you pictured your shot veering left or right and landing in the woods — and then put it there? A positive forecast will create a positive result.

If you watch good players or professional golfers preparing to hit, you'll see that the very first thing they do is stand directly behind the ball, in line with their target. At this point they are presenting a clear image of the target to their conscious mind. If, say, it's a tee shot, then a spot in the fairway, or a bush or tree on the horizon, will be visually impressed upon the mind. During the entire address pattern (see pages 19–21 for specific information), this target will remain clearly in their mind's eye. It's the same with every shot. You must have a clear mental impression of where you are going to hit, pitch, chip, or putt the ball — otherwise you chances of success are slim.

Forecast a Successful Outcome

The next step in the positive visualization process is to project a successful outcome in your mind. At the point that you implant the target image (at the start of your address pattern, when you are standing directly behind the ball), you must also preview the shot you are about to hit. You must literally "see" in your mind a clear image of the swing and the entire shot. Picture your swing at its best (a lovely flowing motion), the complete flight pattern and trajectory of the shot, and the ball landing by the hole.

Use your visualization power creatively. For example, if the pin is tucked over on the right side, visualize a fade, the ball landing, spinning to the right, then rolling to the hole. The more positive your

In a bunker, the two greatest fears for the average player are leaving the ball in the trap or hitting it over the green. Dismiss those fears! Replace them with good, positive thoughts: visualize the swing you must make and picture the ball landing on the spot you select.

input is — the more you program optimistically — the more positive your output will be. Positive thought breeds positive action; negative thought inspires negative action.

Countless times I have seen players hit beautiful shots in practice, one after the other, as straight as an arrow. Then they stroll to the first tee and hit their drive into the woods! On the practice range there was no fear of failure. If they missed a shot, there was always another ball to take its place. On the first tee it's different. The shot *means* something. The player tenses up and sees the out-of-bounds dominating on the right, woods looming on the left, and a microscopic sliver of fairway somewhere in between. The mind starts programming the out-of-bound markers and issuing commands: "I've got to stay to the left because of the woods," or "I must stay to the right because of the out-of-bounds." Negative thoughts, negative image. Does he "think fairway"? Unfortunately, no! He sees himself fail in advance — the preview is of a shot going into the woods. And often, the vision becomes reality.

Are you intimidated by water hazards? The normal reaction is extreme tension. By focusing on positive aspects and picturing a successful result on the hole, you will eliminate the disastrous visions that too often invade your mind and ruin the shot.

Perhaps a player faces a second shot over water in the club championship. She's played this hole all year and has had no trouble. Now the shot means something. "Got to get it over the water," she wishes. Negative thought. Splash!

There is but one way to prevent negativity: be positive. Focus intensely on your target, on your swing, and on the flight pattern of the shot before you hit. If you work hard enough on this there will be nothing else in your mind to spoil the outcome. The combined total of all this mental programming is the most important psychological by-product of all concentration.

And concentration, plus all you have learned about each shot's execution, will produce what this book has tried to help you achieve: a lower score, along with confidence and control over shots and situations you *previously* had feared or flubbed.